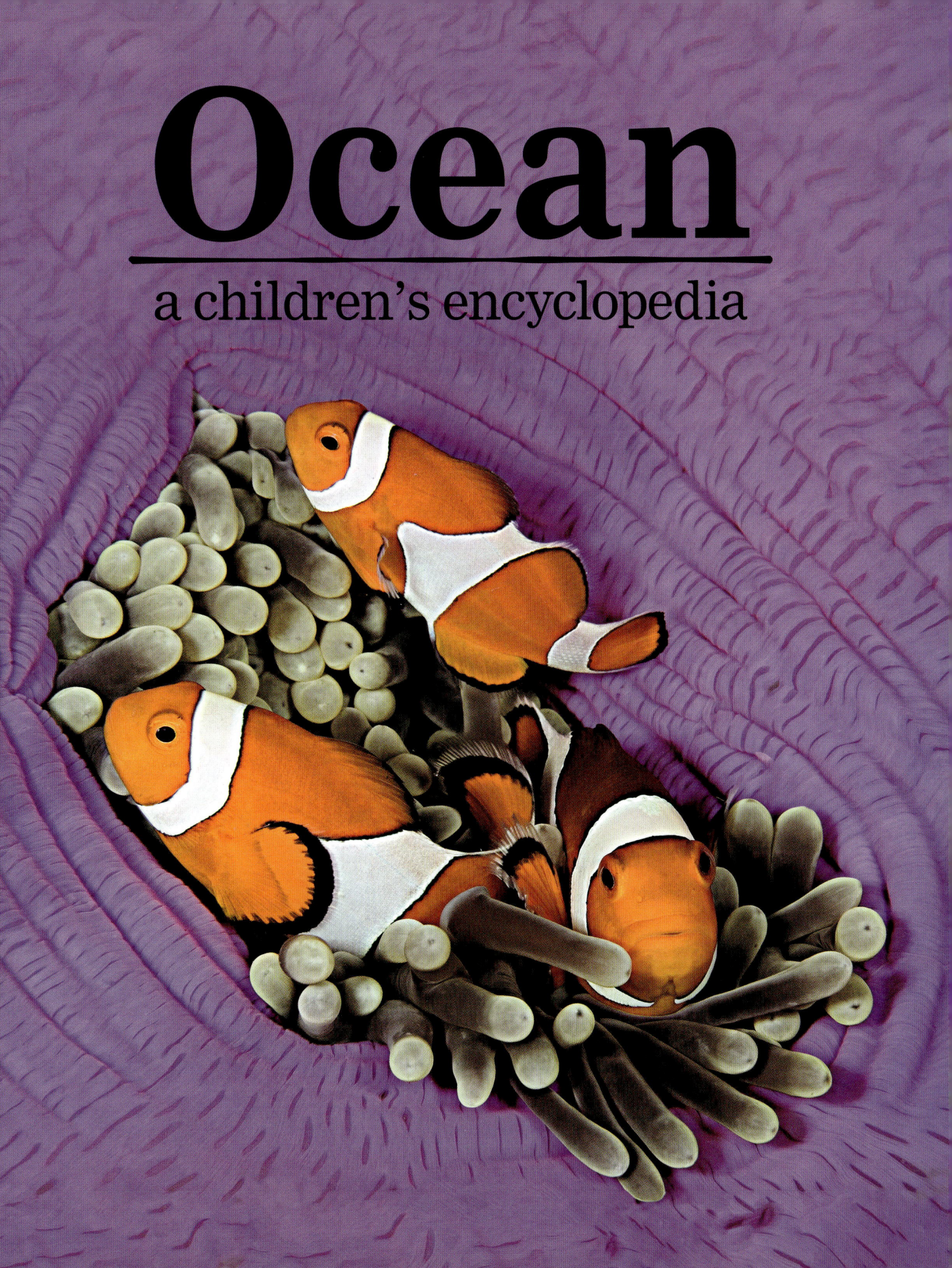

# Ocean
## a children's encyclopedia

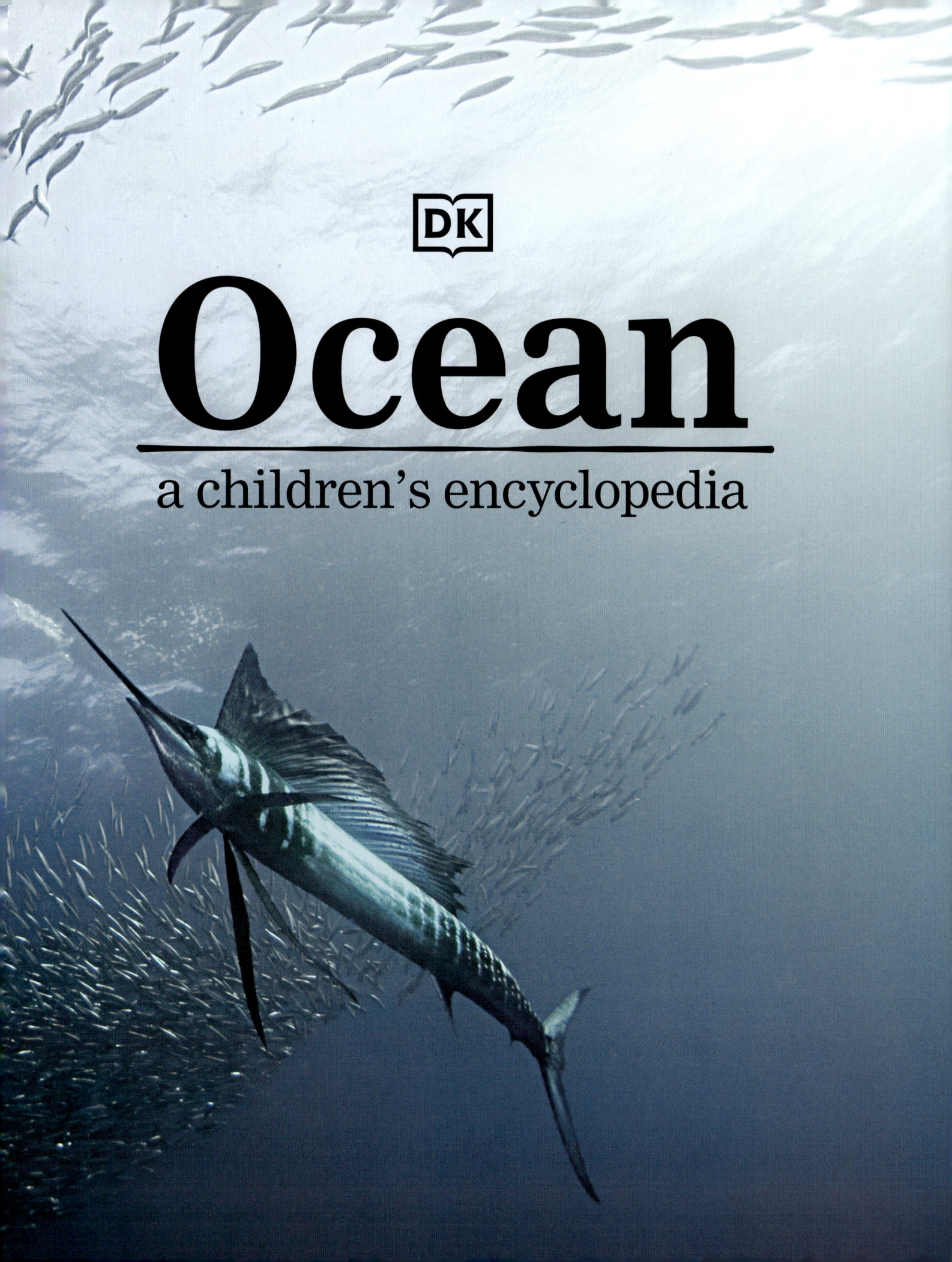
# Ocean
a children's encyclopedia

**Written by** John Woodward
**Consultant** Professor Dorrik Stow

**Second Edition**

**DK Delhi**
**Senior Editor** Neha Ruth Samuel  **Senior Art Editor** Vikas Chauhan
**Editor** Aashirwad Jain  **Art Editor** Prateek Maurya
**Team Lead, Picture Research** Sumedha Chopra
**Deputy Manager, Picture Research** Virien Chopra
**Deputy Managing Art Editor** Shreya Anand
**Managing Editor** Kingshuk Ghoshal
**Managing Art Editor** Govind Mittal
**Pre-Production Designer** Pawan Kumar
**Pre-Production Image Editor** Vikram Singh
**Pre-production Manager** Balwant Singh
**Pre-Production Image Manager** Pankaj Sharma
**Project Jackets Art Editor** Vidushi Chaudhry
**Creative Head** Malavika Talukder

**DK London**
**Editor** Zaina Budaly  **Designer** Anna Pond
**Managing Editor** Rachel Fox  **Managing Art Editor** Owen Peyton Jones
**Production Editor** Gillian Reid
**Senior Production Controller** Leanne Burke
**Publisher** Andrew Macintyre
**Art Director** Mabel Chan

**Consultant** Dr Helen Scales

This edition published in 2025
First published in Great Britain in 2015 by
Dorling Kindersley Limited,
20 Vauxhall Bridge Road, London, SW1V 2SA

The authorised representative in the EEA is
Dorling Kindersley Verlag GmbH.
Arnulfstr. 124, 80636 Munich, Germany

Copyright © 2015, 2025 Dorling Kindersley Limited
A Penguin Random House Company
10 9 8 7 6 5 4 3 2 1
004–349722–March/2026

All rights reserved. No part of this publication may be reproduced, stored in or introduced into a retrieval system, or transmitted, in any form, or by any means (electronic, mechanical, photocopying, recording, or otherwise), without the prior written permission of the copyright owner.
DK values and supports copyright. Thank you for respecting intellectual property laws by not reproducing, scanning or distributing any part of this publication by any means without permission. By purchasing an authorised edition, you are supporting writers and artists and enabling DK to continue to publish books that inform and inspire readers. No part of this publication may be used or reproduced in any manner for the purpose of training artificial intelligence technologies or systems. In accordance with Article 4(3) of the DSM Directive 2019/790, DK expressly reserves this work from the text and data mining exception.

A CIP catalogue record for this book is available from the British Library.
ISBN: 978-0-2417-4174-0

Printed and bound in China

www.dk.com

This book was made with Forest Stewardship Council™ certified paper – one small step in DK's commitment to a sustainable future. Learn more at www.dk.com/uk/information/sustainability

# Contents

## ATLAS OF THE OCEANS — 6

| | |
|---|---|
| Oceans of the world | 8 |
| Arctic Ocean | 10 |
| Atlantic Ocean | 12 |
| Indian Ocean | 14 |
| Pacific Ocean | 16 |
| Southern Ocean | 18 |

## BLUE PLANET — 20

| | |
|---|---|
| Planet ocean | 22 |
| How oceans formed | 24 |
| New land | 26 |
| Ocean floor | 28 |
| Mid-ocean ridges | 30 |
| The deepest depths | 32 |
| Grinding plates | 34 |
| Evolving oceans | 36 |
| Tsunamis | 38 |
| Hotspots | 40 |
| Lava flow | 42 |
| Continental shelves | 44 |
| Changing sea levels | 46 |
| Ocean water | 48 |
| Light, heat, and sound | 50 |
| Oceanic winds | 52 |
| Oceanic storms | 54 |
| Waves | 56 |
| Plunging breaker | 58 |
| Surface currents | 60 |
| Sargasso Sea | 62 |
| Upwelling zones | 64 |
| Deepwater currents | 66 |

## THE OPEN OCEAN — 68

| | |
|---|---|
| Depth zones | 70 |
| Sunlit zone | 72 |
| Zooplankton | 74 |
| Drifting jellies | 76 |
| The food chain | 78 |
| Hungry shoals | 80 |

| | |
|---|---|
| Oceanic hunters | 82 |
| Bait ball | 84 |
| Sharks | 86 |
| Filter-feeding giants | 88 |
| Baleen whales | 90 |
| Bubble-net feeding | 92 |
| Toothed whales and dolphins | 94 |
| Ocean birds | 96 |
| Twilight zone | 98 |
| Midnight zone | 100 |
| Ocean floor life | 102 |
| Life on black smokers | 104 |

## SHALLOW SEAS 106

| | |
|---|---|
| Fertile waters | 108 |
| The seabed | 110 |
| Seaweeds | 112 |
| Kelp forests | 114 |
| Sea otter | 116 |
| Seafloor fish | 118 |
| Sea snails and clams | 120 |
| Squid, octopus, and cuttlefish | 122 |
| Hatching octopus | 124 |
| Prawns, lobsters, and crabs | 126 |
| Starfish, sea urchins, and sea cucumbers | 128 |
| Jellyfish and anemones | 130 |
| Corals and coral reefs | 132 |
| The Great Barrier Reef | 134 |
| Reef fish | 136 |
| Reef invertebrates | 138 |
| Giant clam | 140 |
| Atolls and lagoons | 142 |

## COAST AND SEASHORE 144

| | |
|---|---|
| Tides | 146 |
| Wave power | 148 |
| Cliffs and caves | 150 |
| Twelve Apostles | 152 |
| Rocky shore life | 154 |
| Tide pools | 156 |
| Beaches, dunes, and spits | 158 |
| Hidden riches | 160 |
| Shorebirds | 162 |
| Oystercatchers | 164 |
| Seabird colonies | 166 |
| Sea turtles | 168 |

| | |
|---|---|
| Shore crabs | 170 |
| Estuaries and mudflats | 172 |
| Deltas | 174 |
| Salt marshes | 176 |
| Mangrove forests | 178 |
| Scarlet ibis | 180 |
| Seagrass beds | 182 |
| Sea snakes and crocodiles | 184 |

## POLAR SEAS 186

| | |
|---|---|
| Polar extremes | 188 |
| Sea ice | 190 |
| Life under the ice | 192 |
| Crabeater seals and penguins | 194 |
| Sleek hunters | 196 |
| Antarctic hunters | 198 |
| Antarctic islands | 200 |
| Glaciers and ice shelves | 202 |
| Icebergs | 204 |
| Blue icebergs | 206 |
| Arctic seals | 208 |
| Icy nurseries | 210 |
| Hunters on the ice | 212 |
| Humans on the ice | 214 |

## OCEANS AND US 216

| | |
|---|---|
| Seafarers and explorers | 218 |
| Ocean science | 220 |
| Scuba diving | 222 |
| Deep-sea exploration | 224 |
| Historic shipwrecks | 226 |
| Minerals from the oceans | 228 |
| Energy from the oceans | 230 |
| Fishing | 232 |
| Stilt fishing | 234 |
| Ocean trade | 236 |
| Climate crisis | 238 |
| Harming the oceans | 240 |
| Oceans in danger | 242 |
| Marine conservation | 244 |
| | |
| Glossary | 246 |
| Index | 250 |
| Acknowledgments | 254 |

# ATLAS OF THE OCEANS

Recent breakthroughs in technology have enabled us to map the oceans in more detail than ever before. The results reveal a hidden world of mountains, volcanoes, and trenches beneath the waves.

# Oceans of the world

More than two-thirds of Earth's surface is covered by seawater. Most of the water lies in the five deep oceans, but there are many shallow coastal seas covering the world's continental shelves. There are also several seas that are almost entirely surrounded by land, such as the Mediterranean and the Red Sea. Within this vast expanse of water lies an amazing variety of life.

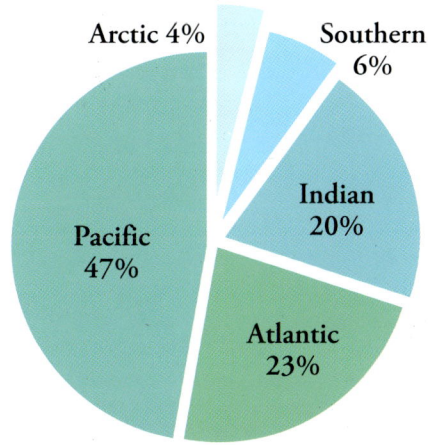

## OCEAN SIZES
The five oceans are connected to one another, and range in size from the Arctic Ocean, the smallest, to the mighty Pacific Ocean, which covers more than a quarter of the planet's surface. This diagram shows how the areas of the five oceans compare, with the Pacific being almost as large as all the other oceans combined.

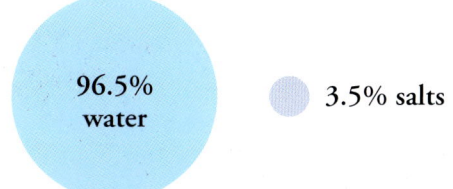

## SALTY WATER
Seawater contains various chemicals called salts. The most important of these is sodium chloride, used to make table salt. Seawater is 96.5% pure water and 3.5% salts.

ATLAS OF THE OCEANS

# Arctic Ocean

Surrounded by North America, Europe, Asia, and Greenland, the Arctic Ocean is the smallest of the oceans. Its water is frozen over near the North Pole throughout the year, and the area covered by sea ice more than doubles in winter. But over recent years, the ice has been shrinking because of climate change.

### FACT FILE
- **Area:** 14,056,000 sq km (5,427,000 sq miles)
- **Average depth:** 1,205 m (3,953 ft)
- **Deepest point:** 5,669 m (18,599 ft)

## ICY ISLANDS

▲ **CHILLING DOWN**
*This satellite view shows sea ice forming around Prince Charles Island, Nunavut.*

The ocean's North American side is dotted with rocky islands. Together with part of the mainland, they form the Canadian territory of Nunavut. In winter, the sea between many of the islands freezes over, so they become part of a vast crust of ice.

## MELTING SEAS

Climate change has made the Arctic one of the fastest warming places on Earth. It is making more of the sea ice melt in summer, opening up shipping routes that were previously blocked. By 2050, summers at the North Pole may be completely ice-free.

## MOVING TARGET

The North Pole lies in the heart of the Arctic Ocean, in a region that is currently covered by sea ice throughout the year. Its position is indicated by a marker, but since the sea ice is constantly drifting with the currents, the marker is always being moved. In the future, melting ice at the North Pole may make placing the marker impossible.

▶ **FROZEN OCEAN**
*The deep ocean basins in the centre of the Arctic Ocean are fringed by broad continental shelves and shallow seas. In winter, much of the ocean is a mass of drifting pack ice (pale blue).*

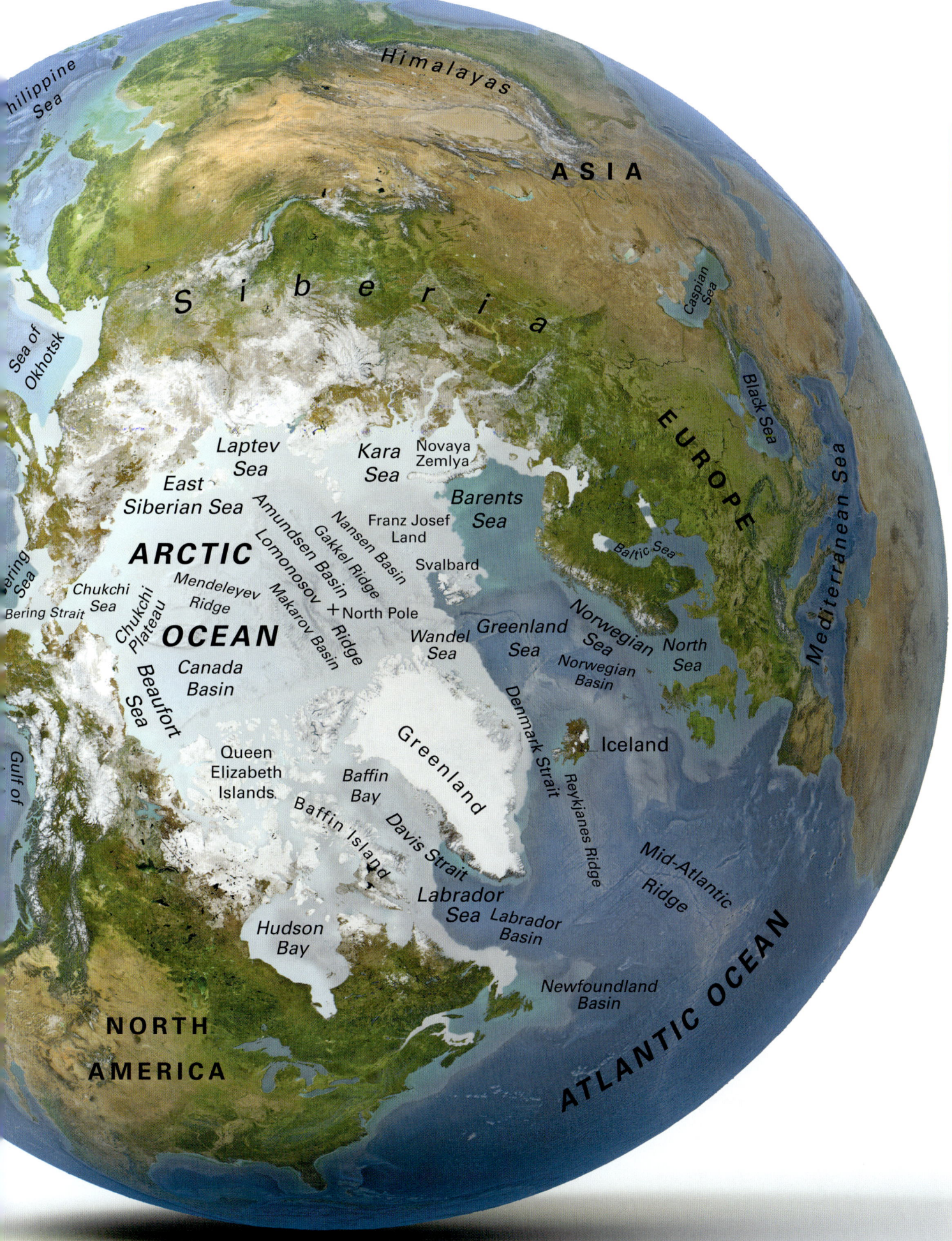

# Atlantic Ocean

Dividing North and South America from Europe and Africa, the Atlantic is the second largest ocean. It is getting wider all the time, at a rate of 4 cm (1.5 in) per year. This is because the Atlantic has a long spreading rift at its heart and there are two subduction zones that destroy the ocean floor.

### FACT FILE

| | |
|---|---|
| Area: | 106,460,000 sq km (41,100,000 sq miles) |
| Average depth: | 3,646 m (11,962 ft) |
| Deepest point: | 8,408 m (27,585 ft) |

## LESSER ANTILLES VOLCANIC ARC

▲ **ACTIVE VOLCANO**
*Steam and gas erupt from Soufrière Hills volcano on Montserrat, Leeward Islands.*

The Windward and Leeward islands, on the fringes of the Caribbean, form an island arc above one of just two subduction zones in the Atlantic. Here, part of the ocean floor is diving beneath the Caribbean, creating the deep Puerto Rico Trench and triggering the eruption of a chain of volcanoes.

## ICELAND HOTSPOT

▲ **SILFRA**
*A diver explores the Silfra fissure at Thingvellir National Park, Iceland.*

The Mid-Atlantic Ridge passes directly through the volcanic island of Iceland forming the Silfra fissure. This flooded rift lies between the North American and European continental plates and gets 2 cm (0.8 in) wider each year.

## MID-ATLANTIC RIDGE

The Atlantic started forming 180 million years ago, as a rift in Earth's crust that divided a vast continent. As the rift opened up, new rock formed the floor of a widening ocean and the rift became the Mid-Atlantic Ridge. New rock is still erupting from cracks in the ridge, such as the one seen below.

▶ **DIVIDING THE WORLD**
*The Atlantic Ocean is about 5,000 km (3,100 miles) wide, and more than 15,000 km (9,320 miles) long. It forms a vast S-shaped gulf, which separates North and South America from Europe and Africa.*

ATLAS OF THE OCEANS

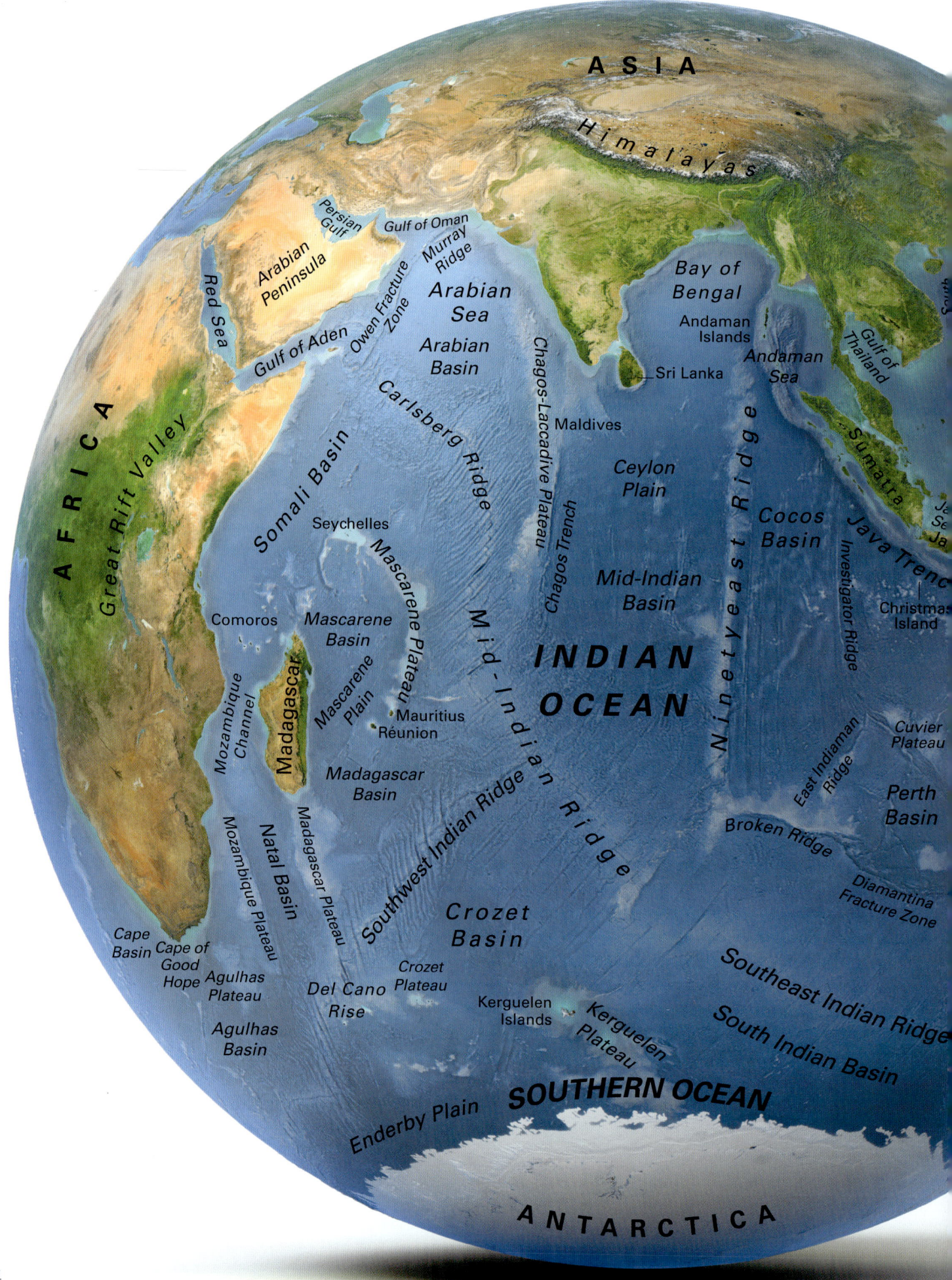

# Indian Ocean

Unlike the Atlantic and Pacific oceans, the Indian Ocean does not extend far north of the equator. Most of its waters are tropical, apart from in the far south. The deep Java Trench on its eastern margin is one of the world's most active earthquake zones, causing catastrophic tsunamis.

### FACT FILE

| | |
|---|---|
| Area: | 70,560,000 sq km (27,240,000 sq miles) |
| Average depth: | 3,741 m (12,274 ft) |
| Deepest point: | 7,187 m (23,579 ft) |

## ISLAND JEWELS

To the south of India, a submerged ridge of rock is capped with the ring-shaped coral atolls of the Maldives. Each atoll is formed of many smaller atolls, and from high above the ocean they look like strings of pearls. These low-lying islands are vulnerable to tsunamis, and are at risk from rising sea levels.

## NEW OCEANS

▲ **RED SEA**
*This sea may owe its name to the blooms of red algae that sometimes form on its surface. Usually, its water is a vivid, glittering blue.*

The Red Sea between Africa and Saudi Arabia is a spreading rift in Earth's crust that is getting wider every year. In the distant future, it will become a new ocean. The rift extends south through east Africa, and this will probably open up to form a new sea.

## MONSOON WINDS

Over most oceans, the wind blows from the same direction all year round. But in the northern Indian Ocean, the wind blows from the dry northeast in winter, and from the rainy southwest in summer. This seasonal wind change is called a monsoon.

*The mainly tropical Indian Ocean is the warmest of the world's five oceans.*

▲ **THIRD LARGEST OCEAN**
*From South Africa to its eastern boundary on the southern tip of Australia, the Indian Ocean is almost 10,000 km (6,200 miles) wide. To its south, it meets the cold, stormy waters of the Southern Ocean.*

# Pacific Ocean

The Pacific is the biggest, oldest, and deepest ocean, stretching nearly halfway round the world at its widest point. It was once even broader, but is steadily shrinking. It is dotted with volcanic islands and submerged seamounts, and its ocean floor is scarred by deep trenches that include the lowest point on the surface of the planet.

| FACT FILE | |
|---|---|
| Area: | 168,723,000 sq km (65,144,000 sq miles) |
| Average depth: | 3,970 m (13,025 ft) |
| Deepest point: | 10,925 m (35,843 ft) |

▼ GIANT OCEAN
*The Pacific is so vast that it takes two maps to show its full extent. The western side near Asia has far more islands than the eastern side, where there are more of the long cracks in the ocean floor known as fracture zones.*

## CORAL ISLANDS

The tropical western Pacific has thousands of coral-fringed islands. Some of these islands are the rocky summits of extinct oceanic volcanoes, but others are formed of coral sand. Built by living organisms, the coral reefs support all kinds of wildlife, and are the richest of all marine habitats.

◀ HIDDEN TREASURE
*The tropical seas of the western Pacific, such as those around Indonesia, contain a wealth of underwater life among the reef's corals.*

## SUBMERGED SEAMOUNTS

Only a fraction of the volcanoes that have erupted from the ocean floor are visible as islands. Most of them form submerged mountains known as seamounts. Some of these were once volcanic islands that became extinct and sank below sea level. Others are still active and growing. Many are in long chains, including the Emperor Seamount chain that stretches across more than 6,000 km (3,730 miles).

▼ VITAL SUPPLIES
*The ocean currents swirling up and over hidden seamounts carry vital food to the surface, and support marine life such as these manta rays.*

## SHRINKING OCEAN

In some places, the Pacific floor is expanding from spreading rifts that create mid-ocean ridges, such as the East Pacific Rise near South America. Some parts of the ocean floor move faster than others, making the rock crack along the sliding faults of fracture zones. But the earthquake zones around the Pacific are destroying ocean floor faster than it is created, so the ocean is shrinking.

# Southern Ocean

The icy Southern Ocean surrounding Antarctica is the windiest, most dangerous ocean on the planet. It is scattered with towering icebergs that have broken off Antarctica's vast ice sheet and glaciers, and in winter its surface is a sea of tumbled pack ice. Cold water flowing from beneath the ice drives powerful deepwater currents that travel all the way round the world.

## FACT FILE

**Area:** 20,327,000 sq km (7,848,000 sq miles)
**Average depth:** 3,270 m (10,728 ft)
**Deepest point:** 7,434 m (24,390 ft)

## ANTARCTIC ICE SHEET

## HOWLING WINDS

Powerful winds blow from west to east over the Southern Ocean throughout the year because there is no land to slow them down. They get stronger the further south they are, reaching storm force near Antarctica. The direction of the winds helps sailors steer their yachts clockwise around Antarctica during *The Ocean Race* as they make their way around the world.

▲ ICE CLIFFS
*The ice sheet breaks off into dramatic cliffs along the northern coastline of Antarctica.*

Most of Antarctica is covered in a huge ice sheet, stretching across an area of 14 million sq km (5.4 million sq miles), with an average thickness of 2.2 km (1.4 miles). The ice sheet spreads over the sea forming ice shelves that break into icebergs. It holds more than half of the world's fresh water.

▲ OCEAN RACERS
*In* The Ocean Race, *sailors make a 59,264-km-long (36,825-mile-long) journey around the globe.*

## RICH WATERS

The ocean's northern limit is known as the Antarctic Convergence, where very cold water sinks beneath the warmer Pacific, Atlantic, and Indian oceans. This encourages the growth of plankton that feed swarms of shrimplike krill, which are eaten by other animals.

◀ SUMMER VISITORS
*These Arctic terns have flown halfway around the world to feed in the rich Antarctic seas.*

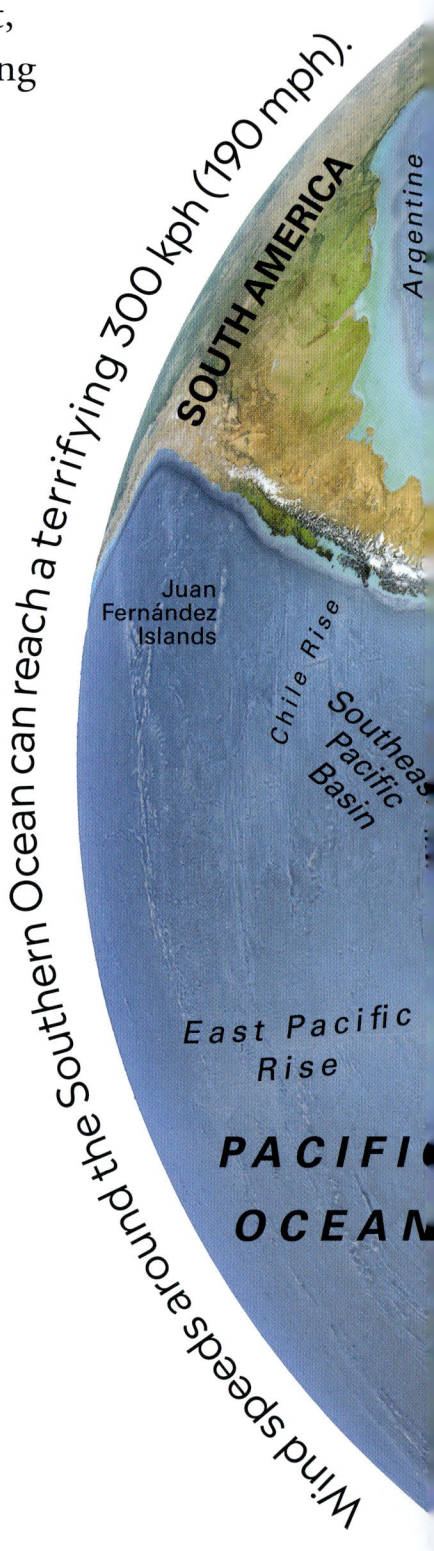

▶ FROZEN OCEAN
*In winter, the Southern Ocean around Antarctica freezes over, creating a vast expanse of pack ice (pale blue). The white dotted line marks the boundary of the ocean at the Antarctic Convergence.*

# BLUE PLANET

Covering most of the globe, the oceans contain 97 per cent of the world's water. They fill vast rocky basins, which continually change shape beneath them.

# Planet ocean

Our planet should be called planet ocean because most of its surface is covered by ocean water. It is the only planet in the solar system that is like this, and the only planet we know about that supports any form of life. This is no coincidence, as water is vital to life. The oceans were probably where life on Earth began.

*This view of Earth shows the Pacific Ocean.*

## BLUE PLANET

If viewed from space, you would see most of Earth's surface covered by water; less than a third of the world's surface is dry land, the rest is covered by oceans. The ocean water has a total volume of 1,330 million cubic km (319 million cubic miles). This is more than a thousand times the volume of land above sea level. Different types of fish and other sea creatures can live anywhere within this mass of water, making it the biggest habitat on Earth.

*If all the oceans were put together, without any land, they would cover a planet two-thirds the Earth's size.*

*If all the land was put together, it would make a planet less than a third of Earth's size.*

## IDEAL DISTANCE

Earth is at just the right distance from the Sun to be warm enough to have oceans of liquid water. If it were nearer, it would be too hot, and the water would evaporate. If it were further away, the water would freeze solid. Our atmosphere also helps by acting like a warm blanket, keeping Earth warmer than the nearby but airless Moon.

*Almost half of all ocean water is found in the Pacific Ocean.*

BLUE PLANET

## WATER OF LIFE
Life depends on liquid water because it can dissolve the chemicals needed to make the proteins and other complex substances that form living things. Seawater in particular contains most of these vital chemicals, and it is likely that life on Earth began in the oceans more than 3.5 billion years ago. The oceans and seas are still ideal habitats for life of all kinds.

**Shoal of striped mackerel**

## GLITTERING VARIETY
The oceans of the world include a huge variety of habitats. They range from icy polar waters to warm coral seas, and from the glittering, sunlit surface to the inky darkness and numbing cold of the ocean depths. The nature of each habitat has shaped the animals that have evolved to live in it, creating an amazing diversity of life.

**Pacific sea nettle**

## FRONTIER ZONE
For centuries, the oceans have been used as trade routes and as a rich source of food and minerals. But they are also incredibly dangerous, and this is one reason why the deep oceans are still largely unexplored. The best maps of the whole seabed only show features bigger than 4.8 km (3 miles) across.

# How oceans formed

An ocean is not just a huge volume of salty water. Its floor is made of a special type of rock that forms in the gaps where Earth's crust has been dragged apart by forces within the planet. This rock is the cool, brittle shell of the deep, hot mantle that lies below. The continents are thicker slabs of lighter rock that float on the mantle like rafts.

### LAYERED EARTH

Earth was formed about 4.6 billion years ago when dust and rocks orbiting the Sun began to clump together. As the planet grew, it attracted iron-rich meteorites, which slammed into Earth, melting on impact. The heat built up until the whole mass of rock and metal melted. The heavier metals, such as iron, then sank towards the centre of the planet to form a hot metallic core surrounded by the thick rocky mantle and cool outer crust.

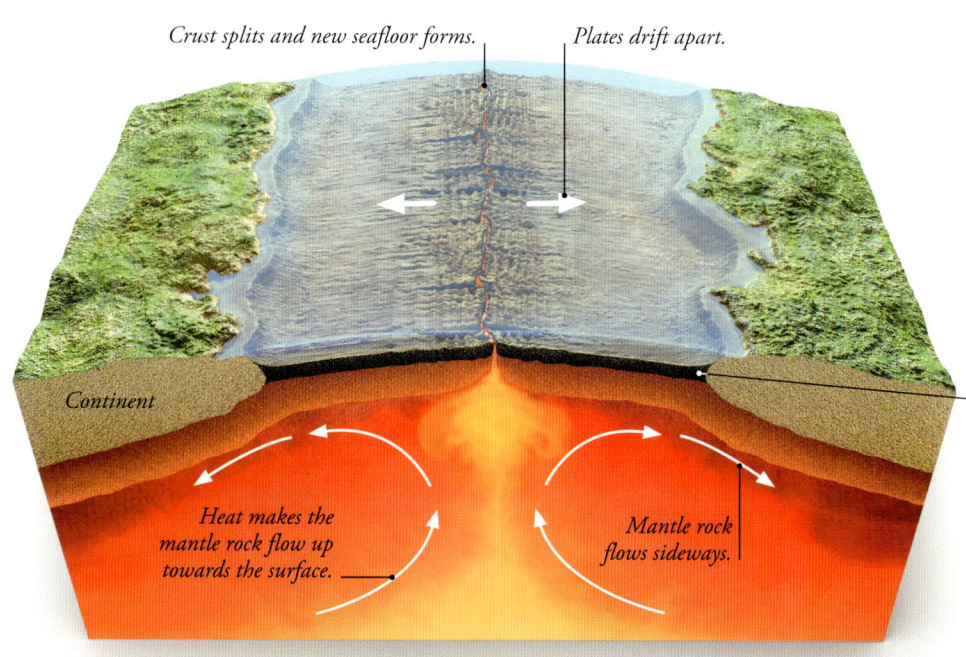

*Crust splits and new seafloor forms.* *Plates drift apart.*
*Continent*
*Heat makes the mantle rock flow up towards the surface.*
*Mantle rock flows sideways.*
*Oceanic crust is dragged sideways, and new crust forms where it splits apart.*

## MOVING PLATES

The breakdown of radioactive elements deep inside the planet keeps the rocky mantle very hot. High pressure stops the rock from melting, but the heat makes it soft enough to flow in currents that rise very slowly, flow sideways near the surface, then sink. As the mantle rock flows sideways, it drags the brittle crust with it. This breaks the crust into many separate, moving plates, which carry the continents. New ocean floor forms where these plates are pulling apart.

## FLOATING ROCK

The mantle is made of a very heavy rock called peridotite. A slightly lighter rock called basalt forms the oceanic crust – the bedrock of the ocean floors. The continents are made of granite and similar rocks, which are even lighter than basalt. This enables the continents to float on the heavy mantle, like ice on water, and is one reason why the continents rise above the ocean floors.

**Peridotite**

**Granite**
**Basalt**

## WATER VAPOUR

Most of the water on the planet probably erupted from huge volcanoes early in Earth's history. Volcanoes still produce a lot of water vapour, as well as other gases. A similar mixture would have formed Earth's first atmosphere. The water vapour turned into clouds that spilled torrential rain on the bare rocky surface of Earth's crust, flooding it to form the first oceans.

BLUE PLANET

**FACT**
Some ocean water may have arrived on Earth in the form of icy comets that melted as they plunged through the planet's atmosphere.

## THE GLOBAL OCEAN

Four billion years ago, there were no continents, and Earth had only a thin crust of the basalt that now forms the ocean floors. So, the first ocean probably covered the whole planet. Over time, volcanoes created the lighter rocks that formed the first continents. As these land masses grew, the water flowed into the low-lying basins between them to fill deep oceans such as those we see today.

# NEW LAND

Molten rock spills into the Pacific Ocean on the shores of Hawai'i, US – a volcanic island that has erupted from the ocean floor. Islands such as this were the first land masses to appear above the waves of the global ocean; over millions of years, they grew and merged together to form the first continents.

# Ocean floor

The ocean floors are not just flat and featureless. The deep blue water of the oceans conceals a hidden landscape of shallow coastal seabeds, rocky reefs, vast muddy plains, incredibly deep chasms, and colossal volcanoes. Long ridges of high mountains stretch for many thousands of kilometres across the ocean floors, forming the longest mountain ranges on the planet. Until very recently, we had no idea that many of these features existed, or why they were there.

**FACT**
There are ocean trenches that are deep enough to swallow some of the highest mountains on Earth.

## UNDERWATER WORLD

As methods of measuring depth have improved, scientists have been able to detect more features of the ocean floor. This section through a typical ocean shows the most important features, together with images that were gathered using the most advanced technology. Colour-coded for depth, they reveal a hidden world beneath the waves.

▲ CONTINENTAL SHELF
*The shallow regions at the fringes of oceans are the continental shelves. At the edge of the shelf, the continental slope descends to the deep ocean floor. This image shows the shallow shelf in red, and the ocean floor in blue.*

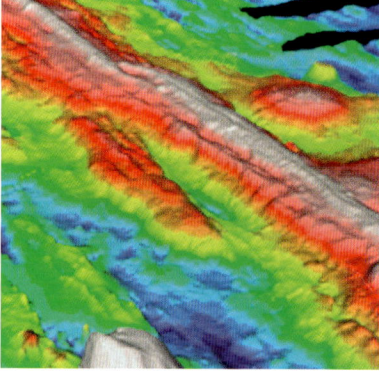

▲ OCEAN RIDGE
*Made using echo-sounding technology, this image shows part of the long ridges (red) that snake across the ocean floors. Forming a network that extends around the globe, these ridges can be up to 3,000 m (9,800 ft) high.*

*Continent, fringed by the shallow continental shelf*

*Submerged seamount*

▲ SOFT SEDIMENTS
*Vast areas of the deep ocean floors are covered with thick layers of soft mud and ooze, forming flat abyssal plains. Some of these soft sediments are the remains of tiny sea life. Others are made of rock particles blown over the ocean by desert storms, such as this Saharan dust storm seen from space.*

## SEEING THE OCEAN FLOOR

The first complete map of the ocean floor was created in the mid-20th century by American geologists Marie Tharp and Bruce Heezen, using simple depth measurements gathered from all over the world. As the map took shape, it revealed a pattern of ocean-floor features that were unknown to science. It inspired both its makers and other scientists to discover more about how these features had been formed.

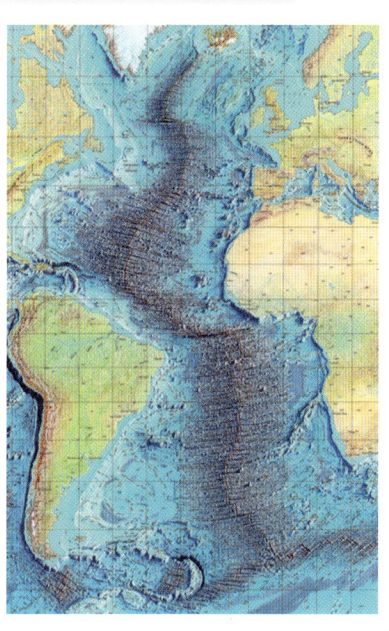

▶ HEEZEN-THARP MAP
*This graphic representation of the Mid-Atlantic Ridge on the Atlantic Ocean floor is part of the map that astounded the world.*

BLUE PLANET

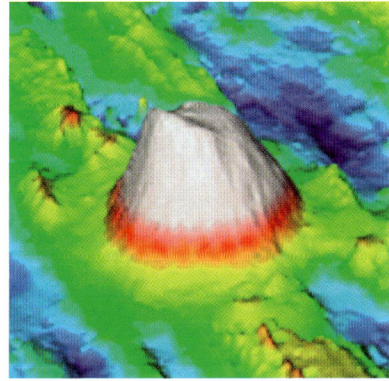

▲ SEAMOUNT
*The ocean floors are peppered with underwater mountains known as seamounts. These are nearly all extinct oceanic volcanoes, though some are still erupting. There are thousands of them in the Pacific.*

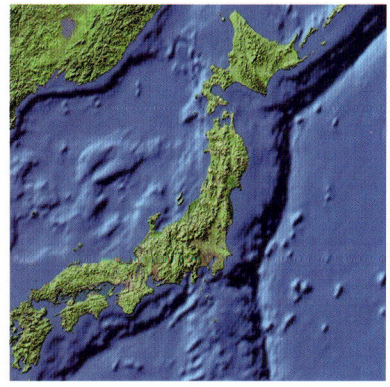

▲ OCEAN TRENCH
*Most ocean trenches lie on the fringes of the Pacific and in the northeast Indian Ocean. Some are more than twice as deep as the average ocean. This satellite image shows the deep trenches (dark blue) off Japan.*

*Volcanic island*

*Magma beneath an active volcano*

# Mid-ocean ridges

The rock beneath Earth's crust is as hot as molten volcanic lava, but it is kept solid by intense pressure. When plates of ocean crust are pulled apart, rifts open up and reduce the pressure, allowing the hot rock to melt and shoot up through the rift. This creates chains of volcanoes that form long ridges of submarine mountains. These mid-ocean ridges are among the largest geological features on the planet.

### PILLOW LAVA

The rock that erupts through cracks in the ocean floor is molten basalt, like the lava that erupts from volcanoes in Hawai'i. When it hits the cold water, it turns solid on the outside, but the molten rock keeps bursting out through the hard shell to form cushion-shaped mounds called pillow lava.

### ▼ RIDGES AND VALLEY
*This cross section through a mid-ocean ridge shows how a rift in the ocean floor creates a valley with underwater mountains on each side of it.*

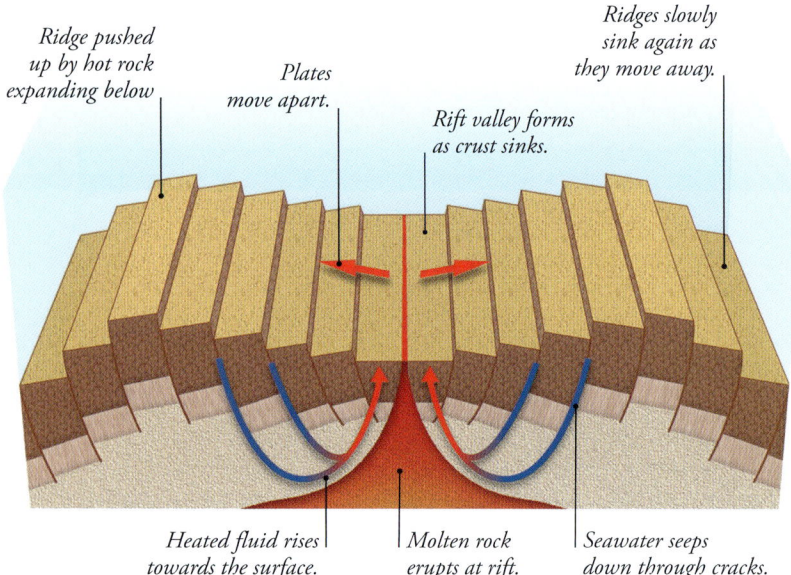

*Ridge pushed up by hot rock expanding below*

*Plates move apart.*

*Ridges slowly sink again as they move away.*

*Rift valley forms as crust sinks.*

*Heated fluid rises towards the surface.*

*Molten rock erupts at rift.*

*Seawater seeps down through cracks.*

### RIFT ZONE
Where plates of oceanic crust are being dragged apart by convection currents in the hot mantle rock below, the ocean floor sinks to form a rift valley. The base of the valley is full of cracks that allow molten rock to erupt and form new ocean floor. Meanwhile, the heat raises blocks of ocean crust on each side of the rift valley to form a double ridge.

### BLACK SMOKERS
Ocean water seeping into the rift zone is heated by contact with the hot rock, but high pressure stops it from boiling. It gets hotter and hotter, reaching up to 400°C (750°F) – four times higher than its normal boiling point. The very hot water dissolves chemicals in the rock, and eventually this chemical-rich fluid is forced back up into the ocean. When it hits the cold ocean water, the chemicals form dark particles that look like smoke billowing from the rift, so these plumes are known as black smokers.

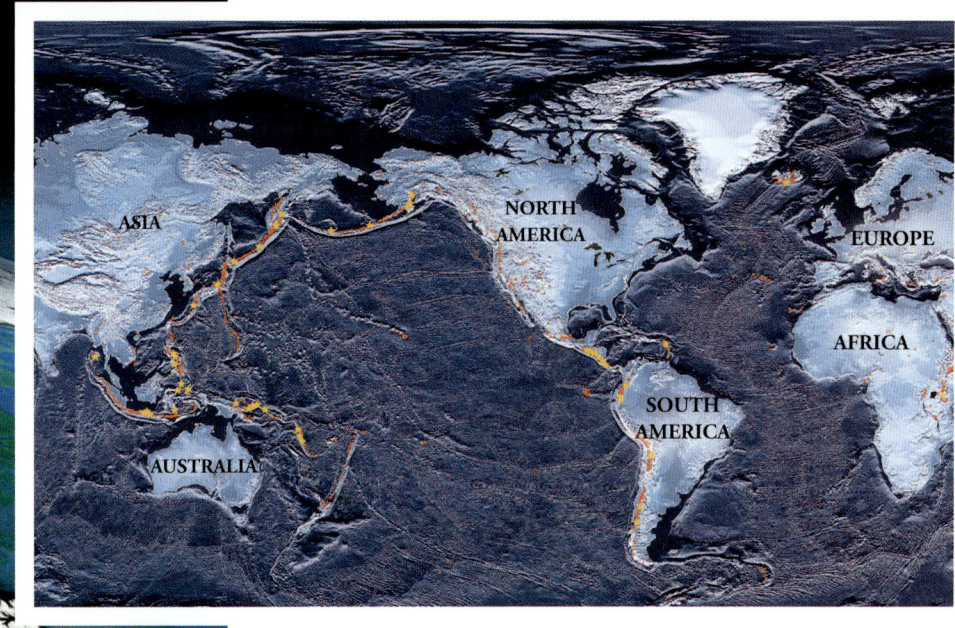

KEY  Most active volcanoes  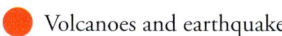 Volcanoes and earthquakes

### RING OF FIRE

Most of the planet's subduction zones lie on the edges of the giant Pacific Ocean. They have created a ring of deep ocean trenches around the Pacific, fringed by a chain of more than 450 volcanoes – the Pacific Ring of Fire. The relentless movement of the plates is gradually destroying the fringes of the ocean floor, shrinking the Pacific Ocean by 0.5 sq km (0.2 sq mile) a year. It also triggers up to 90 per cent of the world's earthquakes.

### DANGER ZONES

The subduction zones, where one plate of Earth's crust is grinding beneath another, are notorious for causing earthquakes. Japan lies in one of these regions. As a result, it suffers more than a thousand earth tremors each year, and every few years a really big earthquake causes massive destruction and loss of life.

# Evolving oceans

### CREATION AND DESTRUCTION
New ocean floor is created in the spreading rifts of mid-ocean ridges and eventually destroyed in the subduction zones beneath ocean trenches. These changes happen at different rates in each of the world's oceans, which are constantly growing and shrinking in size.

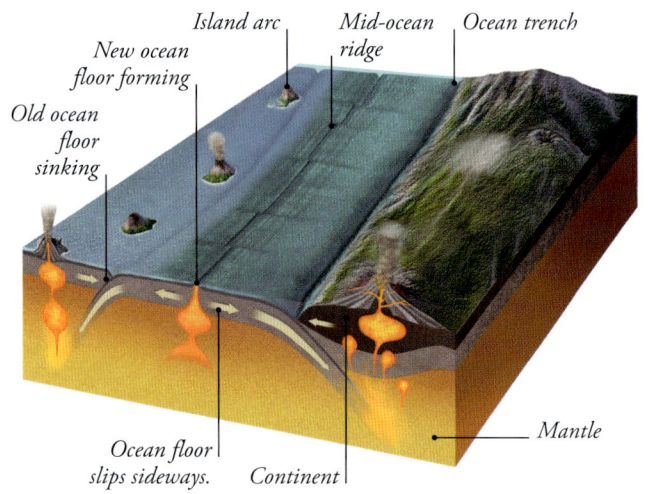

▲ **CONTINUOUS PROCESS**
*This illustration shows how the ocean floor forms at the mid-ocean ridge, moves away from the ridge, and eventually sinks back into the hot mantle beneath Earth's crust.*

As fast as new ocean floor is created in some parts of the world, old ocean floor is destroyed in others. The two processes balance out, so the planet does not get any bigger or smaller. But this does mean that some oceans are expanding while others are shrinking. Over many millions of years, these movements shift the continents around the globe, pulling them apart to create new oceans, and pushing them together to squeeze older oceans out of existence.

### SEAS OF CHANGE
Over hundreds of millions of years, the Pacific Ocean has been shrinking, because its ocean floor is being destroyed in subduction zones all around the Pacific Ring of Fire. Meanwhile, the Atlantic Ocean has very few subduction zones, and has been steadily growing.

### CONTINENTAL DRIFT
As oceans expand and contract, they push continents apart or draw them together. Over the 4.5 billion years of Earth's existence, this has changed the map of the world many times. Until about 100 million years ago, the continents would have been unrecognizable. It was only towards the end of the Mesozoic age of dinosaurs, about 66 million years ago, that the world as we know it began to form.

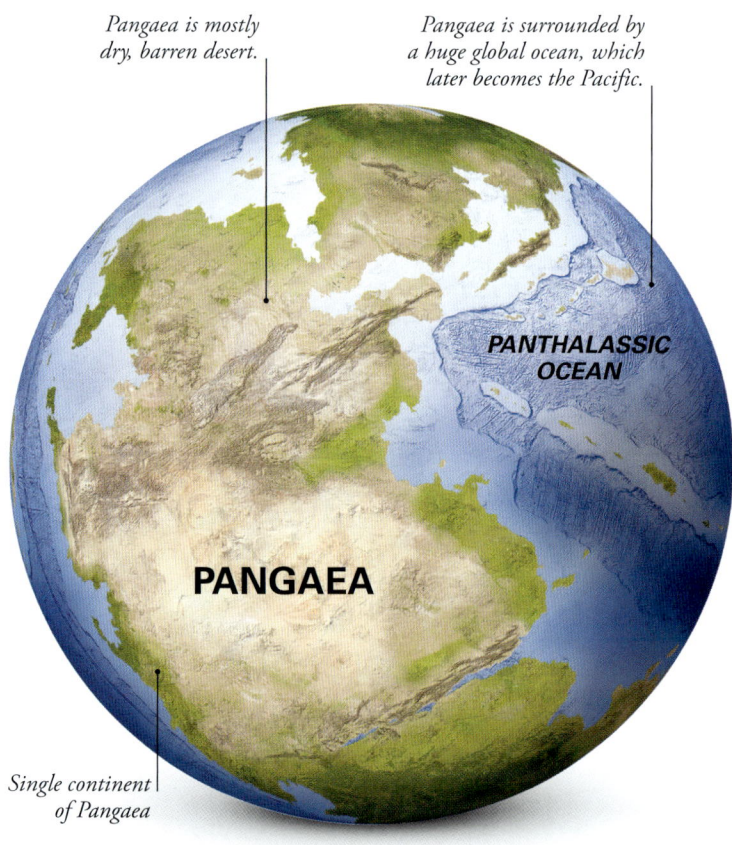

▲ **250 MILLION YEARS AGO**
*At the beginning of the age of dinosaurs, 250 million years ago, all the land had been pushed together into a vast supercontinent.*

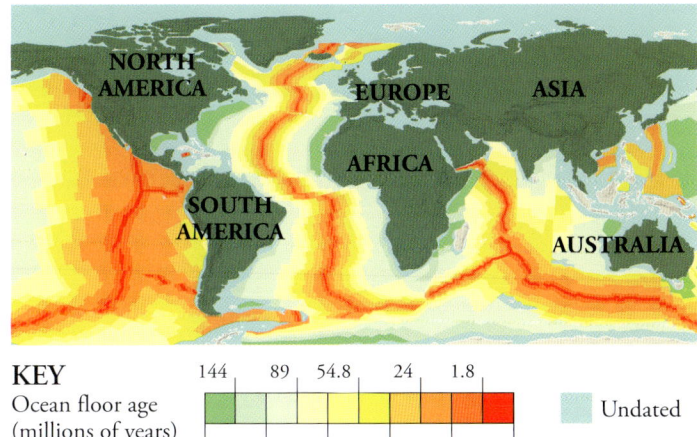

**KEY**
Ocean floor age (millions of years)

144 | 89 | 54.8 | 24 | 1.8
154 | 127 | 65 | 33.5 | 5 | 0

Undated

## RECYCLED ROCK

Scientists have sampled the rocks of the ocean floors and measured their age. The data shows that the youngest rocks are at the mid-ocean ridges (shaded in red), and that they get older the further they are from the ridge. This proves that the rocks are forming at the ridges and gradually moving away from them. Some of the oldest ocean-floor rocks are being dragged into the subduction zones beneath deep ocean trenches, where they are melted and recycled.

### EARTHQUAKE ZONES

The relentless movements of Earth's crust that reshape oceans and move continents also trigger countless earthquakes. Many are felt on land, and sometimes have catastrophic effects. But many more occur beneath the oceans, in the regions where ocean floors are being created at mid-ocean ridges, or destroyed in subduction zones. As a result, the locations of these earthquakes form lines that follow the network of ocean-floor ridges and trenches.

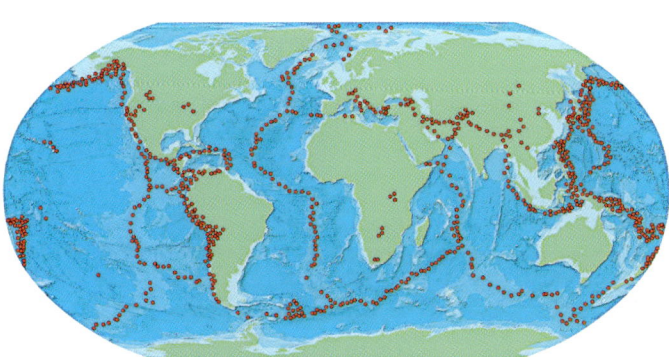

▲ **TREMBLING EARTH**
*The red dots on this map mark the sites of all the earthquakes detected over the last 50 years. The mid-ocean earthquakes form a pattern that matches that of the youngest ocean-floor rocks.*

BLUE PLANET

▲ **180 MILLION YEARS AGO**
*During the Jurassic Period, the supercontinent split in two, and the outline of North America began to appear.*

▲ **66 MILLION YEARS AGO**
*By the end of the age of dinosaurs, the Atlantic Ocean had opened up, pushing the Americas away from Europe and Africa.*

# Tsunamis

Every few years, a big earthquake on the ocean floor causes a massive rock movement that is transferred to the water and generates giant waves, known as tsunamis. Out on the open ocean the waves are broad and low, covering a huge area. But when a tsunami reaches shallower water, the wave piles up like an extra-high tide that surges ashore and floods the land in just a few minutes. These waves are incredibly destructive and deadly.

## WHY TSUNAMIS HAPPEN

The biggest recent tsunamis have occurred in places where one plate of ocean floor is slipping beneath another, as shown below. The plates became locked together, then suddenly gave way, triggering oceanic earthquakes. But tsunamis can also be caused by volcanic eruptions, coastal landslides, and even collapsing ice shelves.

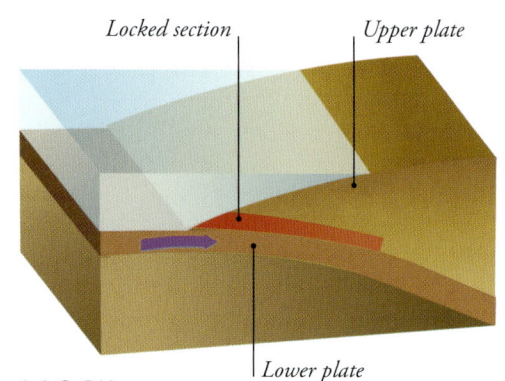

▲ 1. LOCK
*As the lower plate pushes beneath the upper one, the sliding rocks become locked at the plate boundary.*

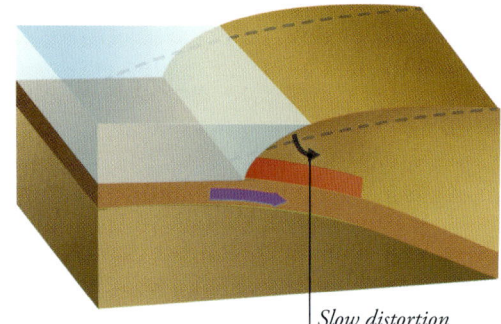

▲ 2. DISTORT
*Eventually, the moving lower plate bends the edge of the upper plate downwards.*

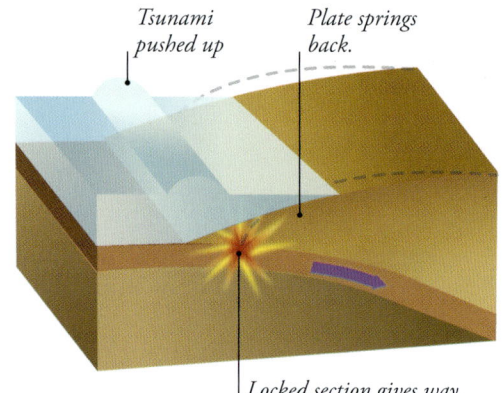

▲ 3. SNAP
*When the tension makes the rocks give way, the edge of the top plate springs upwards, pushing the water up into a giant heap.*

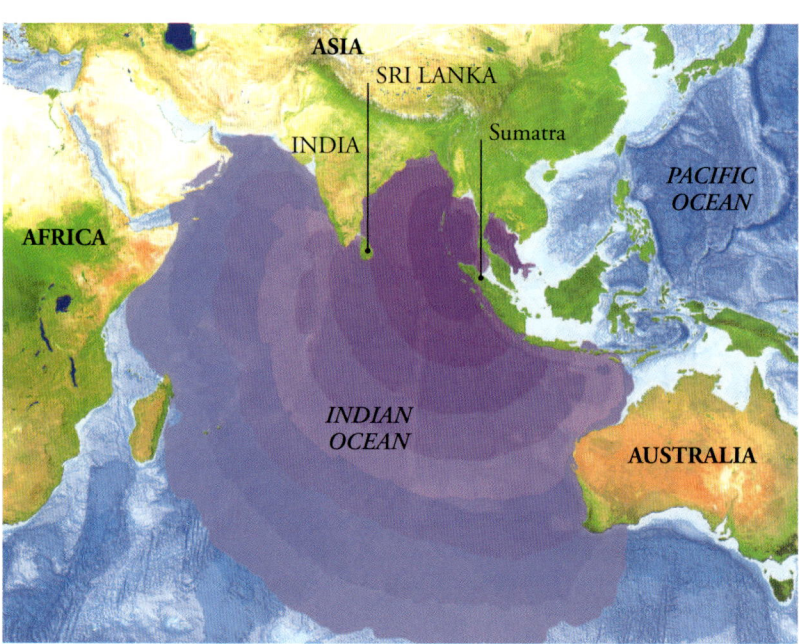

### RACING WAVES
Tsunami waves race across the ocean at incredibly high speeds. In December 2004, an earthquake off the northern tip of Sumatra caused a catastrophic tsunami that travelled outwards across the Indian Ocean. It struck India and Sri Lanka just two hours later. This means that it travelled at about 800 kph (500 mph).

▲ 2004 TSUNAMI WAVES
*Each colour band on this map of the Indian Ocean shows the distance the tsunami waves travelled in one hour. The waves even reached the coast of Antarctica, although they were only about a metre (3 ft) high by the time they got there.*

**FACT**
The 2011 Japanese tsunami raised the sea level by 40.5 m (133 ft) at Miyako in northeast Japan, and sent waves 10 km (6 miles) inland.

## LANDFALL
When a tsunami reaches shallower water, the length of its wave shortens and the height steepens. This creates a very high but broad wave peak and an equally deep trough. The trough usually reaches the coast first, making the sea draw back like a very low tide. But this is soon followed by the tsunami peak, which surges ashore and floods the landscape.

▲ **TSUNAMI SURGE**
*The relentlessly rising water of the 2011 Japanese tsunami surges over the sea wall at Miyako.*

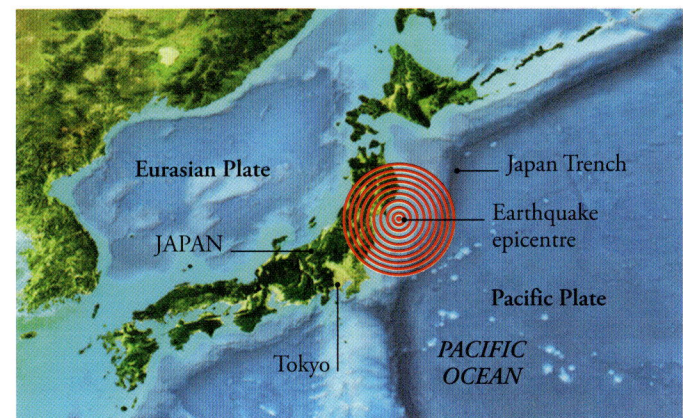

## POWERFUL EARTHQUAKE
During the earthquake that caused the 2011 Japanese tsunami, the Pacific floor slipped west into the Japan Trench by more than 20 m (66 ft). Meanwhile, the main island of Japan shifted eastwards by 2.4 m (8 ft). A long stretch of its eastern coast sank by 60 cm (2 ft), and this allowed the tsunami waves to flood even more of the land. Some of the debris that was swept out to sea drifted across the Pacific Ocean as far as the US.

## DISASTER ZONE
As the tsunami rushes over the land, the water behaves like a giant liquid bulldozer, destroying everything in its path. The moving water becomes thick with floating debris, including sea-going ships that often end up stranded in the middle of wrecked coastal cities.

# Hotspots

In some parts of the world, plates of oceanic crust are moving slowly over extra-hot parts of the mantle called hotspots. Each hotspot creates a volcano in the moving crust. Once the volcano moves off the hotspot, it becomes extinct, and a new volcano erupts in its place. Over millions of years, this process creates a chain of islands.

## Hawai'i
*Longest island chain*

**Location** Central Pacific
**Highest point** 4,205 m (13,796 ft)
**Last eruption** Constant activity

The Hawai'ian islands were formed by a hotspot in the middle of the Pacific plate, which is moving northwest over the hotspot at the rate of 9 cm (3.5 in) a year. For more than 80 million years, the heat has been making volcanoes erupt through the moving plate. This has formed a chain of islands and submerged seamounts stretching about 6,000 km (3,700 miles) across the Pacific Ocean.

▶ **FIRE FOUNTAIN**
*The Hawai'ian hotspot now lies beneath the most southerly island of Hawai'i, where the most active volcano on Earth, Kīlauea, has been erupting almost continuously since 1983.*

## Iceland
*Spreading rift*

**Location** North Atlantic
**Highest point** 2,110 m (6,923 ft)
**Last eruption** Constant activity

Iceland is a vast mass of basalt lava that has erupted from a hotspot lying below the Mid-Atlantic Ridge. The plates of the crust are moving apart beneath the island, causing the eruption of many volcanoes and geysers. But since the hotspot is not under a moving plate, it has not created an island chain.

## Réunion
*Tropical hotspot*

**Location** Western Indian Ocean
**Highest point** 3,070 m (10,072 ft)
**Last eruption** Constant activity

Réunion is at the southern end of a short chain of volcanic islands in the Indian Ocean that also include Mauritius. The chain extends further north underwater, and underlies the coral islands of the Maldives. The hotspot now lies under the southeast corner of Réunion, causing the regular eruption of the Piton de la Fournaise volcano.

---

### VOLCANIC CHAINS

A hotspot beneath the crust heats the rock so that it expands and rises. Some rock melts and erupts as basalt lava, forming a volcanic island. When plate movement carries the volcano off the hotspot, it stops erupting. As the rock beneath it cools and contracts, the island sinks and eventually becomes a submerged seamount. Some hotspots have created hundreds of volcanic islands and seamounts.

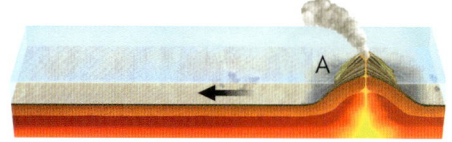

▲ **1. ERUPTION**
*A stationary hotspot melts a hole through the Earth's moving crust, creating a volcano (A), which erupts and forms an island.*

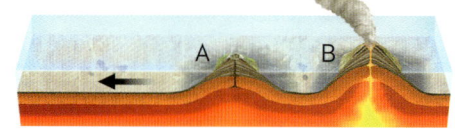

▲ **2. EXTINCTION**
*Over millions of years, the island moves off the hotspot and starts sinking, while a new volcano (B) erupts.*

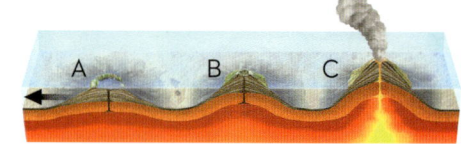

▲ **3. SUBSIDENCE**
*As the first island in the chain sinks below the waves, the second moves off the hotspot, and a third volcano (C) erupts.*

## Ascension Island
*Young volcanoes*

**Location** South Atlantic
**Highest point** 859 m (2,818 ft)
**Last eruption** 500 years ago

Ascension Island is a hotspot island near the Mid-Atlantic Ridge between Brazil and West Africa. It began forming around six million years ago – young by geological standards – and is not part of a hotspot chain, although it may be in the future. Its surface is peppered with volcanic craters such as the one shown here, but its volcanoes are dormant.

## Easter Island (Rapa Nui)
*Triple peak*

**Location** Southeast Pacific
**Highest point** 507 m (1,663 ft)
**Last eruption** 10,000 years ago

Formed from three volcanoes that have become joined together, Easter Island (Rapa Nui) lies at the western end of a chain of seamounts extending 4,000 km (2,485 miles) east to South America. The chain was created by the ocean floor slipping west over a hotspot near Easter Island, but the volcanoes on the island itself are now extinct.

BLUE PLANET

## Galápagos
*Mobile islands*

**Location** East Pacific
**Highest point** 1,707 m (5,600 ft)
**Last eruption** 2024

Lying on the equator off the Pacific coast of South America, the Galápagos are a group of 21 volcanic islands and many smaller islets that have formed over a hotspot on the Pacific ocean floor. They are being carried east off the hotspot at the rate of 6.4 cm (2.5 in) a year, and the oldest, most easterly volcanoes are now extinct and sinking. The youngest volcanoes on Fernandina and Isabela islands are still active, creating barren landscapes of dark basalt lava. The islands are also famous for their unique wildlife.

▲ **STONE STATUES**
*Easter Island (Rapa Nui) is famous for its many huge statues, carved centuries ago from rock cut from the slopes of one of its volcanoes.*

▼ **FLOODED CRATER**
*The small islet of Rocas Bainbridge off the east coast of San Salvador island is the tip of a submerged volcanic cone.*

## LAVA FLOW
The lava that erupts from a hotspot volcano is molten basalt, with a temperature of more than 1,000°C (1,800°F). It flows fast, pouring down the flanks of the volcano like a river. As it cools, a crust of black basalt forms, but molten rock often bursts through it, as shown here on the slopes of Kīlauea in Hawai'i, US.

# Continental shelves

**FACT** The widest continental shelf extends 1,210 km (752 miles) north of Siberia into the Arctic Ocean.

The oceans are fringed by coastal seas that are much shallower than the open oceans. This is because the seabed here is not the deep ocean floor, but the flooded edge of a continent. The edge is cut away at sea level by wave erosion, creating a shallow seabed of continental rock. This is the continental shelf. At its outer edge it falls away as the continental slope, which descends to the ocean floor.

## COASTAL EROSION

The edges of continents are eaten away by the sea waves in a relentless process that turns solid rock into the shingle and sand that form beaches. This coastal erosion creates the shallow seabed of the continental shelf. It is made of the same solid bedrock as the land, covered with sedimentary rock.

## SHELF, SLOPE, AND RISE

On average, the continental shelf extends about 80 km (50 miles) from the coast. The outside edge is called the shelf break, and beyond this, the gradient falls away as the continental slope. At the foot of the slope, a layer of rocky debris called the continental rise hides the transition from continental rock to the basalt of the true ocean floor.

## SHALLOW SEABED

The seabed of the continental shelf has an average depth of 150 m (492 ft). It has a very shallow gradient, and is mostly covered with soft sand and mud. A lot of this is the result of coastal erosion, but some of the sand and mud is swept into the sea by rivers. It is mixed with the remains of microscopic marine plankton.

## MUDFLOWS AND CANYONS

Vast amounts of sand, silt, and mud are carried off the land by big rivers and swept onto the seabed. These sediments pour off the continental shelf in powerful flows called turbidity currents, carving canyons in the continental slope. Some of these canyons can be more than 4,000 m (13,123 ft) deep.

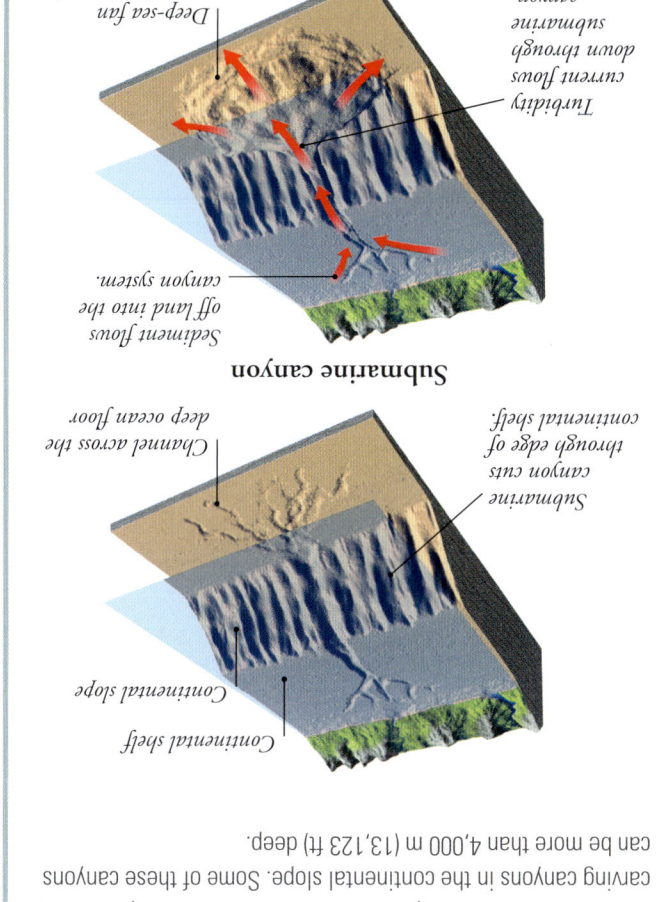

Submarine canyon
- Continental shelf
- Continental slope
- Submarine canyon cuts through edge of continental shelf
- Channel across the deep ocean floor

Turbidity current
- Sediment flows off land into the canyon system.
- Turbidity current flows down through submarine canyon.
- Deep-sea fan created at base of continental slope.

## REEFS AND SANDBANKS

The seabed is dotted with rocky reefs, and, in places, the currents create shallow banks of sand and gravel. These hidden shallows have always been hazards for ships, especially in the days before there were accurate ways of measuring ocean depth. As a result, the seabed of the continental shelf is littered with shipwrecks.

# Changing sea levels

Throughout Earth's history, global sea levels have always been rising and falling, often because of climate change. In many places, the seabed itself has risen, or the land has sunk beneath the waves. As a result, seabed rocks that contain fossil fish and seashells are now found on land, and some regions that were once land are now shallow seas.

## ANCIENT OCEANS

We know that many rocks once lay beneath the sea because they contain fossil seashells and fish skeletons. Such fossils have even been found in limestone rocks at the top of Mount Everest, more than 8,600 m (28,215 ft) above sea level. The fossils show that the rocks were formed on the bed of a shallow tropical sea more than 400 million years ago.

► FOSSILIZED AMMONITES
These shells are the remains of sea creatures related to living squid. They are often found in rocks on land.

## SINKING SEAS

During the last ice age, which ended about 10,000 years ago, so much rainwater turned into snow and ice that global sea levels fell by about 120 m (394 ft). This exposed vast areas of the continental shelves, which became home to people and land animals such as mammoths. Today, their remains lie under the sea.

◄ MAMMOTH TOOTH
Fossils of mammoth teeth have been found by fishers off the Atlantic coast.

► DRY LAND
The red dotted lines mark the Atlantic coastlines of ice-age America 22,000 years ago, when mammoths roamed on what is now the continental shelf. The pale blue areas are now shallow seas.

## RISING ROCKS

Many of the rocks that now form much of the land were once soft sediments such as sand and mud, which were laid down on the seabed. They have been turned into rocks — sandstone, shale, and limestone. In places such as the Grand Canyon, US, you can see many layers of these rocks, all raised high above sea level by the forces that build mountains. Long ago they were under the sea.

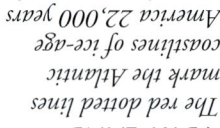

◄ GRAND CANYON
Rock layers revealed in the wall of the Grand Canyon, Arizona, US.

# BLUE PLANET

## FLOODED VALLEYS

As the ice age ended and the ice sheets melted, all the meltwater flowed into the sea, raising global sea levels. By 6,000 years ago, seas had reached the same level as today, drowning many landscapes that had formed during the ice age. For example, deep valleys that had once contained icy glaciers were flooded to create steep-sided fjords.

▲ GEIRANGERFJORD
During the ice age, this flooded fjord on the coast of Norway lay high above sea level.

### FACT
Until 6,000 years ago, stone age hunter-gatherers roamed a huge area in northwest Europe known as Doggerland – which now lies 15–30 m (50–100 ft) underwater in the North Sea.

## BOUNCING BACK

During the last ice age, when many parts of the northern continents were covered by thick ice, the weight of ice pressed down on the Earth's crust, pushing aside the softer mantle rock below. When the ice melted, the crust started rising, but slowly. As a result, shores that were once beaches are now high above sea level, and are still rising.

Ice weighs down the land
- Heavy ice sheet
- Hot, soft mantle rock pushed aside

Ice melts and land rises
- Crust slowly rises.
- Mantle rock flows back.

# Ocean water

What is water? We are so used to it that we don't give it much thought, but water is a remarkable substance with some unique properties. It is also vital to life, and seawater especially contains most of the chemicals that living things need to grow and multiply.

## WATER MOLECULE

Water is also known as $H_2O$. This describes a single molecule of water, which consists of two atoms of hydrogen (H) bonded to one atom of oxygen (O). Electrostatic bonds make the water molecules cling to each other to form a liquid. These molecules are tiny; in one drop of water, there are more than one billion molecules.

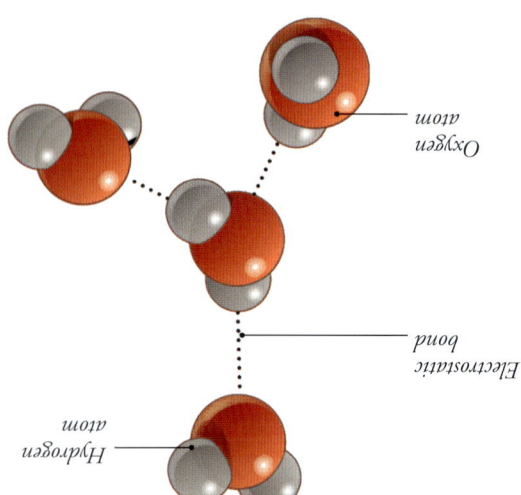

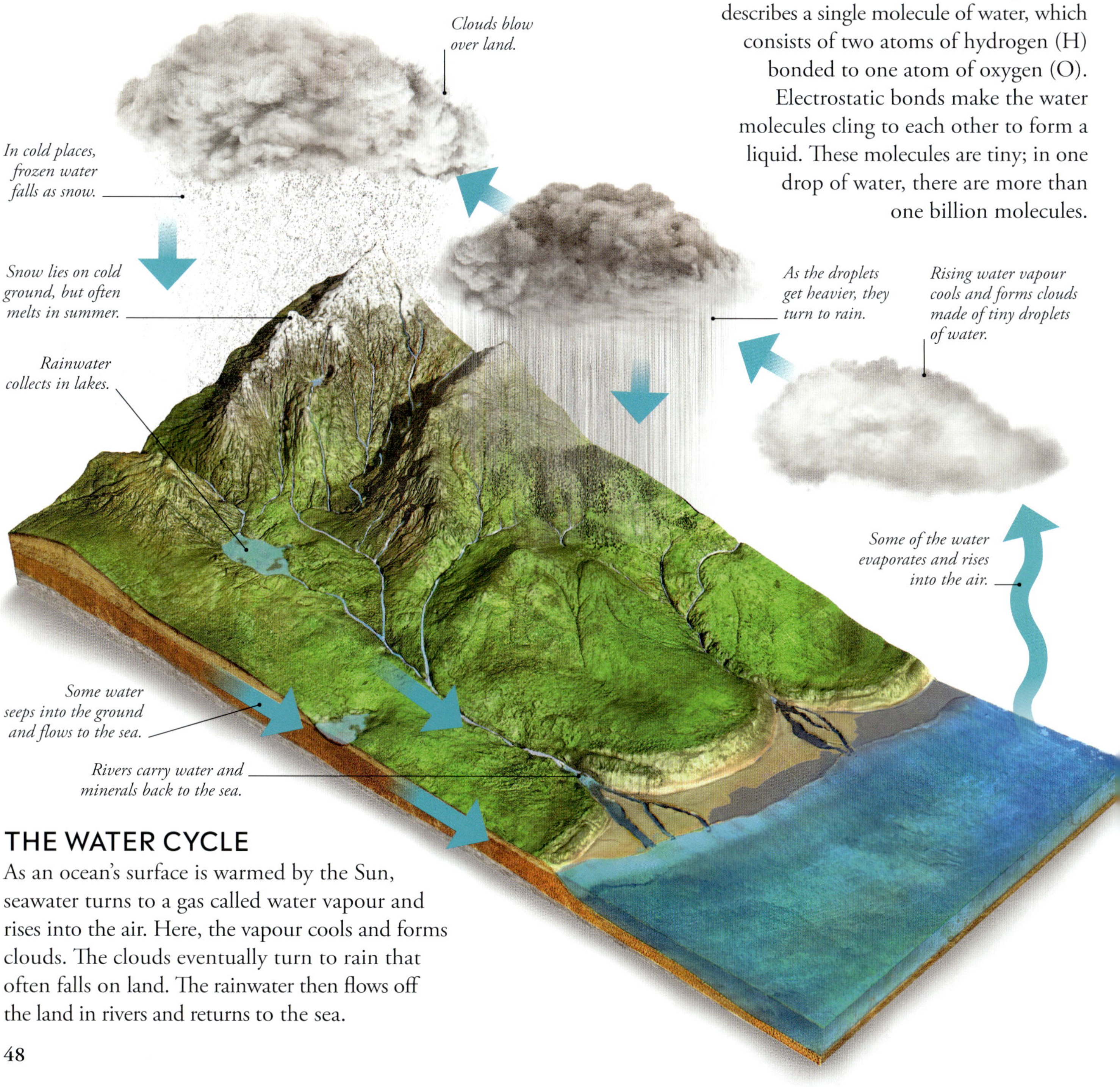

*Hydrogen atom*

*Electrostatic bond*

*Oxygen atom*

## THE WATER CYCLE

As an ocean's surface is warmed by the Sun, seawater turns to a gas called water vapour and rises into the air. Here, the vapour cools and forms clouds. The clouds eventually turn to rain that often falls on land. The rainwater then flows off the land in rivers and returns to the sea.

*Rivers carry water and minerals back to the sea.*

*Some water seeps into the ground and flows to the sea.*

*Some of the water evaporates and rises into the air.*

*Rising water vapour cools and forms clouds made of tiny droplets of water.*

*As the droplets get heavier, they turn to rain.*

*Rainwater collects in lakes.*

*Snow lies on cold ground, but often melts in summer.*

*In cold places, frozen water falls as snow.*

*Clouds blow over land.*

**BLUE PLANET**

48

## CHEMISTRY OF LIFE

As well as the minerals that make it salty, ocean water also contains other dissolved substances, including carbon, oxygen, nitrogen, phosphorus, calcium, and iron. These are essential ingredients of complex molecules such as proteins, which are vital to life in all its forms. This makes ocean water an ideal habitat — fossil evidence suggests that the first life on Earth developed in the oceans. The seas and oceans are still teeming with an incredible array of animals.

## SALTY SEAS

Water is very good at dissolving substances, such as the minerals that form rocks. Water flowing off the land in rivers picks up many of these dissolved minerals, known as salts, from the rocks as well as particles of sand and mud made from rock fragments. They are carried down to the sea, where they have built up over billions of years. Most of the salt is sodium chloride, which is the same as table salt. This is why seawater tastes salty.

▶ SALTY LAKES
*In hot regions, water flowing off the land can evaporate to leave salt crystals such as these on the edge of a salty lake. In oceans the salt is dissolved and invisible.*

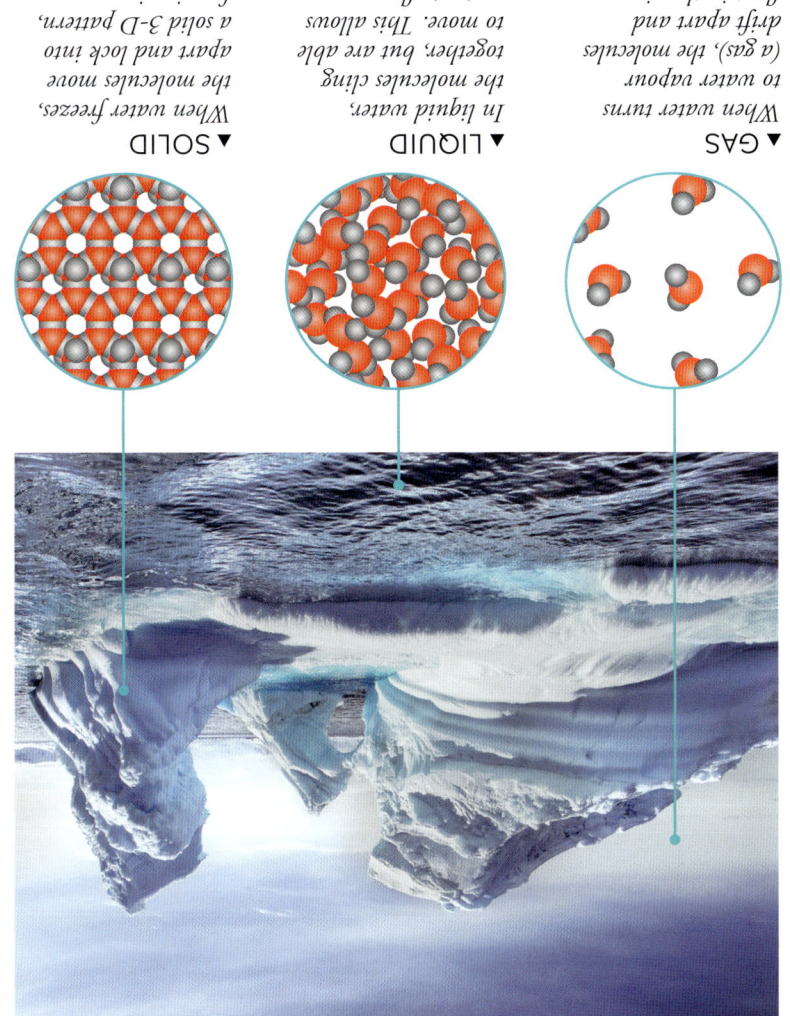

▶ GAS
*When water turns to water vapour (a gas), the molecules drift apart and float in the air.*

▶ LIQUID
*In liquid water, the molecules cling together, but are able to move. This allows water to flow.*

▶ SOLID
*When water freezes, the molecules move apart and lock into a solid 3-D pattern, forming ice.*

## SOLID, LIQUID, AND GAS

At very low temperatures, water molecules lock together to form solid ice. At higher temperatures, the molecules come unstuck so they drift apart to form water vapour. Ice floats because water molecules pack together less tightly than in liquid water, making ice less dense.

BLUE PLANET

# Light, heat, and sound

Water absorbs light and heat. This means that neither can penetrate far into the ocean depths – unlike sound, which travels well through water. Ocean water is also slow to warm up and cool down. This has a big effect on the climates of nearby shores, and it also allows ocean currents to carry heat to other parts of the globe.

## BLUE WATER

Even shallow seawater looks blue or blue-green. This is because the water absorbs all the other colours from the sunlight. Red light is absorbed first, followed by yellow, green, and violet. Blue light is reflected back, so this is the colour we see. The colour of the water may change depending on the particles in it.

▲ NATURAL LIGHT
*This photo of a coral reef shows it lit by natural blue-green underwater light.*

▲ FLASH LIGHT
*The pure white light of a camera flash reveals the true colours of the coral reef.*

## OCEAN TEMPERATURES

The Sun shines straight down on the equator, warming the surface waters of tropical oceans to temperatures of up to 30°C (86°F). But in the polar regions, the Sun is lower in the sky and less powerful, even in summer. In winter there is so little warm sunlight that the seas freeze over. But warm currents flowing towards the poles stop the sea getting even colder, and cold currents flowing away from polar seas help to cool the tropics.

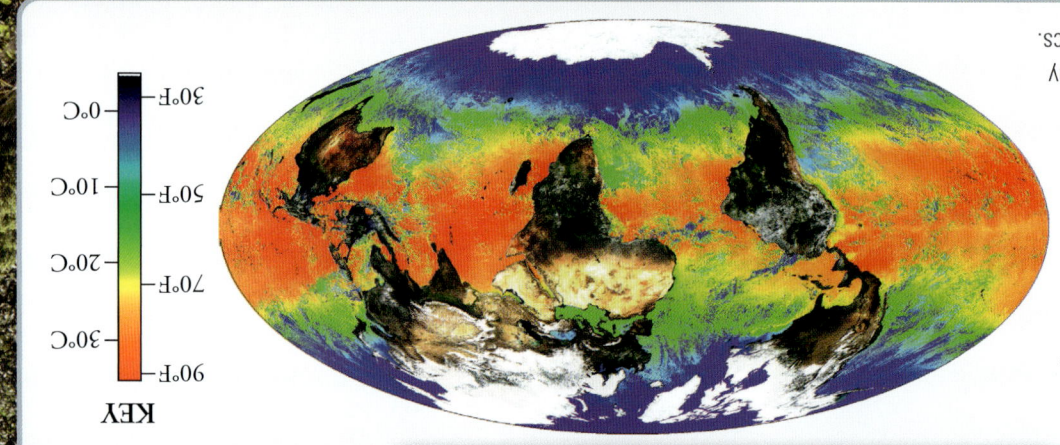

KEY
- 0°C / 30°F
- 10°C / 50°F
- 20°C / 70°F
- 30°C / 90°F

# BLUE PLANET

## OCEANS AND CONTINENTS

Ocean water never gets as hot or cold as the land, because it gains and loses heat so slowly. This affects the climate on islands and coastal regions, making it milder than the climate at the heart of a continent. So in summer, people living on an island never get as hot as people living in the middle of a nearby continent, nor do they get as cold in winter.

▼ **MARITIME CLIMATE**
*The surrounding Pacific Ocean gives the islands of New Zealand a mild, moist climate.*

▼ **HUMPBACK WHALE**
*These whales communicate by "singing" to each other. This consists of a sequence of howls, moans, and cries, which can last for hours.*

## SPEEDY SOUND

The speed of sound in water is more than four times faster than the speed of sound in air. This enables marine animals such as whales to call to each other over incredible distances. In some parts of the ocean, sound transmission is so efficient that a whale call generated on one side of an ocean could be picked up on the other side, thousands of kilometres away.

## DEADLY SOUND

The speed of sound in water allows animals such as this remarkable little pistol shrimp to use it as a weapon. The shrimp has a specialized claw that it can lock open. When prey comes close, the shrimp snaps the claw shut creating tiny bubbles that collapse creating a shock wave that's louder than a bullet and powerful enough to kill its victim.

# Oceanic winds

As the Sun warms the atmosphere, it creates global air currents that are swept east or west by the way Earth spins in space. The air flows over the oceans in a broadly predictable pattern, creating oceanic winds that usually blow from one direction. Known as prevailing winds, they include the tropical trade winds and the stronger westerlies of cooler oceans.

### TRADE WINDS

The spin and swerve effect makes the prevailing winds blow roughly from east to west over tropical oceans near the equator. They are called the trade winds because, before the invention of steamships, the tall ships that traded between the continents used them to sail west across the oceans. Trade winds are mostly gentle breezes rather than strong winds.

### CIRCULATING AIR

In the tropics, warm air rises and flows north or south, then cools, sinks, and flows back towards the equator at low level. In temperate regions, air rises and flows towards the equator before sinking and flowing away again. At the poles, cool air sinks and flows towards the warmer temperate zones.

*Low-level air flows towards poles in temperate zones.*

*Air flows towards equator in tropics.*

*Rising and sinking air forms circulation cells.*

### SPIN AND SWERVE

Earth's spin makes moving air veer off course. North of the equator the airflow swerves right, while south of the equator it swerves left. As a result, low-level air flowing towards the equator in the tropics swerves west, while air flowing away from the equator in the temperate zone swerves east. This creates the prevailing winds that blow over oceans.

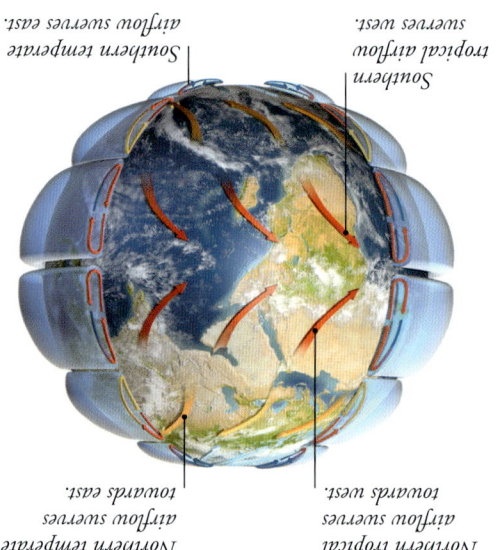

*Northern tropical airflow swerves towards west.*

*Northern temperate airflow swerves towards east.*

*Southern tropical airflow swerves west.*

*Southern temperate airflow swerves east.*

## POWERFUL WESTERLIES

Over the cooler oceans of the temperate zones, the prevailing winds blow from west to east. Since winds are always named according to where they blow from, they are known as westerlies. Near the polar regions they blow more strongly, especially in the Southern Ocean around Antarctica.

◀ **SOUTHERN OCEAN**
*In the far south, where there are no continents to hamper airflow, the strong westerlies are called the Roaring Forties.*

## POLAR EASTERLIES

Over the icy seas near the North and South poles, air flowing away from the poles towards the warmer temperate zones veers west. This means that the prevailing winds over the cold polar oceans blow from east to west. They drive the floating pack ice west too, especially in the Arctic Ocean and the Antarctic Weddell and Ross seas.

▼ **ANTARCTIC BLIZZARD**
*A cold polar easterly picks up loose snow and hurls it at these tents pitched on the sea ice near the shores of Antarctica.*

## CALM ZONES

Between the tropical trade wind zones and the westerly wind belts lie calm zones where there is very little wind from any direction. Similar calm regions, called the doldrums, occur near the equator. These windless zones were a serious problem in the days of sailing ships with no engines. Ships could be trapped in the doldrums for weeks, and often ran out of food and fresh water.

# Oceanic storms

Although open oceans are swept by winds from one direction most of the time, they are also affected by local weather systems that change the wind pattern, and often bring heavy rain. These weather systems are generated by warm, moist air rising off the oceans. They form zones of circulating air called cyclones, which can cause destructive storms.

## STORM CLOUDS

Warm air rising from sun-warmed oceans carries a lot of invisible water vapour with it. As it rises, the air cools. This makes some of the vapour turn back into the tiny water droplets that form clouds. Where a lot of warm, moist air is rising, this process builds up giant storm clouds that contain a huge weight of water. Eventually, the water spills out of them as heavy rain.

BLUE PLANET

## SWIRLING CYCLONES

As warm air rises, it reduces the weight of air at sea level, creating a zone of low air pressure. Surrounding air swirls into the low-pressure zone to replace the rising air. The faster the warm air rises and the lower the pressure, the faster more air moves in, causing strong winds. These weather systems are called cyclones or depressions. They swirl anticlockwise in the northern hemisphere, and clockwise in the southern hemisphere.

*Air swirls into the low-pressure zone.*

*Rising warm air reduces pressure.*

*Low pressure*

## FRONTAL STORMS

In the temperate regions just north and south of the tropics, warm tropical air is pushed up by cold polar air at an invisible boundary called the polar front. This helps generate cyclones over cool oceans such as the north Atlantic. The cyclones are swept east by westerly winds, and sometimes cause powerful storms, such as this one lashing a town on the Atlantic coast of Britain.

## HURRICANES

Huge cyclones form over tropical oceans, where intense heat causes the build-up of colossal clouds around a zone of very low air pressure. Air swirling into the low-pressure zone at high speed starts the clouds spinning, creating a tropical revolving hurricane. These storms, the most violent on Earth, are also known as typhoons or tropical cyclones.

◀ **SPIRALLING CLOUDS**
*This satellite view shows a hurricane going past Florida, US. Winds near the centre of a hurricane can reach speeds of 350 kph (220 mph), causing immense destruction.*

## STORM SURGES

Extremely low air pressure at the centre of a hurricane also makes the sea heap up like a tsunami wave – an effect called a storm surge. If the storm moves over land, it drags the storm surge with it, and if the surge is high enough, it can swamp coastal defences and cause catastrophic flooding.

▶ **FLOODED CITY**
*These houses in New Orleans, US, were flooded by a storm surge swept ashore by Hurricane Katrina in August 2005.*

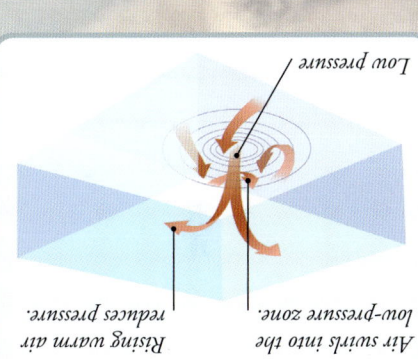

# Waves

Waves start out as tiny ripples on the water, created by wind blowing over the smooth surface. If the wind keeps blowing, the ripples grow and develop into a confused wave pattern called a chop, with waves of many different sizes and shapes. Gradually, this chaotic effect becomes more ordered, and eventually settles into a regular series of large waves called a swell, which can travel vast distances across the ocean.

As the wind blows over the ocean, it whips up waves on the surface. The stronger the wind, and the longer it blows, the bigger the waves get. They also grow as they travel, so the biggest waves are the ones that travel long distances over vast oceans, especially the Pacific. Such waves can be destructive when they break on shore. Out on the ocean they cause less damage, but rare extra-large waves can be dangerous to ships at sea.

## MAKING WAVES

Waves are caused by the way the wind drags on the surface of the ocean. The wind pushes the wave forwards, but the water within the wave stays where it is. In fact, each drop of water moves in a circle, rolling forwards and then back as the wave passes. This is why objects floating on the water, such as these ducks, stay in the same place as the waves roll under them.

### FACT
In 1995, the ocean liner *Queen Elizabeth 2* was hit by a rogue wave during a hurricane in the Atlantic. The wave was about 29 m (95 ft) high.

## WAVE PATTERN

▼ RIPPLES
Moving air drags on the surface of the water to push up ripples. These tiny waves are less than 25 mm (1 in) high.

▼ CHOP
Ripples may eventually turn into a chop – a disordered mass of small waves that are up to half a metre (20 in) high.

▼ SWELL
Over time, waves start rolling across the ocean in a regular swell, with wave crests often towering high above the troughs.

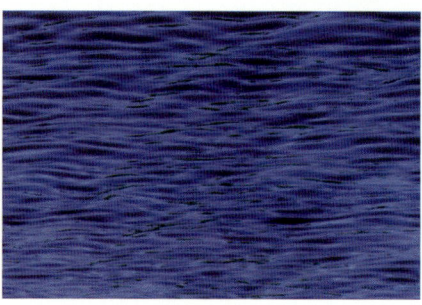

BLUE PLANET

# BLUE PLANET

## ATLANTIC STORM
Howling winds blow spray off the crests of the giant waves threatening this fishing boat.

## WAVE HEIGHT
The further a wave travels, the bigger it can get. A gale (strong wind) blowing over a small lake will create only small waves, but a wind of the same strength blowing over an ocean can create waves that are more than 10 m (33 ft) high. Some of the biggest waves build up in the Southern Ocean, where there is no land to stop them sweeping around Antarctica, driven by the westerly wind.

## ROGUE WAVES
Out at sea, regular swells can be very high without being particularly dangerous. But if two swells come together, they can clash to form colossal rogue waves more than 20 m (66 ft) high. These also form where a series of storm waves meet a strong opposing current. Such waves can wash right over big ships, and may even sink them.

## BREAKERS
As waves approach the shore and move into shallower water, the bottom of the waves rub against the seabed and slow down, while the water at the surface keeps moving forward. This makes the waves shorter, steeper, and top-heavy, until finally the crest topples forwards in a foaming mass of water called a breaker. The steeper the shore, the more dramatically the waves break, hurling water up the beach.

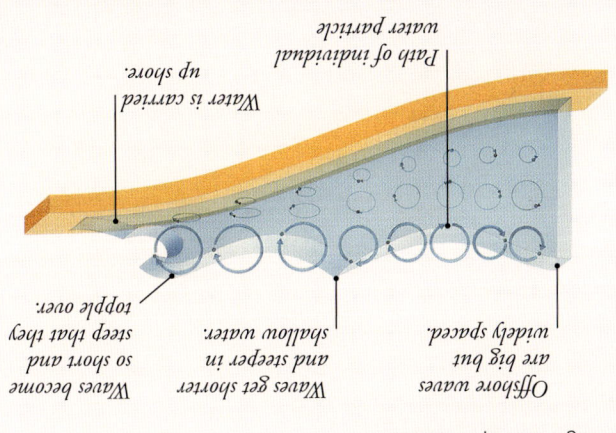

Offshore waves are big but widely spaced.

Waves get shorter and steeper in shallow water.

Waves become so short and steep that they topple over.

Water is carried up shore.

Path of individual water particle

## PLUNGING BREAKER
The crests of gigantic waves rolling in from the Pacific Ocean topple and crash in spectacular breakers on the beaches of Hawai'i, US. This wave may have travelled more than 4,000 km (2,500 miles), growing all the time, before being swept into shallow water where it falls dramatically.

# Surface currents

The wind that whips up waves also drives powerful surface currents. The main driving forces are the winds generated by global airflow and deflected by Earth's spin – the prevailing winds. The spin effect also influences the currents themselves, making them swerve right or left. As a result, they form huge rotating gyres that swirl around the oceans, carrying cold water into the tropics and warm water towards the poles.

**FACT**
Currents flowing around the ocean sped up by 15 per cent from 1990 to 2013 because warming surface waters flow faster.

*Wind*
*Drag on ocean water*
*Water moves in this direction.*
*Drag from upper layer*
*Direction of water movement in lower layer*
*Water movement in even lower layer*
*Drag*

## EKMAN TRANSPORT

The spinning Earth effect that makes the wind swerve off-course does the same to ocean currents. They veer to the right in the northern hemisphere, and to the left in the southern hemisphere. Moving water at the surface drags deeper water with it, which swerves even further right or left. As a result, the current's direction changes with depth – a pattern called Ekman transport.

## ROUND AND ROUND

The trade winds in the tropical Atlantic north of the equator blow towards the southwest, but Ekman transport pushes water westward. The current veers right as it comes up against North America, to become the Gulf Stream. This flows eastward, driven by prevailing winds blowing towards the northeast, then swerves south as the Canary Current. The resulting circulation is called the north Atlantic gyre. Similar gyres occur in all other oceans.

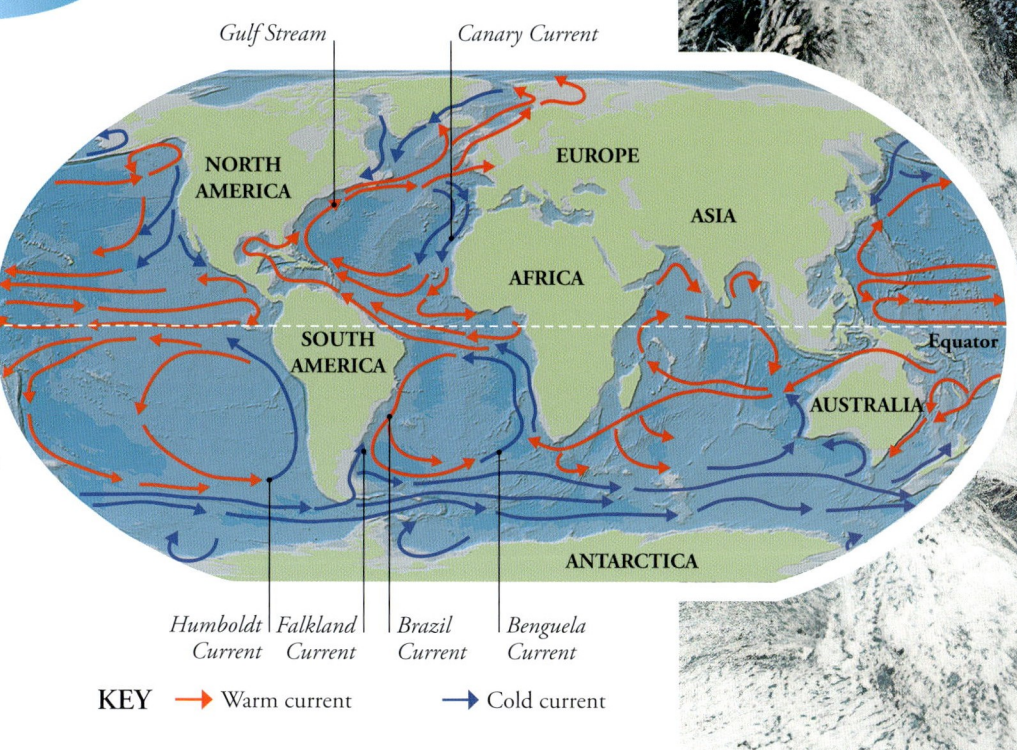

*Gulf Stream*  *Canary Current*
NORTH AMERICA  EUROPE  ASIA  AFRICA  SOUTH AMERICA  Equator  AUSTRALIA  ANTARCTICA

*Humboldt Current*  *Falkland Current*  *Brazil Current*  *Benguela Current*

KEY  → Warm current   → Cold current

## HEAT PUMPS

All the currents near the equator flow westward, then turn north and south in western boundary currents such as the Gulf Stream and Brazil Current. These carry warm water to cooler regions, making their winters milder. Meanwhile, eastern boundary currents such as the Humboldt Current and the Benguela Current carry cool polar water into the tropics.

BLUE PLANET

▲ TROPICAL GARDENS
*The Gulf Stream gives the Scilly Isles in the north Atlantic a surprisingly warm climate.*

## VISIBLE FLOW

Where warm and cold currents meet, the cold water pushes below the warm water, stirring up minerals from the seafloor that are vital for tiny drifting algae called plankton. This fuels plankton growth, providing food for fish and other animals. This effect is most marked in shallow continental shelf seas, because the seabed is nearer the surface. Sometimes the two currents are made visible by different-coloured plankton blooms.

◀ COLOUR-CODED
*Seen from space, these plankton blooms mark where the warm Brazil Current (carrying the blue plankton) meets the colder Falklands Current (carrying the green plankton).*

# Sargasso Sea

Near the centre of the north Atlantic is a region of warm, still water called the Sargasso Sea. It lies in the middle of the surface currents that swirl clockwise around the ocean to the north of the equator. These currents push drifting seaweed into the Sargasso Sea, forming a unique ecosystem of floating marine life.

### CIRCLING CURRENTS

The powerful currents of the great oceanic gyres flow around broad areas of water that are not moving at all. Since the flowing surface water pushes deeper water sideways, the currents also drive water into the middle of the gyre. In the north Atlantic, this effect has created the Sargasso Sea.

### FLOATING GARDEN

The seaweed of the Sargasso Sea is unusual because it is not attached to rocks, but thrives drifting free on the surface of the deep ocean. Called sargassum weed, it forms a shallow floating forest in the warm water just beneath the waves. Some types have gas-filled bladders on the fronds that act as floats. This layer of drifting seaweed is only a few centimetres deep, but it is a habitat for many specialized creatures that do not live anywhere else.

### EEL NURSERY

The Sargasso Sea is the breeding site for eels that live in European and North American rivers. Adult eels migrate down-river and swim across the ocean to the Sargasso Sea. Here, they lay their eggs, which hatch as tiny leaf-shaped young. They drift on the Gulf Stream current flowing east across the ocean. Eventually, they reach either North America or Europe, by which time they have turned into tiny transparent eels.

### FLOTSAM AND JETSAM

Unfortunately, it is not just floating seaweed that is driven into the Sargasso Sea. The currents also gather up rubbish that has been thrown from ships or carried down rivers into the ocean. These currents push the rubbish into the middle of the Sargasso Sea, where it forms a floating rubbish dump.

BLUE PLANET

### LURKING KILLER

The sargassum fish is a master of disguise. It is adorned with flaps and tassels that look just like seaweed fronds, so it can hide among the floating weed and ambush its prey. It has a huge mouth that allows it to swallow fish almost as big as itself, including other sargassum fish.

### SARGASSUM CRAB

Most crabs live on the seabed, but the sargassum swimming crab is adapted for swimming in open water among the floating sargassum weed. The crab's excellent camouflage makes it hard to see among the weed, and enables it to pounce on unwary shrimps, worms, sea slugs, and other small prey.

### BABY TURTLES

When north Atlantic loggerhead turtles hatch on tropical beaches, they head for the Sargasso Sea. Here, the young turtles hide among the floating seaweed, safe from their enemies. They feed on small animals living in the weed until they are about 45 cm (18 in) long, then they leave for shallow coastal seas.

BLUE PLANET

▼ ON THE PROWL
*The rich pickings in an upwelling zone attract hundreds of big, hungry hunters, including these hammerhead sharks.*

### RICH SEAS
Deep water drawn up from the seabed by upwelling contains dissolved nutrients that act as fertilizer for plantlike algae called phytoplankton. This causes vigorous growth, which feeds swarms of tiny animals. These support huge shoals of small fish such as anchovy, which attract bigger fish, sharks, dolphins, and other oceanic predators.

# Upwelling zones

In some parts of the world, the prevailing wind drives the surface water of the ocean away from the shore. This forces deeper water to well up from below to take its place. The water contains chemicals and minerals that fuel the growth of plankton, providing food for fish. Similar upwelling effects create food-rich zones over submerged seamounts and near the equator. Upwelling zones support rich fisheries that provide a lot of the world's seafood.

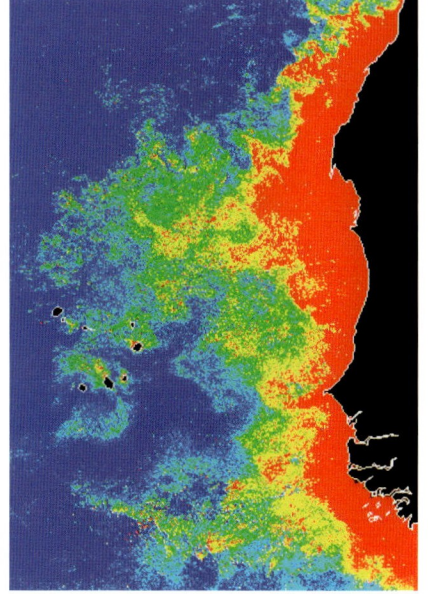

▲ PLANKTON GROWTH
*This satellite image of an upwelling zone off the west coast of Africa shows regions of dense plankton growth in red and yellow.*

## SEAMOUNTS

Upwelling zones are also created when deep currents hit submerged volcanoes, known as seamounts, and flow upwards, bringing nutrient-rich water to the surface. These isolated hotspots often have their own unique wildlife.

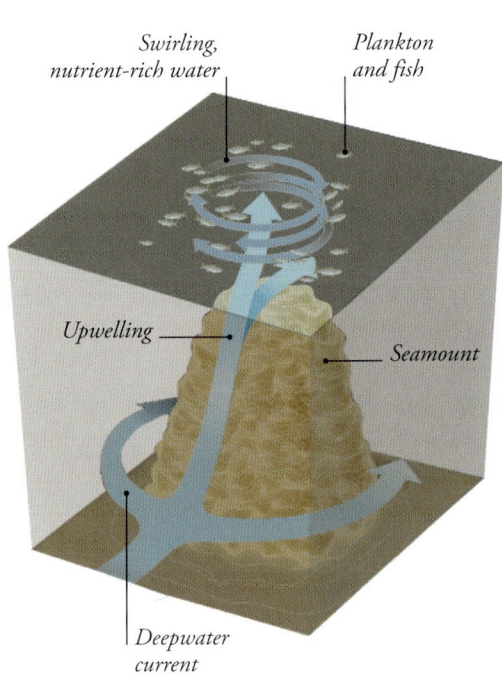

*Swirling, nutrient-rich water*
*Plankton and fish*
*Upwelling*
*Seamount*
*Deepwater current*

## EL NIÑO

If upwelling stops, it has a big impact on ocean life. Sometimes the trade winds over the Pacific weaken, allowing warm surface water to flow east and smother an upwelling zone off tropical South America. Known as the El Niño effect, this reduces the plankton growth, so the fish vanish – a disaster for fish-eating birds such as these blue-footed boobies.

### HOW IT WORKS

The Ekman transport effect can make strong winds blowing along the coast drag water away from the shore, creating an upwelling zone. Wind blowing in the opposite direction can cause downwelling. The pattern shown would be reversed in the northern hemisphere. The Ekman transport effect also draws surface water away from the equator, so cool, rich water wells up from below.

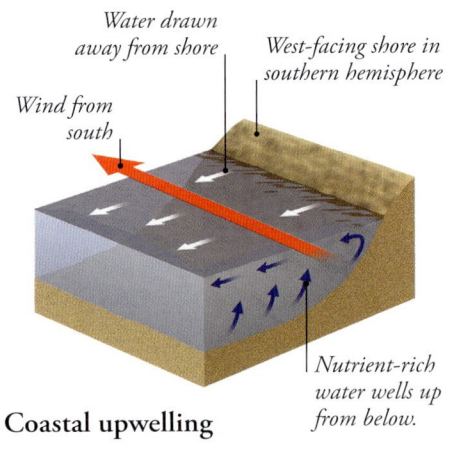

*Water drawn away from shore*
*West-facing shore in southern hemisphere*
*Wind from south*
*Nutrient-rich water wells up from below.*

**Coastal upwelling**

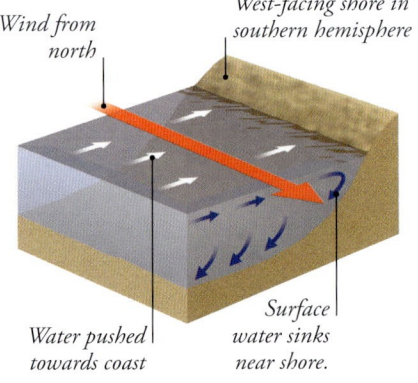

*Wind from north*
*West-facing shore in southern hemisphere*
*Water pushed towards coast*
*Surface water sinks near shore.*

**Coastal downwelling**

*Surface water dragged away from equator by Ekman transport effect*
*Trade wind*
*Cool water wells up from below.*
*Equator*

**Equatorial upwelling**

BLUE PLANET

# Deepwater currents

## SINKING WATERS

In the polar regions, cold air and floating ice makes the water beneath it very cold. This makes the water molecules move closer together, so the water becomes denser (heavier per litre). Extra salt expelled from the sea ice as it forms makes this cold water even denser and heavier, so it sinks towards the ocean floor.

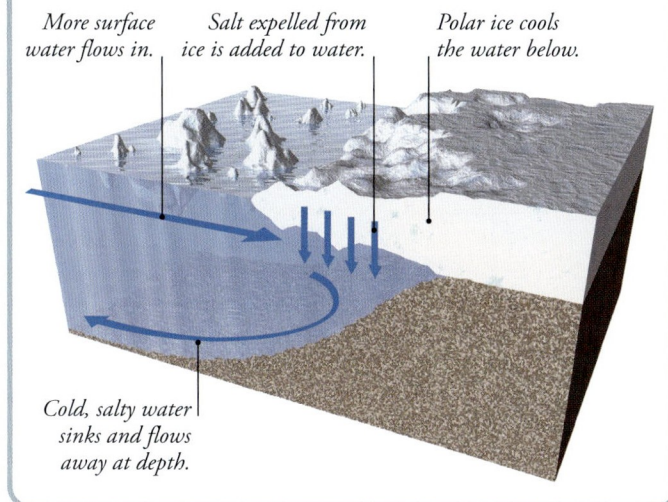

*More surface water flows in.*

*Salt expelled from ice is added to water.*

*Polar ice cools the water below.*

*Cold, salty water sinks and flows away at depth.*

The surface currents that swirl around the world's oceans are linked to a network of deepwater currents. These are driven by cool, salty water sinking towards the ocean floor and flowing beneath the warmer surface water, until they eventually come back to the surface. Together, the deepwater currents and surface currents carry ocean water all around the world.

## DEEP CHILL

The coldest deepwater current is called Antarctic Bottom Water, which flows from beneath the ice that covers the Antarctic Weddell Sea. A similar flow comes from the Ross Sea on the other side of Antarctica. In the north, sinking water near Greenland propels the North Atlantic Deep Water, which flows south and helps drive a deepwater current around the globe.

▼ ANTARCTIC ICE
*Sea ice forming on the Weddell and Ross seas close to the South Pole makes cold, salty ocean water even colder and saltier, driving powerful deepwater currents.*

**FACT**
It takes about 1,000 years for a single drop of ocean water to travel all around the world in the global conveyor.

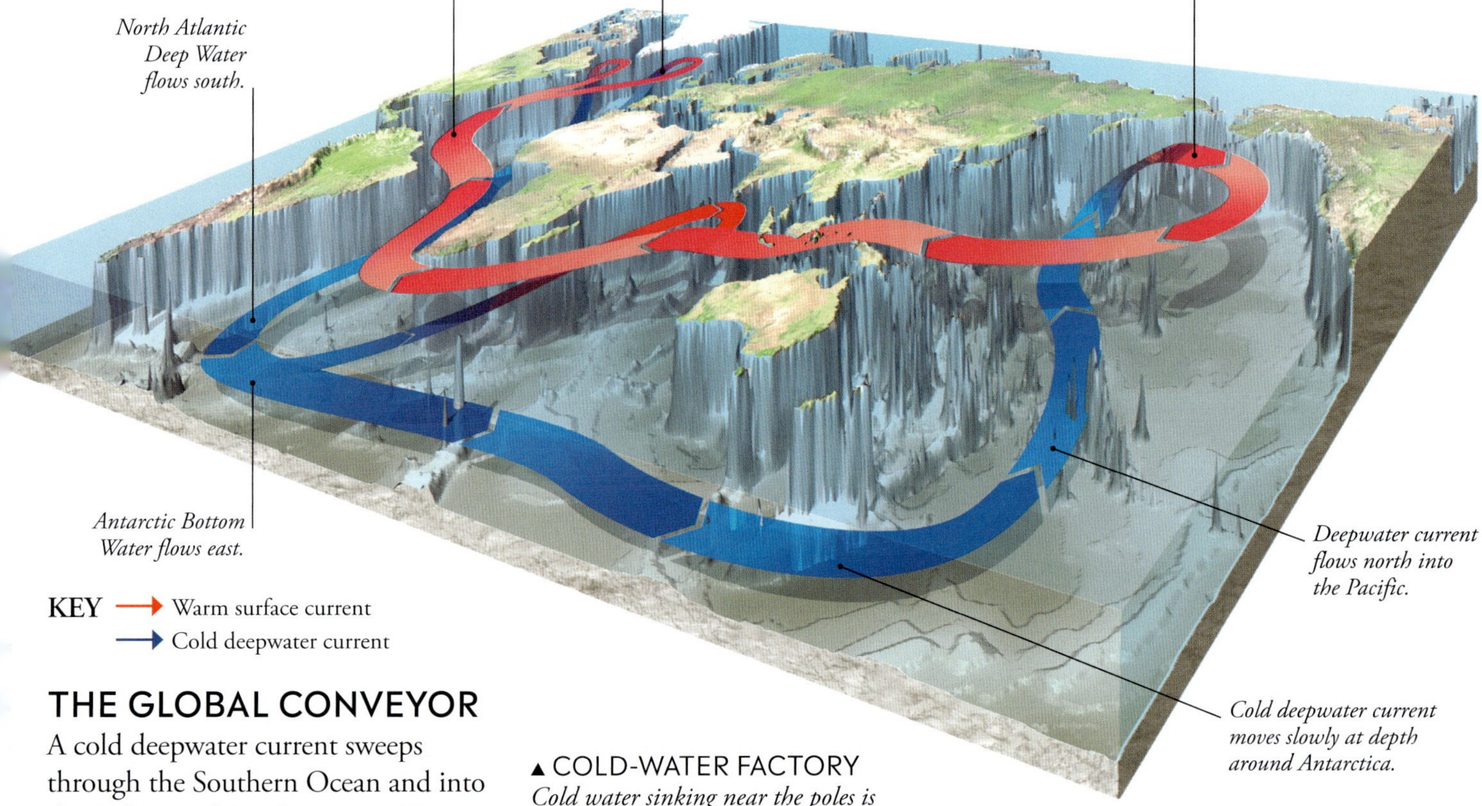

*Warm Atlantic Gulf Stream flows north.*

*Cold, salty water sinks in the north Atlantic.*

*Deep water rises to the surface and flows across the equator.*

*North Atlantic Deep Water flows south.*

*Antarctic Bottom Water flows east.*

KEY → Warm surface current
→ Cold deepwater current

*Deepwater current flows north into the Pacific.*

*Cold deepwater current moves slowly at depth around Antarctica.*

## THE GLOBAL CONVEYOR

A cold deepwater current sweeps through the Southern Ocean and into the Indian and Pacific oceans. Here, some of it rises to feed into the surface currents. These link with the warm Atlantic Gulf Stream, which eventually cools and sinks in the far north to drive the flow. The whole network is often called the global conveyor, because it transports ocean water all around the globe.

▲ **COLD-WATER FACTORY**
*Cold water sinking near the poles is the main driving force behind this never-ending circulation pattern.*

### FAST FACTS

- Scientists describe the global conveyor as the thermohaline circulation, driven by heat (*thermos*) and saltiness (*haline*).
- The global conveyor moves masses of water more than 100 times the volume of the flow of the Amazon River.
- Deepwater currents flow faster where they squeeze between the continents.

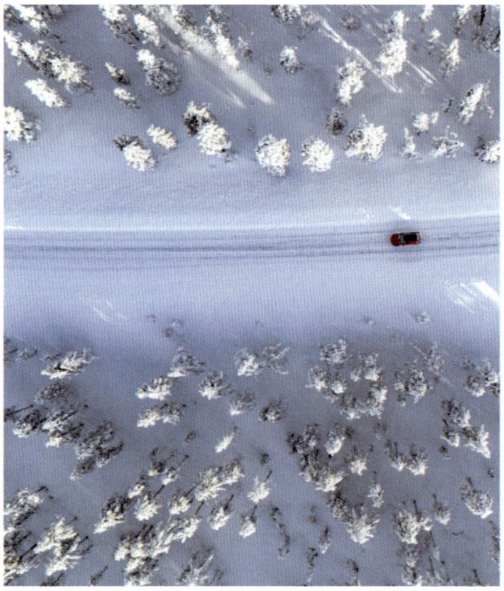

## ESSENTIAL SUPPLIES

The global conveyor carries ocean water around the world, along with dissolved oxygen and nutrients that are vital to oceanic life. A lot of these nutrients are scoured from the ocean floor by the deepwater currents, which carry them up to the sunlit surface. Here, they nourish the plankton that feed animals such as these humpback whales.

## GLOBAL IMPACT

Climate change could affect the global conveyor. Global warming is melting Arctic ice, adding fresh water to the sea. This is making the North Atlantic seawater less salty and less likely to sink and drive deepwater currents. Since the sinking water draws the warm Gulf Stream north towards Europe, this could lead to Europe getting colder.

BLUE PLANET

# THE OPEN OCEAN

The oceans are the largest wildlife habitat on Earth. Most creatures live near the surface, but there is life even in the deepest, darkest, coldest depths.

# Depth zones

The world's oceans have an average depth of almost 4,000 m (13,120 ft). But just a few metres below the surface, they start changing dramatically because of the way the light fades with depth. From the glittering, sunlit surface to the permanent darkness of the deep ocean, the dwindling light affects visibility, colour, temperature, and the availability of food.

**SUNLIT ZONE**
The top 200 m (660 ft) of the ocean is lit up with enough sunlight to support the plantlike plankton that need light to live and multiply. Since these are the main source of food in the oceans, this zone is where most marine animals live.

Sunlit zone
0–200 m
(0–660 ft)

**TWILIGHT ZONE**
Below 200 m (660 ft) there is not enough sunlight to support the organisms that rely on it for energy. The only light filtering down from the surface is a faint blue glow, so this part of the ocean is called the twilight zone. Animals live here, but far fewer than in the sunlit zone.

Twilight zone
200–1,000 m
(660–3,300 ft)

**MIDNIGHT ZONE**
Below 1,000 m (3,300 ft) lies the midnight zone, with no light except the glow produced by deep-sea animals. Since the oceans are often much deeper than 1,000 m (3,300 ft), most of the world's ocean water is in total darkness. Below the midnight zone is the abyss, with no sunlight and fewer animals.

Midnight zone
Below
1,000–4,000 m
(3,300–13,120 ft)

## THERMOCLINE

Tropical oceans are warm at the surface, reaching 30°C (86°F). But the temperature falls rapidly with depth to 4°C (39°F) in the twilight zone, and almost freezing in the midnight zone. In the tropics, the warm surface water rarely mixes with the colder water below it, and the boundary between the two is called the thermocline.

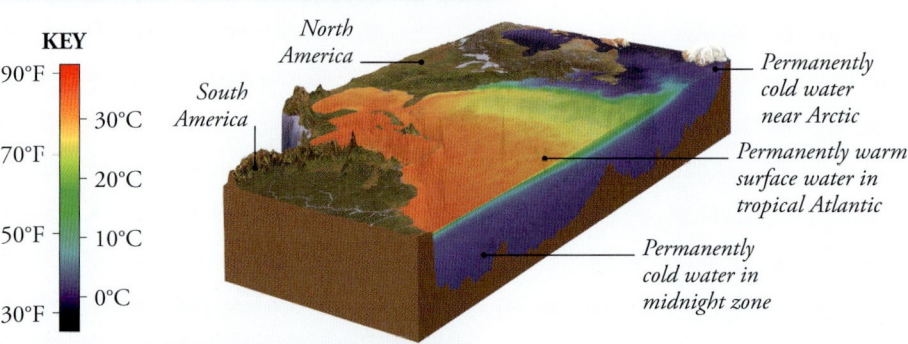

Sooty shearwater
Anchovies
Common dolphins
Blue shark
Comb jelly
Hatchetfish
Vampire squid
Deep-sea squids
Anglerfish
Red krill

▲ CLEAR BLUE WATER
*In open tropical oceans the thermocline usually stops dissolved minerals reaching the sunlit surface water, where they would encourage the growth of microscopic plankton. As a result, there is very little plankton in most tropical seas. This is why the water is crystal clear. In cooler seas, the thermocline breaks down in winter, allowing nutrients to fuel plankton growth.*

▲ SPECIALLY ADAPTED
*Ocean water contains a lot of oxygen, which is vital to animal life. The colder the water, the more oxygen it has. But deep in the twilight zone there is a region where most of the oxygen has been used up by bacteria feeding on dead plankton sinking from above. The only animals that can survive in this region are specially adapted creatures such as this vampire squid.*

THE OPEN OCEAN

THE OPEN OCEAN

# Sunlit zone

Most of the animals in the oceans live in the sunlit zone near the surface. They live here because, ultimately, nearly all animal life depends on the food made by plantlike seaweeds and tiny drifting organisms called phytoplankton. Just like land plants, these organisms use sunlight to make food. This means they have to live in the top 200 m (660 ft) of the ocean, where the light level is high enough for them to grow and multiply.

## DEEP BLUE

Sunlight is made up of all the colours of the rainbow. Just beneath the waves all these colours combine to form white light, but as the light penetrates deeper into the ocean some of the colours are filtered out. Red, orange, and yellow are first to go, leaving only green, blue, and violet. Eventually, only blue light is left, but there is still enough of this to support plantlike life down to an average depth of 200 m (660 ft).

## VITAL LIGHT

The plantlike organisms that live in the sunlit zone use the energy of light to make sugar compounds, which they turn into living tissue that can be eaten by animals. Most of these organisms are microscopic algae and special forms of bacteria that drift as phytoplankton in the open sea. But they also include the much bigger algae that we call seaweeds. Most of these seaweeds and the seagrass live attached to the seabed in shallow coastal water.

▶ GREEN GLOW
*The light glowing through these seaweed fronds provides the essential energy that the seaweed needs to grow.*

**FACT**
Photosynthesis in the oceans not only makes food, but it also releases about 50 per cent of the oxygen on Earth.

## PHOTOSYNTHESIS

Seaweeds, seagrass, and phytoplankton make food by converting water and carbon dioxide into oxygen and sugar. This process is called photosynthesis. It happens inside microscopic structures called chloroplasts. These contain a green substance called chlorophyll that can absorb solar energy. The energy triggers the chemical reaction that makes the sugar, so if there is not enough light, photosynthesis cannot take place.

## SUNLIT DRIFTERS

Like seaweeds, the tiny drifting organisms of the phytoplankton can live only in the upper, sunlit zone of the ocean, where there is enough light for them to make sugar. But unlike seaweeds, they all consist of just one living cell. They range from very simple bacteria to complex single-celled algae, including diatoms, dinoflagellates, and coccolithophores. Diatoms, seen here under a microscope, have intricate skeletons made of glassy silica. Coccolithophores have similar skeletons made of chalky calcite.

▲ SUGAR FACTORIES
*The fronds of big seaweeds are made up of millions of microscopic cells linked together like bricks in a wall. Each cell contains many green chloroplasts that use light to make sugar compounds.*

## BLOOMING OCEANS

Although the individual organisms that make up phytoplankton are only microscopic, they can form dense blooms near the ocean's surface that are sometimes visible from space. These usually develop where the sea is rich in minerals, drawn up from deeper water by ocean currents. The diatoms and other organisms absorb these minerals and use them to make their skeletons. They also combine them with sugar compounds to make other substances vital to their survival.

## LIVING LIGHT

Since phytoplankton are too small to be seen without a microscope, we normally see the organisms as a cloudiness in the water. The richer the sea, the more phytoplankton it can support, and the cloudier it is. But some of these drifting organisms, such as certain types of dinoflagellate, can glow with a blue-green chemical light when they are disturbed. This creates dazzling effects at night, as seen on this tropical shore.

THE OPEN OCEAN

# Zooplankton

The tiny drifting algae that form the phytoplankton are eaten by swarms of small animals and other organisms that cannot make their own food by photosynthesis. These organisms are known as zooplankton because they also drift with the currents, but many of them can swim. This ability enables zooplankton to hide in the dark depths by day and move up to the surface to feed at night.

THE OPEN OCEAN

### PROTOZOANS
The smallest types of zooplankton have bodies made up of a single cell – unlike true animals, which have many cells. But they feed on other living things in the same way as animals, and some are known as protozoans (meaning "near animals"). They include these radiolarians, which gather food using their long flexible spines.

### COPEPODS
Zooplankton animals are much bigger than protozoans, but many of them are still very small. The most numerous and widespread of these animals are copepods. These tiny crustaceans – relatives of shrimps and crabs – swim through the water using their enormously long antennae, which act like paddles. They eat microscopic single-celled algae and protozoans.

### FACT
So many Antarctic krill live in the Southern Ocean that their total weight is greater than that of the human population of the world.

◀ TEEMING KRILL
This krill swarm off the Pacific coast of California, US, has attracted a shoal of hungry fish.

▲ KRILL
Antarctic krill look like shrimps and grow up to 6 cm (2.4 in) long.

## KRILL SWARMS

Shrimplike krill are a lot larger than copepods. They live in all the world's oceans, but are most abundant in the cold Southern Ocean where they form vast swarms that turn the ocean red. Like copepods, they feed on microscopic life, but are in turn preyed upon by Antarctic whales, as well as many fish, seals, and penguins.

## UP AND DOWN

Copepods and many other types of zooplankton sink into the twilight zone by day to hide from fish that hunt by sight. As night falls, they swim up to the surface again to feed on phytoplankton. But some fish such as these herring have evolved ways of catching copepods in the dark, and every night dense shoals of herring gather at the ocean's surface to feast on the swarms of small animals.

## EGGS AND BABIES

Many marine animals such as fish, crabs, and clams produce eggs that drift in the sunlit zone. The eggs hatch as tiny larvae that feed on phytoplankton, just as copepods do. Eventually, the larvae turn into bigger adults. Many of these animals settle on the seabed and never move far again. So this drifting stage of their life is the only way they can spread to different parts of the ocean.

THE OPEN OCEAN

# Drifting jellies

Most of the animals that drift in the sunlit zone as zooplankton are tiny and almost weightless. But some are much bigger. They include jellyfish and unusual creatures such as comb jellies and salps. Although many can swim to some extent, they drift with the currents, feeding on the smaller animals as well as on each other. Some even catch fish.

*Bell-shaped body is mostly made of springy jelly.*

**THE OPEN OCEAN**

### STINGING TENTACLES
Many jellyfish live among the plankton. As they drift with the current, they swim by contracting their circular bodies to push water behind them and drive themselves along. They trail long, almost invisible tentacles armed with microscopic stinging cells, snaring and paralyzing other animals, which they can then reel in and eat. Some are giants – more than 2 m (6.6 ft) wide.

### FLOATING KILLER
The notoriously venomous Portuguese man-of-war may look like a jellyfish but its body is made up of tiny animals called zooids. Each zooid has a specific job: one is the float with a sail that makes it drift in the wind, while others gather food, produce young, or defend the colony.

▶ **LION'S MANE JELLYFISH**
*One of the biggest jellyfish, this oceanic drifter can have venomous tentacles more than 30 m (98 ft) long.*

## SWIMMING SLUG

Despite its deadly sting, the Portuguese man-of-war is preyed upon by another animal that also lives among the plankton – the blue sea slug. Unlike most sea slugs, it swims in open water, attacking and eating other animals. Amazingly, the blue sea slug recycles the stinging cells of its venomous prey and uses them for its own defence.

*Each tentacle carries hundreds of stinging cells.*

## GLITTERING JELLIES

Although they look like jellyfish, the comb jellies are very different. Their name refers to the shimmering rows of mobile "combs" along their bodies. By flicking these back and forth, the animals push themselves through the water. Some have long tentacles for snaring prey.

THE OPEN OCEAN

## DRIFTING CHAINS

Salps are tubular, transparent open-water relatives of the sea squirts that live attached to rocks. They move by pumping water through their bodies, and also filter the water for phytoplankton. For part of their lifecycle, salps live alone, but breed by producing long chains of identical, cloned animals that drift in the sunlit zone of the ocean. Eventually, each member of the chain produces another generation of solitary salps.

# The food chain

THE OPEN OCEAN

In the ocean, nearly all life depends on the food made by seaweeds and the microscopic drifting algae called phytoplankton. They use the energy of sunlight to build living tissue. Tiny animals eat this and turn it into muscle, skin, and other parts of their bodies. Many of these animals are eaten by other animals, which use the food to build their own bodies. They are eaten by even bigger animals, in a food chain that leads to top predators such as sharks.

## EAT AND BE EATEN

Seaweeds and phytoplankton make complex living tissue out of simple chemicals – they are food producers. But animals cannot make their own food; they survive by eating this living (or dead) tissue, so they are food consumers. Animals that eat the algae are primary consumers, while the larger animals that prey on the primary consumers are secondary consumers. These are eaten by even bigger hunters, which fall prey to powerful top predators.

▲ PRODUCER
*This seaweed uses solar energy to turn water and carbon dioxide into sugar. It adds other chemicals to turn sugar into living tissue.*

▲ PRIMARY CONSUMER
*A limpet eats seaweed. In its stomach, the seaweed is digested and used to make substances that help it to grow.*

▲ SECONDARY CONSUMER
*Crabs cannot digest seaweed. Instead, this shore crab eats limpets that have already turned the seaweed into animal tissue.*

### FAST FACTS

- The coldest oceans are often the richest in animal life, because cold, stormy waters contain more oxygen and nutrients, which encourage the growth of plankton.
- Animals are scarce in open tropical oceans, because the clear, almost pure water has very little phytoplankton.
- On tropical coral reefs, nearly all the food that supports the reefs is made by tiny algae that live inside the corals.
- In parts of the deep ocean, bacteria make food using energy from volcanic chemicals erupting from the ocean floor.

## FOOD PYRAMIDS

This diagram shows that it takes a huge amount of plankton at the bottom of the food chain to support just one top predator, such as this Arctic polar bear. This is because a lot of food is converted into energy and used up before it can be passed up to the next level in the chain.

*A polar bear eats dozens of seals per year.*

*Seals eat thousands of fish per year.*

*Fish eat trillions of zooplankton.*

*Zooplankton feed on countless phytoplankton.*

*Phytoplankton make their own food.*

▲ BIG MOUTHFUL
*A shoal of small fish desperately try to escape the gaping jaws of a hungry Bryde's whale. It could easily swallow the entire shoal in one mouthful.*

## SHORT CUTS

Some big oceanic animals short-cut the food chain by targeting very small animals. They include giant filter-feeding whales, which eat small fish and shrimplike krill instead of hunting bigger prey such as tuna. The whales get to eat more this way, because the smaller animals lower down the food chain are much more numerous than the tuna, and easier to catch. This is one reason why these whales – and other giant filter feeders such as the manta ray – can grow so big.

▲ TERTIARY CONSUMER
*A crab makes a perfect meal for this octopus. It digests the meat and turns it into nutrients and energy. But the octopus may get eaten too.*

▲ TOP PREDATOR
*A big, powerful shark might eat the octopus. But the shark has no predators, so it is at the top of the oceanic food chain.*

## OCEANIC FOOD WEB

Simple food chains such as the one shown above are unusual, because many animals eat a variety of prey from different parts of the chain. Even top predators are eaten by other animals when they die, and these include tiny worms and snails. So in practice most living things are part of a complex food web, rather than a chain. This diagram shows a simplified food web for the Arctic Ocean, from phytoplankton to polar bear and killer whale. The arrows go from prey to predator in each case.

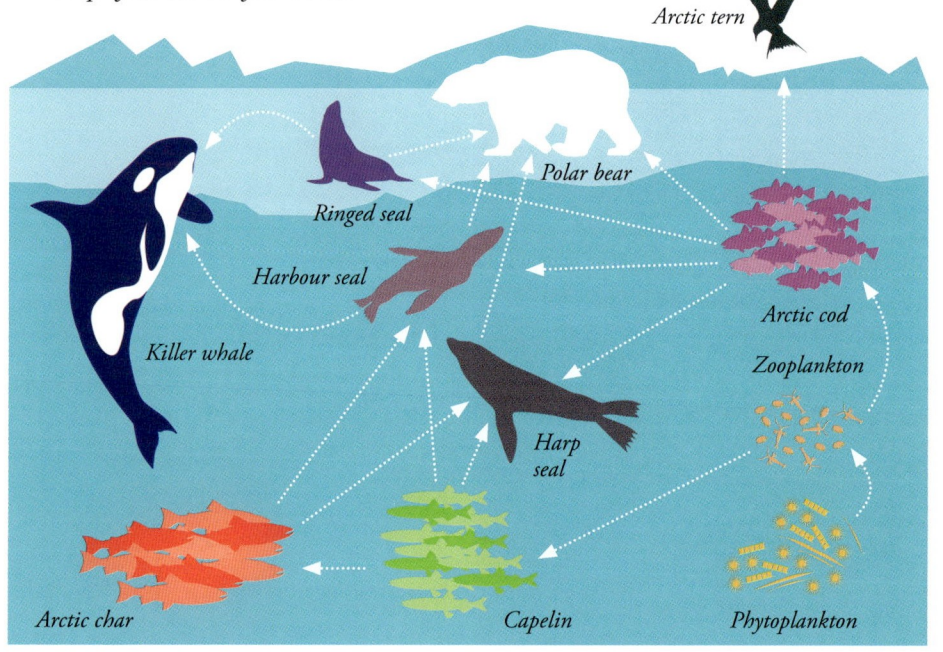

# Hungry shoals

The swarms of small animals that form the zooplankton are preyed upon by fish such as anchovy, sardine, and herring. They swim in shoals of thousands, all moving together as if they were a single giant creature. Swimming like this helps them catch their tiny prey, and also makes the fish less easily caught by their own enemies.

### SAFETY IN NUMBERS
Fish that live in open water near the surface can often find plenty to eat, but they are in serious danger of being eaten themselves. Big fish can take the risk, but smaller ones such as these herrings swim in large shoals. If attacked, a fast-moving, swirling shoal is a confusing target for a predator such as a shark or tuna; it is harder to isolate and catch a single fish.

### SLEEK ENEMIES
These mackerel swim with their mouths open, filtering masses of zooplankton from the water. They also swallow small fish such as sand eels. Mackerel have highly streamlined bodies for fast swimming, and streak through the oceans at speed in search of big shoals of fish to prey on.

### FILTER FEEDERS
A fish "breathes" by gathering oxygen from the water, which flows into its mouth and through oxygen-absorbing gills at the back of its head. Plankton-feeding fish use their gill rakers to strain the water for prey as they swim through plankton swarms with their mouths wide open. The trapped prey is collected in the back of the fish's mouth and passes down its throat and into its stomach.

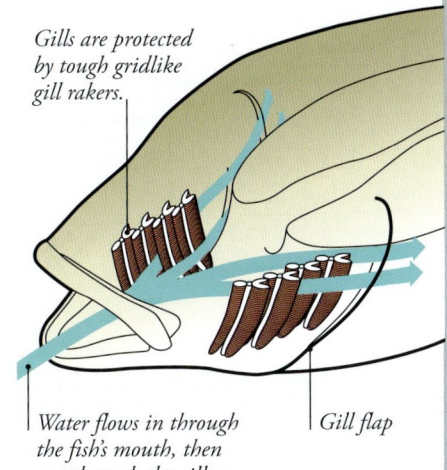

*Gills are protected by tough gridlike gill rakers.*

*Water flows in through the fish's mouth, then out through the gills.*

*Gill flap*

## SCHOOL DISCIPLINE

Many fish swim in formation – a type of behaviour known as schooling. They align themselves by watching each other, using visual clues such as brightly coloured markings and patterns. They can also sense the pressure waves in the water generated by the movement of their neighbours. This helps them stay spaced out in perfect formation when they change direction.

▲ **COLOUR-CODED CLUES**
*The vivid yellow tails of these fusiliers flash instant signals to the rest of the school, enabling all the fish to switch direction at the same time.*

**FACT**
Mega-shoals containing hundreds of millions of Atlantic herring, and covering dozens of square kilometres, could be the biggest known groups of animals on Earth.

## SUPERORGANISM

Fish that swim in big schools often move together in such perfect harmony that they are like one giant animal – a superorganism. Swimming in such tight formation makes it hard for predators to catch them.

# Oceanic hunters

Shoaling fish are hunted by bigger fish. Some of these big fish also swim in shoals, but others live alone. They include tuna, which hunt in packs, and sharp-snouted billfish. These oceanic hunters are fast enough to outrun a powerful speedboat. They owe their speed to their streamlined bodies, powerful muscles, and incredibly efficient ways of generating energy. They are among the most specialized hunters on the planet.

**FACT**
The sailfish is the fastest fish in the sea – one was timed at an astonishing 110 kph (68 mph) as it streaked in to attack.

### SLEEK AND SPEEDY

Tuna can swim incredibly fast because of a combination of special adaptations. Not only are they super-streamlined, their huge flank muscles drive their crescent-shaped tail fin from side to side at such high speed that it almost acts like the propeller of a powerboat. The faster they swim, the faster the water flows through their gills, and this provides extra oxygen to turn blood sugar into energy. These fish can also raise their body temperatures to well above the temperature of the water, making their muscles even more efficient.

*Tall, narrow tail fin*
*Streamlined body*
*Gill flap*

### TUNA PACKS

Tuna travel in shoals that mount coordinated attacks on smaller shoaling fish. They are fast, powerful hunters, capable of amazing speeds of up to 75 kph (47 mph). Some also grow to astonishing sizes – the Atlantic bluefin tuna can reach 4.6 m (15 ft). But overfishing has made some species rare, and the Atlantic bluefin have been threatened with extinction.

▲ HERRING PREY
*Herded together by the frenzied attack of a shoal of hungry tuna, herrings leap into the air in a desperate bid to escape.*

## FEEDING FRENZY

When one of these oceanic hunters runs into a shoal of fish, it accelerates to strike at high speed, giving its victims little chance of escape. Tuna launch a mass attack, snapping at anything that moves. Prey fish often try to hide behind each other to avoid being picked out, forming a tightly packed, swirling mass. They may even try to get away by bursting up through the ocean's surface.

▼ SWORDFISH
*The sharp bill of the swordfish makes a useful weapon when attacking a fast-moving, dense ball of fish, but its main job is to make the swordfish perfectly streamlined.*

THE OPEN OCEAN

*Swordlike bill pierces water as fish rockets after its prey.*

*Smooth skin has no scales to slow it down.*

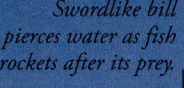

## FORMIDABLE PREDATORS

The swordfish has an acute sense of vision, and its sharp bill is the longest among all billfish. Like the other billfish, it uses its powerful muscles to slice through the water at an incredible speed as it chases after smaller fish and squid. When it overtakes its prey, the swordfish sometimes uses its long bill to slash at its victims, stunning or injuring them so they are easier to catch.

## OCEAN RACERS

While tuna hunt in packs, the big predators, known as billfish, hunt alone. These include marlins and swordfish. They all have long, bony, sharp-pointed upper jaws, or bills. Like tuna, they are built for speed, but many are even faster. The sailfish folds away its big sail-like dorsal fin when it is swimming fast. It travels huge distances through the ocean in search of prey.

◀ SAILFISH
*These fish are found near the ocean's surface, targeting shoals of fish. But they will also prey on squid and octopus.*

### BAIT BALL
Targeted by a roving pod of common dolphins, a large shoal of blue jack mackerel bunch together in a swirling mass of glittering silver – a bait ball. By forming this shape, the fish aim to confuse their enemies and make it harder for them to pick out a victim, but these dolphins are not put off so easily.

# Sharks

The most notorious oceanic hunters are the predatory sharks with their terrifyingly sharp teeth. In fact, not all sharks are like this. Some are lazy shellfish feeders, and others eat only very small animals. But many are powerful killers that combine lethal teeth with acute senses and amazing speed. They have few enemies apart from other, bigger sharks.

## ALL SHAPES AND SIZES

Sharks have lived in the world's oceans for more than 400 million years. Today, there are more than 500 species. Many are fast, streamlined open-water hunters, but other sharks have strange adaptations that equip them for life on the seabed, or in the dark, cold depths of the deep ocean.

▲ SAW SHARK
*An effective weapon, the swordlike snout of this shark is edged with razor-sharp teeth.*

▲ THRESHER SHARK
*The upper lobe of the thresher's tail is as long as its body. It uses it like a whip to stun its prey.*

▲ WOBBEGONG
*This ambush killer lies on the seabed, relying on its camouflage to hide from its prey.*

▲ FRILLED SHARK
*The eel-like frilled shark looks like the earliest ancestors of all sharks.*

*Tall triangular dorsal fin helps keep the shark upright as it swims.*

*Crescent-shaped tail fin is adapted for speed.*

*Powerful streamlined body*

**FACT**
A great white shark has 300 teeth, and since they are always being replaced, it may get through 30,000 teeth in its lifetime.

▲ GREAT WHITE SHARK
*The massively powerful great white reaches lengths of up to 7 m (23 ft). It is found in all tropical and temperate oceans, mainly near coasts.*

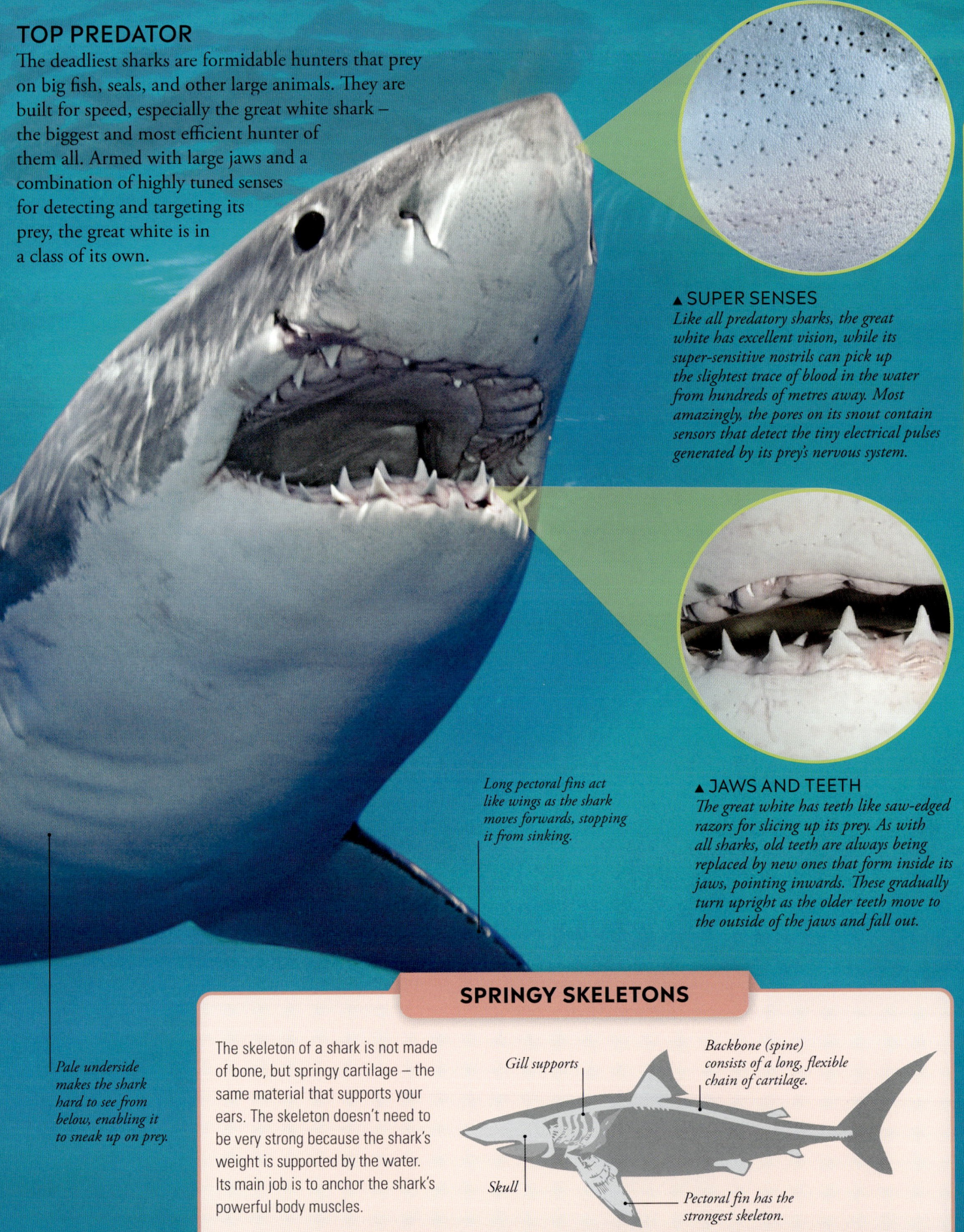

## TOP PREDATOR

The deadliest sharks are formidable hunters that prey on big fish, seals, and other large animals. They are built for speed, especially the great white shark – the biggest and most efficient hunter of them all. Armed with large jaws and a combination of highly tuned senses for detecting and targeting its prey, the great white is in a class of its own.

**▲ SUPER SENSES**
Like all predatory sharks, the great white has excellent vision, while its super-sensitive nostrils can pick up the slightest trace of blood in the water from hundreds of metres away. Most amazingly, the pores on its snout contain sensors that detect the tiny electrical pulses generated by its prey's nervous system.

THE OPEN OCEAN

Long pectoral fins act like wings as the shark moves forwards, stopping it from sinking.

**▲ JAWS AND TEETH**
The great white has teeth like saw-edged razors for slicing up its prey. As with all sharks, old teeth are always being replaced by new ones that form inside its jaws, pointing inwards. These gradually turn upright as the older teeth move to the outside of the jaws and fall out.

Pale underside makes the shark hard to see from below, enabling it to sneak up on prey.

### SPRINGY SKELETONS

The skeleton of a shark is not made of bone, but springy cartilage – the same material that supports your ears. The skeleton doesn't need to be very strong because the shark's weight is supported by the water. Its main job is to anchor the shark's powerful body muscles.

Gill supports

Backbone (spine) consists of a long, flexible chain of cartilage.

Skull

Pectoral fin has the strongest skeleton.

# Filter-feeding giants

The biggest fish in the sea are not sharp-toothed hunters, but placid, slow-moving animals that feed by straining plankton-rich seawater for food. They use the same filter-feeding system as shoaling fish such as herring and anchovy, allowing the water to flow through their gills so the food is trapped by their tough gill rakers.

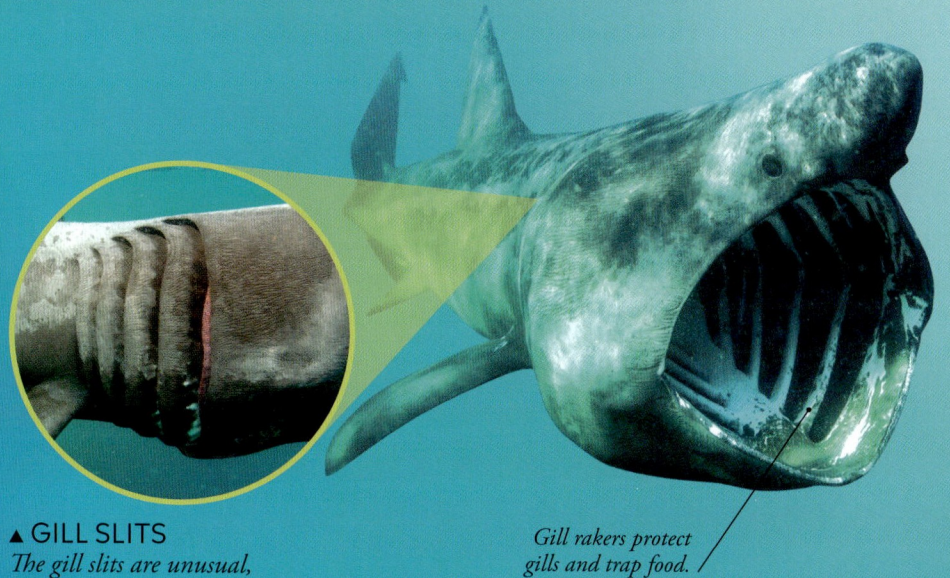

## BASKING SHARK

Three of the giant filter feeders are sharks – the basking shark, whale shark, and megamouth shark. The basking shark feeds in cool oceans, which are often cloudy with plankton. When feeding, it swims with its mouth wide open so the plankton-rich water flows through the mesh of gill rakers. These trap the food, while the water flows out through the huge gill slits at the back of the shark's head.

▲ GILL SLITS
*The gill slits are unusual, in that they are so big, they almost encircle the neck.*

*Gill rakers protect gills and trap food.*

*Prominent ridges along its body*

## RECORD BREAKER

The basking shark is a giant fish that can grow to an enormous 15 m (49 ft) long, but it is smaller than the whale shark. This tropical plankton feeder may be up to 20 m (66 ft) long. Like the basking shark, the whale shark catches its food by straining water through its gill rakers. It can also actively take in a mouthful of water, closing its mouth, and forcing the water out through its gills.

▲ WHALE SHARK
*A diver swims alongside the colossal but harmless whale shark. This fish travels huge distances across warm oceans in search of plankton-rich waters.*

THE OPEN OCEAN

*Huge mouth for gulping large amounts of tiny prey*

## MYSTERY SHARK
Basking and whale sharks have been known for centuries, but the megamouth shark was discovered more recently in 1976. No one knew it existed because it spends its days in the dark depths of the ocean, and comes up to the surface only at night. It follows the movements of the tiny zooplankton, which also migrate to the surface at night and go back into the depths by day.

**FACT**
Some whale sharks may weigh 30,000 kg (66,000 lb) – more than a fully loaded school bus.

*Each whale shark can be identified from its unique pattern of white spots and stripes.*

*The whale shark is the biggest fish in the ocean.*

*Winglike pectoral fins beat up and down as it swims.*

*Two long lobes help channel plankton into its mouth.*

*Gill slits*

## GIANT RAY
With its huge pectoral wings and two hornlike lobes, the manta ray is also known as the devil fish. It is the biggest of the rays, spanning up to 7 m (23 ft) from tip to tip of its big pectoral fins. The manta ray uses these like wings to "fly" through warm oceans in search of plankton. It feeds like a basking shark, swimming with its mouth open so food-rich water flows through its gills.

▲ **FLYING FILTER FEEDER**
*This view of a feeding manta ray from below shows how its big gill slits gape open as the water flows through them.*

# Baleen whales

The biggest animals in the oceans are the baleen whales, with the largest group known as rorquals. They are called baleen whales because, instead of teeth, they have fine comblike plates made of a fibrous material called baleen. These whales, similar to the giant filter-feeding sharks and manta rays, use the plates to strain small animals from the water. But each species has a different way of catching its food. They are highly intelligent, and some regularly work together to round up prey. They can communicate using a wide variety of moans, wails, and clicks.

### BALEEN PLATES

A whale's baleen plates are made of keratin – the same material as human hair and fingernails. The plates form long, bristly combs attached to each side of the upper jaw, and they hang down so they fill the gap between the whale's upper and lower jaw when its mouth is open. When feeding, the whale uses various techniques to fill its mouth with water and force it out through the plates. These then trap any small prey such as copepods, krill, and small fish.

## Bowhead whale
*Arctic specialist*

**Length** Up to 20 m (66 ft)
**Weight** Up to 90 tonnes
**Habitat or range** Arctic

Named for its upwardly arched jaw, the bowhead specializes in gathering tiny copepods from the icy waters of the Arctic Ocean and nearby cold seas. Thick blubber (fat under the skin) keeps bowhead whales warm. They use their huge heads to break through sea ice up to 1 m (3.3 ft) thick to breathe.

## Gray whale
*Seafloor feeder*

**Length** Up to 15 m (49 ft)
**Weight** Up to 45 tonnes
**Habitat or range** Coastal north Pacific

Uniquely for a baleen whale, the gray whale feeds on animals that it gathers from the seabed. It does this by swimming along the bottom on its side to plough up soft mud. The whale draws the sediments into its mouth, then pumps it out through its baleen to trap prey.

## Humpback whale
*Lunge feeder*

**Length** Up to 15 m (49 ft)
**Weight** Up to 30 tonnes
**Habitat or range** Worldwide

Given its name for the way it arches its back before diving, the humpback has longer flippers than other whales, and a snout that is covered with bumps called tubercles. It is a rorqual, with an expandable throat that allows it to gulp enormous mouthfuls of prey-filled water. It eats krill and small fish, often rounding them up in groups by blowing walls of bubbles around them and lunging up to gulp an entire shoal at once.

THE OPEN OCEAN

## Minke whale
*Expanding throat*

**Length** Up to 10 m (33 ft)
**Weight** Up to 10 tonnes
**Habitat or range** Worldwide

The minke is the smallest rorqual whale – a type of baleen whale that feeds by forcing a huge volume of seawater into its mouth and pumping it out through its filtering baleen. Pleats beneath the whale's lower jaw allow its throat to expand to hold the water, which it pumps out with its massive, muscular tongue.

## Pygmy right whale
*Antarctic krill-feeder*

**Length** Up to 6.5 m (21 ft)
**Weight** Up to 3.5 tonnes
**Habitat or range** Southern Ocean

This Antarctic whale is the smallest of all the baleen whales, yet it can still weigh twice as much as an average car. It feeds in the cold Southern Ocean, moving north as far as Australia and South Africa as the sea around Antarctica freezes over in winter. It feeds mainly on krill and similar small animals.

## Blue whale
*Streamlined giant*

**Length** Up to 31 m (102 ft)
**Weight** Up to 180 tonnes
**Habitat or range** Worldwide

The biggest animal on the planet, the blue whale is a giant rorqual that feeds in the same way as the minke. It eats mainly shrimplike krill, especially in the Southern Ocean where it can devour 40 million krill a day in summer. Sleek and fast, the blue whale migrates to warmer oceans in winter to breed.

### BUBBLE-NET FEEDING
A pod of humpback whales uses a specialized hunting strategy called bubble-net feeding. One whale blows air bubbles from their blowhole encircling a shoal of fish. The rising bubbles form a cylindrical wall that traps fish and krill, while another whale from the pod calls loudly to the others so they can gulp down the captured prey.

# Toothed whales and dolphins

Most of the world's whales are not filter-feeding baleen whales, but fish-eating toothed whales. There are 77 different species, which include the giant sperm whale, the long-tusked narwhal, and many types of dolphins and porpoises. Unlike the filter-feeding whales, toothed whales chase and catch individual animals such as large fish, squid, seals, and even other whales.

## WHALE TEETH

Unlike the teeth of most mammals, whale teeth are simple conical pegs, similar to those of crocodiles. They are good for grabbing prey such as fish, but not for cutting it up or chewing it. Some whales have more than 100 teeth, others hardly any. The biggest teeth belong to the sperm whale, shown below, weighing up to 1 kg (2.2 lb) each.

## SLEEK HUNTERS

The most well-known toothed whales are dolphins. These sleek, powerful, high-speed hunters are sociable and intelligent animals. They travel in large groups, and work together to round up shoals of fish and squid. Dolphins are known for the wide variety of sounds they make, including clicks and squeaks, which they use to stay in touch while hunting. Each dolphin also has its own special whistle, which acts like its name and is used by other dolphins to attract its attention.

### FACT
Bottlenose dolphins in Australia have learned to carry sea sponges to protect their faces while they rummage for prey in the seabed.

## ECHOLOCATION

Dolphins and other toothed whales locate their prey by emitting loud clicks that echo off the target. The returning echoes create a "sound image" of the prey's location. The dolphin's clicks are generated in nasal sacs near its blowhole (nostril), and focused by an organ in its forehead called the melon. The echoes are picked up by nerves in its lower jaw and carried to its ears.

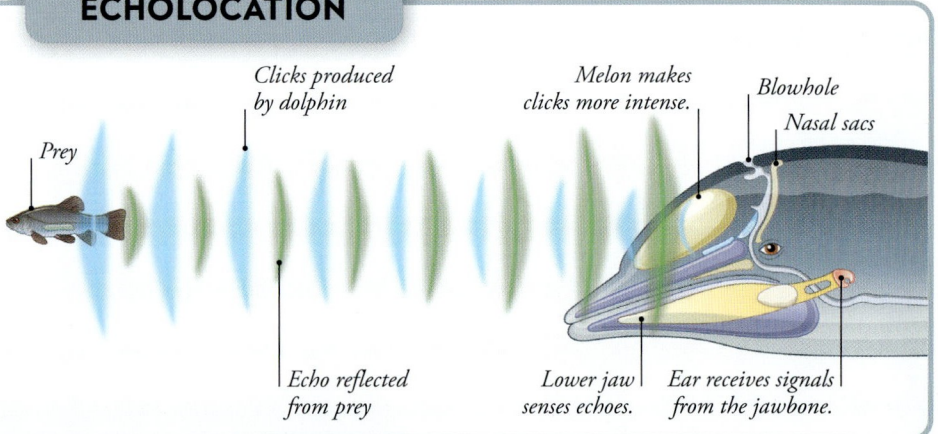

THE OPEN OCEAN

## TOOTHED GIANT

Most toothed whales are much smaller than the average baleen whale, but the sperm whale is a giant. It can grow up to 18 m (59 ft) long, and has a huge box-shaped head that is mostly filled with a waxy substance called spermaceti. This may help sperm whales transmit sounds into the water to search and hunt for prey.

◀ SPERM WHALE
*A hunting sperm whale may dive 3 km (2 miles) below the waves in search of prey. It can stay underwater for more than an hour before surfacing to breathe.*

## HORNED WHALE

The narwhal is a medium-sized whale that lives in the Arctic Ocean. Its unique feature is a spiral tusk that projects for up to 3 m (10 ft) from the male's upper jaw. The exact function of this tusk is still a mystery. It was once extremely valuable, because people who had never seen a narwhal thought the tusk was the horn of the legendary unicorn, and had magical powers.

▲ NARWHALS
*Narwhals often gather in large groups – sometimes several hundred strong. They stay close to broken pack ice with plenty of breathing holes.*

95

### Albatrosses
*Ocean wanderers*

**Wingspan** Up to 3.6 m (12 ft)
**Range** Southern oceans; North Pacific
**Hunting technique** Surface feeding

The biggest, most spectacular ocean birds are the albatrosses of southern oceans, with their enormously long wings. They have special adaptations that allow them to stay on the wing for days or even weeks at a time. The birds watch for squid and fish swimming near the surface and dip down to seize their prey in flight, but they may also settle on the water to feed.

# Ocean birds

Some birds spend most of their lives out on the open ocean. The only reason they return to land is to find somewhere to nest, because they have to lay their eggs on solid ground. At sea they eat fish, squid, krill, and other sea creatures, and have evolved a variety of techniques for catching them. These range from snatching prey while flying over the surface to plummeting into the sea, and even "flying" underwater.

### Cormorants
*Coastal hunters*

**Wingspan** Up to 1.5 m (5 ft)
**Range** Coastal seas worldwide
**Hunting technique** Underwater pursuit

These coastal fish-eaters are specialized for hunting underwater, where they use their big webbed feet to drive themselves along. A cormorant's feathers absorb more water than those of most seabirds. This makes it less buoyant, helping it to stay submerged. As the bird gets very wet, it often has to hold its wings outspread to dry them off.

### Gannets and boobies
*High divers*

**Wingspan** Up to 1.8 m (6 ft)
**Range** All tropical oceans; North Atlantic
**Hunting technique** Plunge diving

The most dramatic feeding technique has been perfected by gannets and boobies, such as this tropical blue-footed booby. They target fish from the air, and hurtle down to slice into the water at high speed with their wings swept back like arrowheads. The birds' vital organs are cushioned from the impact by air sacs under the skin. Once underwater, they seize their prey in their long, sharp bills before bursting back up into the air.

▲ **WANDERING ALBATROSS**
*An albatross holds its long, narrow wings outspread and soars on the wind. It can cover vast distances without once beating its wings.*

## Auks
*Underwater fliers*

**Wingspan** Up to 73 cm (29 in)
**Range** All northern oceans
**Hunting technique** Underwater pursuit

The auks have unusually short, strong wings specialized for "flying" underwater. This allows guillemots, razorbills, and this Atlantic puffin to catch fish by chasing after them beneath the surface. These stubby wings are not so suitable for flying through the air, so the auks have to use fast, whirring wingbeats to stay airborne.

## Penguins
*Flightless swimmers*

**Wingspan** Up to 0.8 m (2.6 ft)
**Range** Southern coastal seas
**Hunting technique** Underwater pursuit

The southern equivalents of the auks are the penguins. These seabirds are highly adapted for hunting underwater, with wings that are so specialized for use as flippers that they cannot fly at all. But this makes them fast, elegant swimmers, and some of the bigger penguins can dive to amazing depths to find deepwater fish and squid. They mostly live in the icy waters of the Southern Ocean around Antarctica.

## Storm petrels
*Tiny but tough*

**Wingspan** Up to 56 cm (22 in)
**Range** All oceans except Arctic Ocean
**Hunting technique** Surface feeding

Ocean birds have to cope with extreme weather and huge waves, yet some are tiny creatures that look too small and fragile to survive. They include storm petrels that are no bigger than sparrows. They spend months at sea, feeding on small animals such as krill. Many live in the Southern Ocean, and breed on the coasts of Antarctica.

▶ **FOOD SNATCHER**
*As frigatebirds cannot dive, they attack smaller birds to steal their catch. This frigatebird is forcing a tern to cough up the fish it has just caught.*

## Frigatebirds
*Pirates of the air*

**Wingspan** Up to 2.4 m (8 ft)
**Range** Most tropical oceans
**Hunting technique** Piracy

A few ocean birds avoid having to catch their own prey by stealing food from other birds. The most notorious of these pirates are the long-winged tropical frigatebirds, which attack their victims in the air and force them to drop their catch. The frigatebirds then swoop down to seize the fish in mid-air before it falls back into the sea.

THE OPEN OCEAN

# Twilight zone

The deeper you go in the ocean, the less light there is. About 200 m (660 ft) below the surface there is only faint blue light left. It is like the light we see at nightfall, so this region of the ocean is called the twilight zone. The light is too dim to support the drifting phytoplankton that feed a lot of marine life in the oceans. So the animals of the twilight zone must either swim up to the sunlit zone to find food, eat scraps, or prey on each other.

### UP FROM THE DEEP
Many animals including copepods and small lantern fish, such as the one shown below, live in the twilight zone during the day, but swim up towards the surface at night to feed on algae and other plankton. At dawn, they sink back into the twilight zone, hoping to avoid being eaten by herring and other shoaling fish. Compared to the fish's size, these are epic journeys, taking up to three hours each way. Since this animal movement happens in most of the world's oceans, every day of the year, this has been called the greatest migration on Earth.

### CHEMICAL LIGHT
The bodies of many twilight-zone animals are dotted with light-producing photophores. They include squid, fish, and jellyfish such as this one, known to scientists as *Atolla*. The light they produce is called bioluminescence. It is created by a chemical reaction that releases energy as light. Some animals use the light to attract prey, but others use it to confuse their enemies.

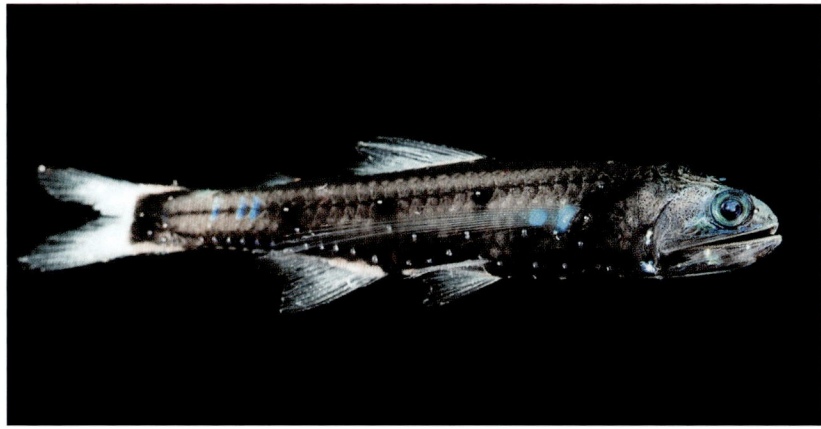

### FATAL ATTRACTION
The small animals that live in the twilight zone by day are hunted by other animals such as this firefly squid. Covered in hundreds of special light-producing organs, it is likely that the firefly squid uses these to attract its prey within range of its long, sucker-covered feeding tentacles.

▼ FIREFLY SQUID
*The photophores of the firefly squid glow bright blue in the dark, but the squid can switch them off to hide from its enemies.*

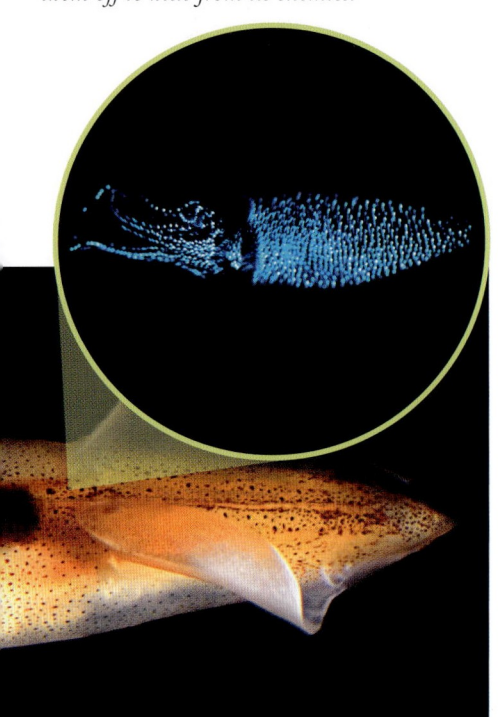

## TRAILING PREDATORS

Some fish that live in the twilight zone are specially adapted for catching animals that migrate to the surface to feed. This hatchetfish has big, bulging eyes that face upwards. This enables it to detect any small fish above it that are silhouetted against the dim blue light filtering down from the ocean's surface. Each evening, the hatchetfish trails its prey up from the depths, sinking back into the twilight zone during the day.

## KILLERS FROM THE DEEP

The twilight zone is the hunting ground of some fearsome-looking predators. They include this viperfish from the Pacific, which is equipped with huge jaws armed with incredibly long, needlelike teeth. Many deep-sea hunters have teeth like this, which can trap their victims. Prey is so scarce in the twilight zone that losing a single meal may mean going for weeks without food.

### FACT
A lot of twilight-zone animals use glowing lights to flash messages at each other in the dark. It's the only way they can keep in touch.

## HIDDEN BY LIGHT

The hatchetfish has rows of glowing photophores on its belly. These help to hide the fish from its enemies, by emitting a blue light that matches the glow from the surface. This eliminates the dark silhouette that would make the fish easy to see from below.

▲ ALL LIT UP
*If the hatchetfish lived in the dark zone, the photophores would show up like beacons.*

▲ MATCHING GLOW
*Seen against the blue glow from the surface, the photophores hide the fish's silhouette, making it almost invisible.*

THE OPEN OCEAN

# Midnight zone

A thousand metres (3,300 ft) below the surface, the faint blue glow of the twilight zone fades out altogether. Here, the only light is made by animals equipped with luminous organs of their own. Many of these are extraordinary-looking hunters with a variety of amazing adaptations for finding, catching, and eating their scarce prey.

THE OPEN OCEAN

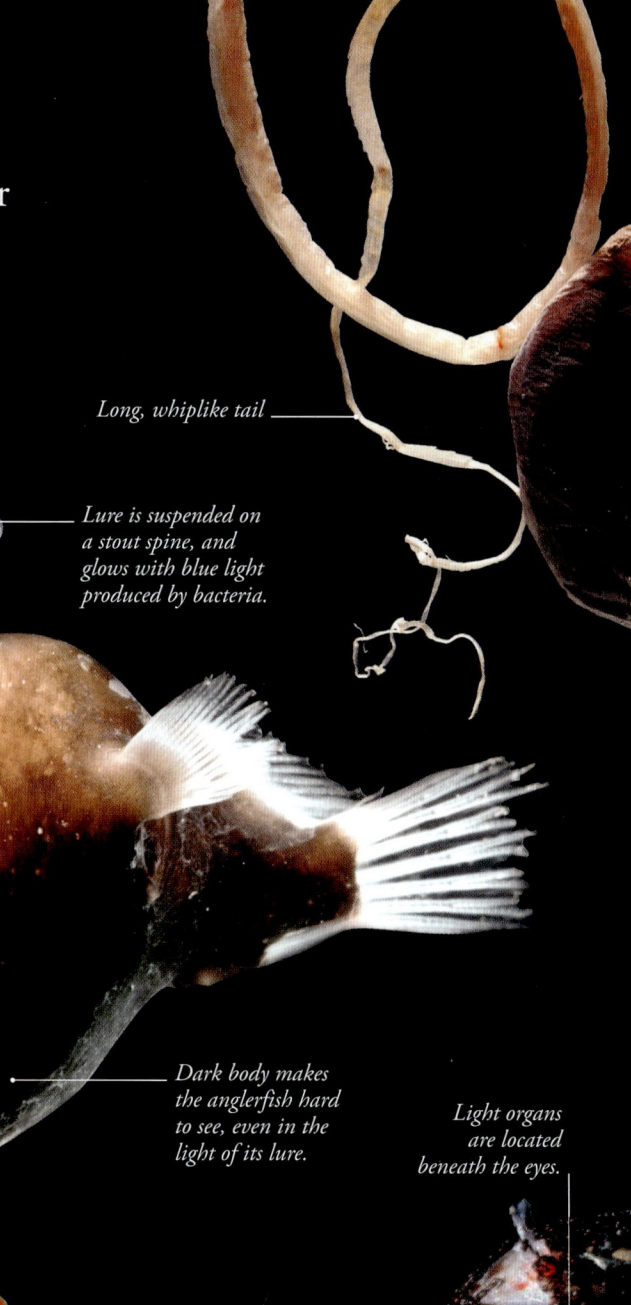

*Long, whiplike tail*

### DEATHTRAP
In the darkness of the deep, some fish are attracted to light. The deep-sea anglerfish makes use of this by holding a glowing lure in front of its enormous mouth. Any fish that comes close to investigate the glow risks being seized and swallowed whole.

*Lure is suspended on a stout spine, and glows with blue light produced by bacteria.*

*Sharp, curved teeth stop prey from escaping.*

*Dark body makes the anglerfish hard to see, even in the light of its lure.*

*Light organs are located beneath the eyes.*

### SEARCHLIGHT
Some predators, such as the stoplight loosejaw fish, have red searchlights for targeting their prey in the dark. Since most deep-sea animals cannot see red light, they do not know they are being stalked until it is too late. The red searchlights are most effective at revealing red-coloured animals that would be invisible if lit up by the blue light produced by other deep-sea animals.

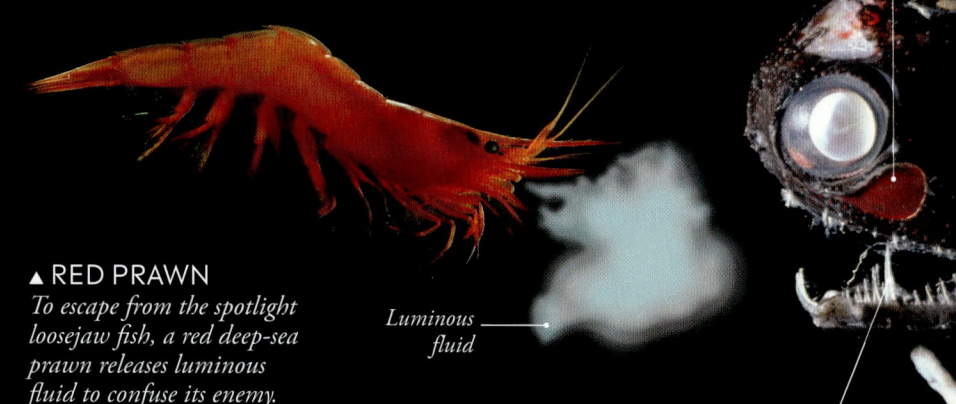

▲ RED PRAWN
*To escape from the spotlight loosejaw fish, a red deep-sea prawn releases luminous fluid to confuse its enemy.*

*Luminous fluid*

*Long, needle-sharp teeth give the fish a deadly grip.*

## HUGE APPETITE

Prey is very hard to find in the midnight zone, so predators must be able to eat almost anything they run into. The amazing gulper eel is one of the most specialized creatures. It has a huge mouth with specially adapted jawbones that allow it to swallow a victim as big as itself. The eel also has an elastic stomach that can expand to hold its outsized meals. The rest of its body has been reduced to a long, slender tail.

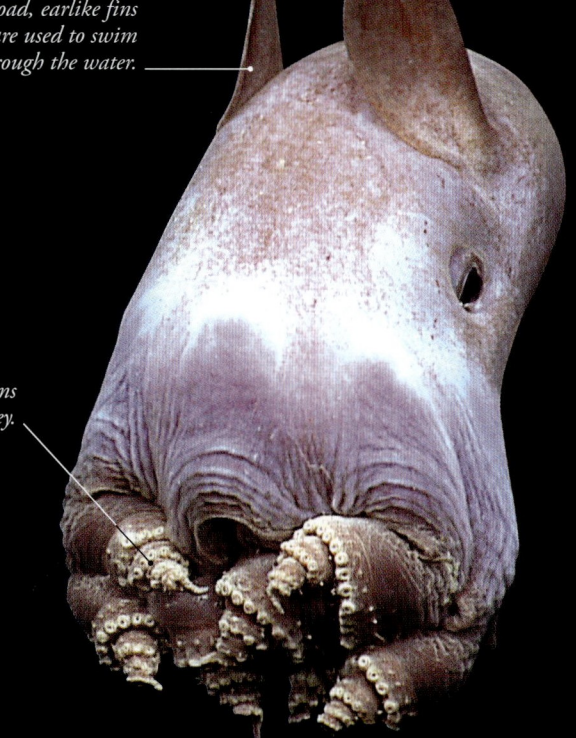

*Broad, earlike fins are used to swim through the water.*

*Sucker-covered arms are used to seize prey.*

*Tiny eyes on tip of snout*

▲ **GULPER EEL**
*Since they live at such depths, very few gulper eels have been seen alive. This is a preserved specimen.*

*Double-hinged jaw enables mouth to open incredibly wide.*

## JELLIES AND OCTOPODS

As well as fish, the open water of the midnight zone is home to many other mysterious animals. They include luminous jellyfish, deep-sea squid, and finned octopods, which are a type of octopus. One of these, the small Dumbo octopus, hovers above the ocean floor at incredible depths of up to 4,000 m (13,000 ft). Although it has poor eyesight, it can spot luminous prey in the water.

### FACT
The giant squid has the biggest eyes of any known animal. They are up to 27 cm (11 in) across – bigger than footballs.

### TITANIC BATTLES

Most midnight-zone animals have small bodies so they can survive without having to eat a lot. But a few are colossal. They include the giant squid, which can grow up to 13 m (43 ft) long. It is preyed on by the even more gigantic sperm whale, and defends itself with sharp-toothed suckers on its arms. The squid uses these to rip at the whale's skin, and many sperm whales show the scars.

Giant squid
13 m (43 ft)

Sperm whale
18 m (59 ft)

*Slender body does not need much food, so the fish can survive long spells without eating.*

**THE OPEN OCEAN**

# Ocean floor life

The deep ocean floor is a permanently dark, numbingly cold world. There are vast plains covered with soft mud and ooze. Much of this is made up of the remains of dead plankton. This provides food for many animals that are specialized for collecting and eating it. There are also a lot of scavengers that feed on dead animals that have sunk to the ocean floor.

### OOZE EATERS

Much of the solid seabed is covered in thick layers of soft sediment, made of mud and sand that washes off land, or the remains of plankton, which sink and settle as soft ooze. Detritivores are organisms that feed on this ooze or detritus (natural waste). They include sea cucumbers, such as the *Amperima* shown here, that swallow the ooze and digest edible material.

### CORAL IN THE DEEP

Corals don't just grow in the sunlit zone. Thousands of coral species live in the deep sea as well. Many of them look like rainbow-coloured bushes and trees, and lots of other animals live among their branches. Deep-sea corals grow very slowly and can live for hundreds and even thousands of years.

### WHALE FALL

When whales die, their enormous bodies fall onto the deep seabed, where they provide a feast that can last for many decades and feed hundreds of species. Scavengers such as sharks and hagfish eat the whale's muscles and blubber. Bone-eating worms, such as the *Osedax* shown here, settle onto the skeleton and use acid to digest the bones.

## SIFTING THE WATER

Some animals sit in one place on the ocean floor and sift the water for drifting food particles. These creatures include sea pens and relatives of starfish called feather stars and basket stars. They attach themselves to the soft seabed, and use their feathery arms to gather anything edible carried past them by the deepwater currents.

THE OPEN OCEAN

**◀ SEA PEN**
*So-called because it looks like a quill pen made from a feather, the sea pen sifts food from the water flowing through its tentacles.*

**▲ BASKET STAR**
*Like its starfish relatives, this basket star uses its short, mobile "tube feet" to pass food to its central mouth.*

## STANDING AROUND

The strange tripodfish has three very long, stiff spines on its lower fins, which it uses to stand on the ocean floor. Facing into the current and high above the soft ooze, it is perfectly placed to seize any food carried its way by the water. So even though it can swim, the tripod fish can get all the food it needs without moving.

**FACT**
Only a tiny fraction of the animals living on the ocean floor are known to science, because the deep ocean is so hard to reach.

# Life on black smokers

The black smokers that boil up from mid-ocean ridges are hotspots teeming with life deep in the ocean. Some extraordinary animals survive here because they have a source of food that does not rely on the energy of sunlight. Instead, the ecosystem is based on chemical energy from the black smokers themselves. Microbes called archaea use this energy to grow and multiply, and in turn feed colonies of animals including shrimps, clams, and giant worms.

## HOT CHEMICALS
The plumes of volcanically heated water that pour from black smokers are full of chemicals dissolved from hot rocks below the ocean floor. Microscopic archaea combine some of the chemicals with oxygen, and this releases the energy the microbes need to make sugar. These archaea use the sugar to build living cells, which provide food for other marine life.

▲ FOOD FACTORY
*Thick mats of pale archaea smother the warm rock around an erupting black smoker.*

## HOT TAIL
The superheated water that erupts from volcanic vents is a source of life-supporting energy, but its high temperature can be deadly. Nevertheless, some animals can live amazingly close to it. This Pompeii worm lives with its head in a burrow where the water is around 20°C (68°F), while the tail end can survive temperatures of 70°C (158°F). This great contrast in temperatures would kill most animals.

## CRABS AND SHRIMPS
The archaea living around the black smokers are grazed by swarms of animals that vary from place to place around the world. White crabs, such as the one shown here, live around black smokers in the Pacific Ocean, and similar white shrimps live on the Mid-Atlantic Ridge. The shrimps and crabs appear to be blind, but some have eyelike organs that may help them locate their food.

## MUSSELS AND CLAMS
While some animals eat the archaea microbes living on the rocks, others feed on colonies of microbes living inside their bodies. These animals include giant mussels and clams that live around the vents, sucking chemically rich water into their shells to supply the microbes that live on their gills.

◀ VOLCANO MUSSELS
*These clusters of giant mussels are living on a vent near the submerged Eifuku volcano in the western Pacific.*

## GIANT WORMS

The most spectacular animals living around black smokers and similar volcanic vents are giant tube worms, which can be 1 m (3.3 ft) long living inside a tube 3 m (9.8 ft) long. The worms form dense colonies around the vents, where they can absorb the chemically rich water. They supply these chemicals to colonies of microbes living in their bodies, and the worms absorb some of the food made by the microbes. This is similar to the system used by the clams and mussels. It allows the worms to grow amazingly quickly, reaching full size in just a few months.

THE OPEN OCEAN

▼ **RED PLUMES**
*Each worm lives in a thin-walled white tube. It has a plume of bright red feathery gills that it uses to absorb oxygen and vital chemicals.*

### FAST FACTS

■ The superheated water erupting from black smokers can have a temperature of 350°C (662°F), but it billows into water that is close to freezing.
■ The smokelike effect is caused by chemicals that have turned into solid black particles. But other chemicals stay dissolved, allowing them to be absorbed by microbes and animals.
■ Other vents in the ocean floor produce methane gas, and are home to similar forms of marine life. The seeping gas can freeze solid when it meets the cold water.

# SHALLOW SEAS

The warm, sunlit shallow seas that fringe continents and islands are teeming with marine life – from luxuriant kelp forests to colourful coral reefs.

## SUNLIT SEAS

The ocean sunlit zone is confined to the top 200 m (660 ft). Since continental shelf seas average 150 m (490 ft) deep, their entire depth lies within the sunlit zone – the region where most marine animals live. In the deep oceans, most of the water is too dark to support the organisms that need the energy of sunlight to make food, so fewer animals can live there.

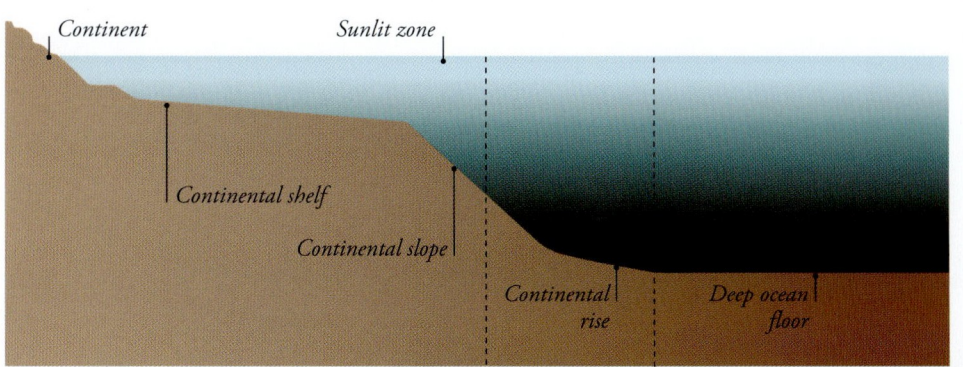

# Fertile waters

Shallow coastal seas are much richer in marine life than the deep oceans. This is partly because the water contains more of the nutrients needed by the tiny plantlike organisms that drift in the water, called phytoplankton. Sunlight also filters all the way down through the shallow water to the seabed, fuelling the growth of phytoplankton and providing food for animal life.

**FACT**
Just seven per cent of the total ocean area is made up of shallow shelf seas, but most of the world's marine life lives in them.

## MINERAL RICHES

Plantlike seaweeds and phytoplankton do not only need light. They need mineral nutrients that they can turn into living tissue – the basic food source for all other marine life. In coastal seas, rivers flowing off the land deliver plenty of these mineral nutrients. Other vital minerals are dissolved from coastal rocks by the waves.

◀ **VITAL MINERALS**
*A satellite view of the mouth of China's Yellow River shows how minerals carried by the river turn the sea itself yellow.*

## STORM POWER

Minerals that settle on the seabed are not far from the surface, and mix easily with the surface waters. This happens mainly during storms that stir up the water, scouring mud off the seabed so it billows up into the sunlit water above. Here, it provides phytoplankton with the nutrients it needs to grow, multiply, and feed other marine life.

**SHALLOW SEAS**

▲ WHALE SHARK
*Filtering the water through its sievelike gills, this whale shark feeds on the swarming microscopic life that makes shallow seas look cloudy.*

## TEEMING LIFE

Phytoplankton multiply fast in shallow coastal seas, where there is sunlit water with plenty of nutrients. The phytoplankton can be so dense that it makes the water look green and cloudy. It may look like pollution, but it is a sign that the water is teeming with microscopic life.

## RICH FISHERIES

The flourishing life in coastal seas supports big shoals of fish such as herrings, sardines, and anchovies. Since these fish are important sources of human food, it means that many of the world's most valuable fisheries are found in shallow coastal waters. Until recently, there was no point in fishing the deep ocean, but overfishing in shallower seas has made many coastal fish scarce.

# The seabed

**SHALLOW SEAS**

Unlike the deep ocean floor, the seabeds of shallow coastal seas are lit up and warmed by sunlight. This allows many forms of life to flourish in large numbers, especially in shallower parts of the sea where the light level is higher. Different types of seabed give the animals a wide variety of places to live.

### RAGGED ROCKS

In places, the hard bedrock of the seabed is exposed to form rocky reefs. These are often teeming with marine life – seaweeds, sponges, sea squirts, and many types of shellfish are attached to these reefs. The ragged and tumbled rocks are also full of holes that make safe refuges for seafloor animals, including eels, crabs, lobsters, and octopuses.

### SHIFTING SANDS

Many seabeds are covered with deep layers of sand and other soft sediments. Most of this is the result of thousands of years of coastal erosion, but a lot is carried out to sea by rivers. Although the sand looks barren, it is full of burrowing worms and clams that are hunted by seafloor animals.

▲ **RIBBON-TAILED STINGRAY**
*The mouth of this tropical stingray is underneath its body so it can easily scoop up prey hidden in the sand.*

### SHIPWRECKS

Many of the shifting sandbanks and rocky reefs of coastal seas lie just below the surface. Before the days of accurate charts and satellite navigation, they caused many shipwrecks. As a result, shallow seabeds are littered with the remains of ships, some dating back more than a thousand years. These wrecks now provide perfect homes for marine life.

## FLAME SHELL

Soft, sandy seabeds are always being stirred up by moving water, making life difficult for many animals. But certain molluscs such as this flame shell anchor themselves to the sand with strong threads, binding the sand together in a tough mat. The mat allows other animals to settle and form reefs that teem with sea life.

## SITTING PRETTY

The sunlight filtering down to the shallow seabed allows a lot of microscopic plankton to live in the water. This supports animals that can survive by sitting in one place on the seabed and simply filtering the water for food. They include mussels and other molluscs such as clams, flowerlike sea anemones, and worms that live in tubes and spread crowns of tentacles to gather food.

◀ **PEACOCK WORM**
*The feathery tentacles of this tubeworm act like a sieve, straining the water for tiny drifting animals and other food.*

**FACT**
In 1987, the US military vessel *Duane* was deliberately sunk off Molasses Reef in Florida, US, to serve as an artificial reef where fish and other marine animals can live.

▲ **GALÁPAGOS SEA LION**
*An agile hunter, the Galápagos sea lion can dive 600 m (1,970 ft), foraging for fish as well as squid and crustaceans.*

## SEAL BANQUET

Seals and sea lions hunt in the sea, but must return to the surface to breathe. Shallow coastal seas are ideal for them, because they can easily dive down to the seabed to look for the rich variety of prey that lives there, then come back up for air. In deeper waters, seals and sea lions often cannot reach the bottom, and have to use a lot more energy hunting fast-moving fish and squid.

**SHALLOW SEAS**

SHALLOW SEAS

*Leaflike frond*

*Soft, flexible stem cannot support itself.*

*Buoyant float (air bladder) holds the stem upright.*

# Seaweeds

Most of the food produced in the oceans is made by tiny phytoplankton that drift in open water. These microscopic algae have much bigger relatives that live in shallow, sunlit water. These are algae too, but we call them seaweeds. Although they look like plants, they are not true plants because they have a different internal structure. They must live underwater, but many are adapted for life on tidal shores.

### MARINE ALGAE
Seaweeds are multi-celled marine relatives of the tiny single-celled algae that form much of the phytoplankton. They are both protists – living things that are neither animals nor plants. But like plants, they are able to absorb solar energy and use it to make sugar from water and carbon dioxide, a process called photosynthesis.

### BUOYED UP
Since seaweeds need sunlight, they must grow near the water's surface. Some float in the ocean, but most are attached to rocks on shallow seabeds and their flexible stems and leaflike fronds are buoyed up by the water. Many seaweeds have gas-filled floats to make sure the light-gathering fronds lie as near to the surface as possible.

## TIDAL SURVIVAL

Seaweeds need water to make the sugar that fuels their growth. They soak it up directly from their surface instead of through roots and veins, like plants. This works only if they are underwater, but many seaweeds that grow in coastal waters are tough enough to survive a few hours of exposure on the shore at low tide. They can dry out under hot sunshine, but recover as the tide rises and submerges them.

## SEAWEED GRAZERS

Seaweeds provide food for a variety of sea creatures, including small crabs, sea urchins, limpets, and many types of fish. Most tropical parrotfish specialize in grazing the seaweed that grows on coral reefs, using their strong teeth to scrape it from the soft rock. This helps stop seaweeds from smothering the coral.

◀ PARROTFISH
*The teeth of parrotfish are fused into a strong "beak" that can crunch through coral rock to get at the small seaweeds growing on it.*

## TYPES OF SEAWEED

There are three types of seaweed: brown, green, and red. The difference is not just their colour – they are not related, and have very different structures. Most brown seaweeds are big, tough wracks and kelps, while green seaweeds include delicate forms such as sea lettuce. The red ones include coralline seaweeds that help build coral reefs.

**Brown seaweed**

**Green seaweed**

**Red seaweed**

SHALLOW SEAS

# Kelp forests

**SHALLOW SEAS**

The shallow coastal waters near the shores of many cool oceans support lush beds of seaweed. In some places, such as coasts off Alaska and California in the US, gigantic seaweeds called giant kelp form tall, dense underwater forests that provide food and shelter for a rich variety of marine animals. Some of these animals eat the kelp, but most of them prey on each other.

## CLEAR SEAS

On coasts where the water is clear, as it is off the Pacific shores of North and South America, giant kelp – a type of seaweed – is able to live in sunlit water up to 40 m (130 ft) deep, and grow as tall as trees on land. Anchored to the seabed, the kelp fronds grow up through the clear water, and their ends trail on the surface. Some fronds can grow to astounding lengths of 50 m (165 ft).

▶ **KELP CANOPY**
*Buoyed up by gas-filled floats, giant kelp fronds off the coast of California, US, grow straight up towards the sunlight.*

## STRONG ANCHOR

The kelp attaches itself to rocks on the seabed by a clawlike structure called a holdfast. Although the holdfast may look like the roots of a plant, it does not absorb nutrients in the same way. Its main function is to anchor the kelp to the seabed, so that it is not swept away by the current. The kelp holdfasts are often covered with sponges, barnacles, mussels, and other animals.

**FACT**
When the growing conditions are right, giant kelp can grow as much as 60 cm (24 in) each day.

## SEA URCHINS

The main enemies of giant kelp are sea urchins, especially a species known as the purple sea urchin. These spiny relatives of starfish have tough teeth on their undersides that they use to nibble away at the kelp fronds and devour them. When conditions are favourable, sea urchins can multiply very fast and their grazing can destroy large areas of kelp forests.

◀ **PRICKLY PROBLEM**
*This group of hungry sea urchins will soon chew through the tough kelp stalks.*

## URCHIN HUNTERS

Luckily for the kelp forest, sea urchins are the favourite prey of the sea otters that hunt in these waters. The otters dive to the seabed to find the urchins, and bring them back up to the surface. They use stones to smash open the urchins so they can feast on the soft flesh inside, avoiding the sharp spines.

## STARRY PREDATOR

Another sea urchin hunter is the sunflower sea star of the Pacific Ocean. These giant sea stars have become very rare after many died out in 2013 from the sea star wasting disease.

## GIANT OCTOPUS

One of the biggest animals that lives among the kelp is the Pacific giant octopus, which has arms that can span up to 5 m (16 ft). It preys on fish and shellfish such as crabs, lobsters, and clams. Like all octopuses, it is very intelligent, with a good memory and sharp senses.

▼ **SHARK SNACK**
*A dead shark on the seabed makes an easy meal for this giant octopus. Like many hunters, the octopus is a scavenger too.*

## SEA OTTER

In the cold water of the north Pacific, sea otters are kept warm by their extremely thick fur. It holds a layer of air that makes the sea otters buoyant, so they can rest and even sleep by floating on their backs. The otters wrap kelp fronds around their bodies to stop themselves being swept away by the current.

# Seafloor fish

An amazing variety of fish live on or near shallow coastal seabeds. Many are specialized for seabed life, with heavy bodies that weigh them down so they can lie on the ocean floor. They are often flattened and so well camouflaged that they are almost invisible when they lie still. Some hunt for seafloor animals such as crabs and clams. Others are ambush predators that wait for prey to come within attacking range.

## AMBUSH KILLERS

Some predatory fish lie half-buried on the seabed, waiting for other fish to swim close enough to catch. Stargazers have eyes on the tops of their heads for spying victims, which they dart up to and seize with their sharp teeth. An anglerfish tempts prey within range using a wriggling lure, like a worm dangling over its enormous mouth.

▲ MARBLED STARGAZER
*Also known as the pop-eyed fish, the venomous stargazer lies in wait with just its eyes and upward-facing mouth showing above the sand.*

## TOUCH SENSITIVE

Soft seabeds are home to a variety of burrowing animals, including small crabs and marine worms. Although they are hidden from sight, some fish such as gurnards are able to find them. These fish have specially adapted pectoral fins with sensitive fingerlike fin rays that can feel for prey buried in the sand as they swim slowly over the bottom.

▲ RED GURNARD
*Sensitive fin rays beneath its head allow this north Atlantic hunter to locate hidden prey.*

## ROCKY REFUGES

On rocky seabeds, many bottom-dwelling fish take refuge in rock crevices and gaps between boulders. These offer small fish protection from their enemies, but they also make perfect hideouts for ambush predators. Some fish such as moray eels may spend most of their lives in one rocky refuge, leaving it only to snatch passing prey.

◀ MORAY EELS
*These powerful hunters have two sets of jaws covered in sharp teeth, which seize and swallow slippery, struggling prey.*

## REMARKABLE FLATFISH

A flatfish such as a plaice or flounder starts life like a normal fish, but gradually changes shape so it can lie on its side on the seabed. Its eyes shift around its head so they are both on the same side, and its mouth twists too. Its upper side is often superbly camouflaged.

◀ **PLAICE**
*Found in oceans throughout the world, flatfish such as this plaice are unique for having both eyes on the same side of their head.*

## WINGED RAYS

While flatfish are flattened from side to side so they can lie on the seabed, rays are flattened from top to bottom. They are relatives of sharks, and swim by flapping their broad pectoral fins like wings. Most of them hunt on the seabed, and many have broad, strong teeth for crushing the shells of crabs and clams.

◀ **SPOTTED EAGLE RAY**
*Two eagle rays glide over a rocky seabed searching for prey. Like many rays, they have stings in their tails.*

**SHALLOW SEAS**

### FACT
The torpedo ray hunts with electricity. It can generate a 200-volt electric shock – enough to kill a small fish instantly.

# Sea snails and clams

The shallow seabed is teeming with invertebrates – animals that do not have internal skeletons with backbones. Many are molluscs – marine relatives of slugs and snails. Some are very snail-like, with coiled shells and obvious heads and tails. Others such as clams and mussels do not have heads, and their bodies are hidden inside two hinged shells.

## STOMACH CRAWLERS
Sea snails seem to crawl on their stomachs, just like garden snails and slugs, and because of this they are called gastropods, which means "stomach foot". Some use their rasping tongues to graze on algae, but others such as the bubble snail are active hunters that attack and eat prey, including marine worms.

▲ **DISTINCTIVE SHELL**
*Easily identified because of its red-lined shell, the bubble snail is found in the Indian and Pacific oceans. If threatened, the snail quickly withdraws into its shell.*

## UNIQUE SHELL
Many sea snails have protective shells. One of the most spectacular and unique shells belongs to the tropical Venus comb, which is covered with needlelike spines that may help protect it from its enemies. It hunts other molluscs, sniffing them out with its long, tubular snout.

## FILTER FEEDERS
Apart from gastropods, the other main group of marine molluscs are bivalves – clams, mussels, and scallops. These have two hinged shells, and live by filtering edible particles from water that they draw through their bodies. Most live in one place, buried in soft seabeds or attached to rocks.

◄ **FAN MUSSEL**
*This big fan-shaped bivalve can be up to 120 cm (47 in) high. It lives in the Mediterranean Sea, with its pointed end buried in the seabed.*

## INSIDE THE SHELL

Gastropods and bivalves share some of the same body structures, but they are modified for different uses. For example, both may have a strong muscular foot, but a gastropod uses it for crawling while a burrowing bivalve uses it to pull itself down into the sand. However, bivalves differ greatly in that their bodies have no head, brain, or obvious sensory organs.

▲ **GASTROPOD**
A sea snail lives like a land snail, crawling around and gathering food with its mouth.

*Labels: Spiral shell, Digestive system, Muscular foot, Gill, Sensory tentacles, Mouth*

▲ **BIVALVE**
A typical bivalve sucks water into its body through a siphon tube, and filters it for food.

*Labels: Digestive system, Gill, Muscular foot, Shell hinge, Shell closing muscle, Siphon*

## COLOURFUL SLUGS

Sea slugs come in an extraordinary array of vivid colours. Many of them prey on animals such as anemones that are armed with venomous stings. Amazingly, some sea slugs are able to swallow the stinging cells, storing them in the tips of their tentacles and using them for their own defence.

*Labels: Hinge, Sensory tentacles, Row of simple eyes*

## SNAPPING SCALLOPS

Most bivalves, such as clams, live like plants, rooted in one place and with few senses. Scallops, however, have shells that are fringed with sensory tentacles and even eyes. If attacked, they escape by snapping their shells shut, which makes them shoot away through the water.

*Some sea slugs have exposed gills, allowing them to take in oxygen from the water.*

▼ **WARNING COLOUR**
The bright colours of this tropical sea slug warn predators that it is dangerous to eat.

*Two hornlike structures at the front help locate food through smell.*

**SHALLOW SEAS**

SHALLOW SEAS

### SHELLED NAUTILUS
Unlike other cephalopods, the nautilus has a coiled snail-like shell. The shell contains gas that makes it buoyant, enabling the nautilus to rise and sink in the water like a submarine. Nautiluses are found in the Indian and Pacific oceans, where they prey on other animals as well as scavenge on the remains of dead ones. Nautiluses have lived in the oceans for about 500 million years – long before the time of the dinosaurs.

# Squid, octopus, and cuttlefish

Most marine molluscs are simple animals; many seem to have only basic senses. But cephalopods – including squid – are different. They are calculating, sharp-eyed hunters, with excellent memories. They have long, flexible arms and tentacles, and some amazing adaptations for hunting, swimming, defence, and communication.

### JET-PROPELLED SQUID
Unlike most of their cuttlefish and octopus relatives, squid live in open water and travel in big shoals. They are very streamlined, and able to streak through the water at high speed by blasting water out of their siphon tubes – a form of jet propulsion. Some even shoot out of the water into the air.

▲ LOW-SPEED OPTION
*To swim at slower speeds, this common squid ripples the fins at the back of its body.*

### EXPERT HUNTERS
Cuttlefish live in shallow coastal waters where they swim slowly over the seabed looking for crabs, shrimps, and other prey to catch with their long tentacles. Like many cephalopods, they have an amazing ability to change colour – switching in a split second from camouflage to dazzling zebra stripes, and even flashing in moving waves of colour like neon signs.

▶ SECRET WEAPON
*This common cuttlefish shoots out its tentacles at lightning speed to seize a crab.*

## CRAB-KILLING OCTOPUS

Most octopuses often live in seabed crevices (cracks). They emerge to seek out prey such as crabs, which they rip apart with their sharp beak and eight suckered arms. Unlike cuttlefish and squid, they do not have an extra pair of tentacles. They are remarkably intelligent and quick to learn.

### ◀ TOXIC TERROR

*Some octopuses kill their prey with a venomous bite. The venom of the tiny tropical blue-ringed octopus is incredibly toxic and can kill a human within a few minutes.*

### INSIDE A CEPHALOPOD

The word cephalopod means "head-limb". It describes the way the arms are attached directly to the animal's head, surrounding its mouth. The mouth has beaklike jaws and a toothed tongue. The eight flexible arms are equipped with rows of suckers, and squid and cuttlefish also have a pair of extendible tentacles.

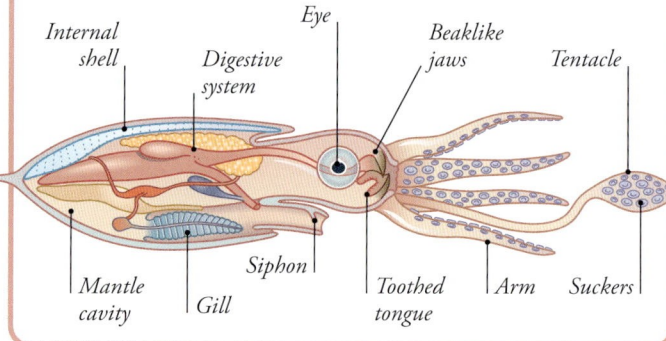

*Internal shell, Digestive system, Eye, Beaklike jaws, Tentacle, Mantle cavity, Gill, Siphon, Toothed tongue, Arm, Suckers*

## INKY DEFENCE

Feeling threatened by an approaching diver, a giant octopus squirts a cloud of dark ink into the water from its siphon tube. The ink billows out in the water like dense smoke, allowing the octopus to escape as it shoots backwards through the water at high speed. Squid and cuttlefish also use this same inky defence tactic.

SHALLOW SEAS

## HATCHING OCTOPUS
No bigger than a grain of rice, this newly hatched octopus will grow into a Pacific giant octopus with an arm span of up to 5 m (16 ft). Like all cephalopods, this species lays eggs. A female can lay up to 400,000 eggs, which she attaches to a rock, and doesn't leave them until they hatch.

# Prawns, lobsters, and crabs

Crustaceans are an important group of marine animals that live in all oceans but are very common in shallow coastal seas. They have jointed, hard-shelled bodies like those of insects, and range from big, heavily armoured types such as lobsters and crabs to the delicate, shrimplike krill and tiny copepods that form much of the oceanic zooplankton.

## JOINTED BODIES
Most crustaceans have bodies like this prawn, with a head, a chain of body segments, and several pairs of legs specialized for different jobs. All the body parts are supported by a hard outer shell (the exoskeleton) made of a tough material called chitin, similar to your fingernails. The rigid segments are linked by mobile joints.

## HEAVY ARMOUR
The external skeleton of some crustaceans, including lobsters, crabs, and crayfish, is strengthened with chalky minerals to form a thick, very hard armour. This gives them protection from their enemies. The exoskeleton's strength also allows some of these animals to have powerful claws for crushing their prey.

*Body has armoured segments.*

*Long antennae sense prey in the dark.*

*Thinner and more flexible chitin forms the joints, allowing the lobster to move its body.*

## DRIFTING LARVAE
All crustaceans lay eggs. The eggs of crabs, for example, hatch as tiny larvae that live in the open ocean. They drift in the plankton, where they feed alongside small adult crustaceans such as copepods. Larvae go through many growth stages, shedding their skin each time and changing shape. Eventually, they change into small adults, which then settle on the seabed.

▲ **CRAB LARVA**
*Crab larvae spread far beyond the home range of their parents by drifting in the plankton and then settling in distant seas.*

▶ **PURPLE REEF LOBSTER**
*This small lobster is brightly coloured, like many inhabitants on tropical coral reefs, where it hunts animals such as crabs and starfish.*

## FACT
The biggest crustacean on Earth is the Japanese giant spider crab, which can have legs spanning almost 4 m (13 ft) from tip to tip.

## NEW SKIN

One problem with having a strong external skeleton is that it will not stretch as the animal grows. This means that a crustacean such as this crab has to keep shedding its shell and growing a new one.

When the crab slips out of its old, hard shell, it has soft skin that has to stretch to a larger size before it hardens. During this time, the crab has no defences and must hide from its enemies.

▲ STAGE 1
*The old shell (orange) splits open at the back, revealing a new, soft shell underneath. The crab then climbs out of its old shell.*

▲ STAGE 2
*The crab expands its soft shell by pumping water into its body; it takes about three days for the shell to harden.*

▶ WHALE BARNACLES
*These crustaceans spend their entire life attached to a whale. Openings in their shells allow them to extend their feathery arms to catch food.*

## SETTLING DOWN

Barnacles are tiny marine animals that look very different from other crustaceans. They begin life like drifting crab larvae, but when they turn into adults, they cement themselves to hard surfaces. Here, the barnacles grow strong plates, and spend the rest of their lives sieving the water for food. Some even attach themselves to the skin of whales.

*Smaller claw has sharp edges and is used for cutting prey.*

SHALLOW SEAS

# Starfish, sea urchins, and sea cucumbers

Echinoderms are animals with bodies that are basically star-shaped, with a mouth in the middle. This five-rayed body plan is obvious in most starfish, but other echinoderms have it too. They live in oceans throughout the world, where they prey on other animals, graze on seaweeds, or feed on the edible debris that settles on the seabed.

## SPINY BALLS

The word echinoderm means "spiny skin". This perfectly describes sea urchins, which are covered with spines. They have the same five-rayed body plan as most starfish, but formed into a ball, like an orange with five segments. They have small, flexible tube feet that they use for moving around and gathering food.

▲ **BODY ARMOUR**
*Slow-moving, sea urchins rely on their spines to deter predators. The spines often break easily, embedding themselves in the attacker's skin.*

## SEA STARS

Most starfish have five arms extending from a central disc but some have as many as 50 arms. They have flexible tube feet, each ending in a tiny sucker. Starfish do not have brains, but they do have simple eyes at the end of each arm. Many starfish feed on animals such as oysters, clamping onto their shells and pulling them apart to get the meat inside.

▲ **VIVID COLOUR**
*Many starfish are brightly coloured, with contrasting patterns of spines or plates on their skin. Their bright colour warns predators that they may taste bad.*

## NEW FOR OLD

One of the most amazing things about starfish is the way they can grow new body parts if they are injured. A starfish can easily grow a new arm to replace a lost limb. If the lost limb still has part of the central disc attached, it will grow a whole new body. This means that if one starfish is sliced in two, it can survive, regrow the missing parts, and become two starfish.

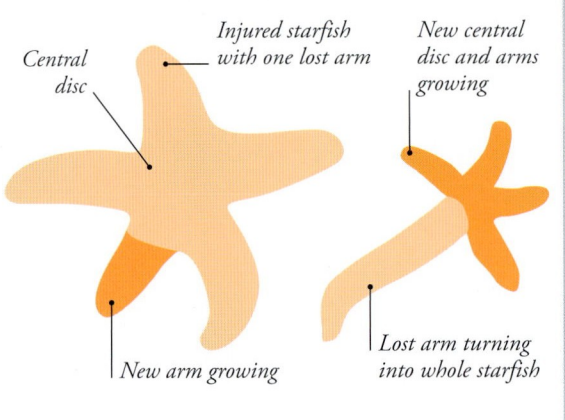

*Central disc*
*Injured starfish with one lost arm*
*New central disc and arms growing*
*New arm growing*
*Lost arm turning into whole starfish*

### STARRY SWARMS

Brittlestars are slender starfish with very flexible arms and small, circular central discs. They live on the seabed, where they use their mobile, spiny arms to crawl over the sand. These colourful starfish feed on small food particles that settle on the bottom. In places where the food supply is plentiful, they can form dense swarms – there can be as many as 2,000 brittlestars in 1 square metre (3 square feet).

**SHALLOW SEAS**

### SIFTING THE WATER

Feather stars are starfish with bodies that have become adapted to living upside down, firmly gripping rocks on the seabed. They feed on tiny plankton and edible particles drifting in the water, which they snare with the tube feet extending from their feathery arms.

### FACT
Starfish have lived in the oceans for at least 480 million years – long before the first dinosaurs roamed the land.

### MUD SWALLOWERS

Sea cucumbers have elongated five-sided bodies, with a mouth and tentacles at one end. They live on the seabed, where they feed by swallowing the soft muddy sediment and digesting any edible material. If threatened, they shoot out their internal organs at the attacker.

*Tentacles around the mouth collect food.*

# Jellyfish and anemones

**SHALLOW SEAS**

The jellyfish that swim gracefully through the oceans are part of a group of animals called cnidarians, which also include sea anemones and corals. These animals look very different from each other, but they have the same basic body structure, and they are armed with stinging cells, which they use to stun prey. They live in all oceans and at all depths, but they are particularly common in shallow coastal seas.

## FLOATING JELLYFISH

The most spectacular cnidarians are jellyfish, which live in open water. A jellyfish swims by squeezing its flexible body to force water out, then relaxing so the body springs back to its original shape. Its bell may have a fringe of tentacles, while bigger feeding arms surround its central mouth. Some jellyfish gather small edible particles, but others snare larger animals using batteries of stinging cells.

## TUBES AND BELLS

All cnidarians have hollow circular or tubular bodies made of an outer and inner skin separated by a layer of jelly. The inner skin acts as a stomach lining. There are two forms: polyps and medusae. Tubular polyps such as anemones live anchored to rocks with their mouth and crown of stinging tentacles facing upwards. By contrast, medusae such as jellyfish are umbrella-shaped, free-swimming animals that live with their mouths and tentacles facing downwards.

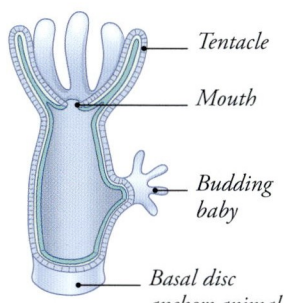

▲ **POLYP**
A polyp is a tube of jelly glued to a rock. Some types of polyp multiply by growing smaller polyps from their sides.

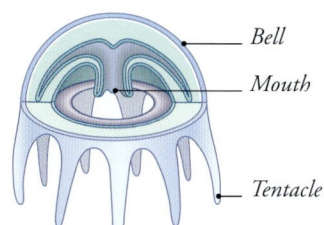

▲ **MEDUSA**
An adult jellyfish is a medusa — a free-swimming cnidarian. Most jellyfish spend part of their lives as polyps, then become medusae.

*Like many jellyfish, the mauve stinger can glow in the dark.*

*Four large feeding arms gather food into the central mouth.*

▲ **MAUVE STINGER**
This jellyfish lives in all the warm and slightly cooler oceans of the world, where it feeds on other drifting animals. It has a painful sting.

*Body is made of springy jelly inside a layer of skin.*

*A ring of muscle squeezes the body during swimming.*

*Small red lumps on the body are clusters of stinging cells.*

*Eight long tentacles are armed with stings to catch prey.*

## STINGING CELLS

Jellyfish, anemones, and other cnidarians are armed with tiny stinging cells. Each cell contains a barbed, venomous harpoon. When it is triggered – usually by touch – the harpoon shoots out and pierces the skin of an enemy or prey, injecting its venom. Each cell is microscopic, but a single jellyfish may have thousands or even millions of them on its long stinging tentacles. The effect of these massed stings on human victims can be incredibly painful, and even lethal.

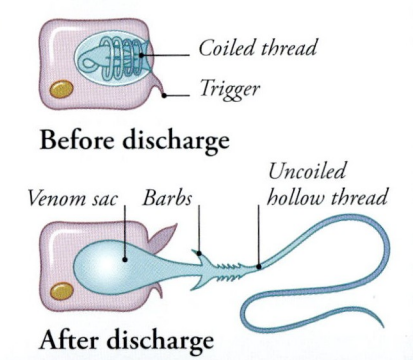

Coiled thread — Trigger

**Before discharge**

Venom sac — Barbs — Uncoiled hollow thread

**After discharge**

## SHALLOW SEAS

## TROPICAL KILLER

Also known as sea wasps, box jellyfish are considered to be among the deadliest animals in the ocean. They live in the tropical coral seas around Australia and Indonesia. The biggest of these is only the size of a basketball, but its tentacles are armed with more than 30 million stings.

## SEA ANEMONES

They may look harmless, but sea anemones are efficient predators. They feed by trapping tiny drifting animals and other food particles with their stinging tentacles. Many, such as these jewel anemones, look like colourful flowers, while others such as the snakelocks anemones resemble writhing clusters of worms. They also vary in size, from about 1.5 cm (0.5 in) to 1 m (3 ft) in diameter.

### FACT
The mauve stinger's body is only 10 cm (4 in) wide, but its stinging tentacles can trail beneath it for more than 3 m (9.9 ft).

## PERFECT PARTNERS

Although sea anemones can catch and kill prey with their stinging cells, the clownfish of tropical coral seas are immune to their venom; mucus on the clownfish's skin likely keeps it from being stung. Clownfish live in partnership with certain species of anemone and shelter among their tentacles, which protects them from predators. In return, clownfish chase off animals that might harm the anemones.

131

# Corals and coral reefs

Corals are close relatives of sea anemones, and have the same tubular body form, called a polyp, with a crown of tentacles surrounding a central mouth. But unlike anemones, many corals form colonies, with each coral connected to many others. Some of these colonial corals have skeletons of limestone that build up to form brilliantly coloured coral reefs that are home to thousands of species of marine animals.

**SHALLOW SEAS**

*Among the fastest growing corals on the reef, the staghorn coral can be pink, blue, or yellow.*

## CORAL REEFS

Hard corals absorb minerals from seawater and use them to make limestone cups that support their soft bodies. When the corals die, their stony skeletons survive, and new corals grow on top of them. Over thousands of years, this builds up a vast depth of coral rock capped by many different types of living coral. These reefs form on tropical coasts and around islands, especially in the western Pacific and Indian oceans, and the Caribbean and Red seas.

*Sea fans have tough but flexible spreading branches.*

### ▶ CORAL COLONIES
*Colonial corals are made up of individual coral polyps (seen here in white) linked to others by tubular stolons, or branches (red). The polyps use their stinging tentacles to gather food, digest it, and share the nutrients.*

### ▶ VITAL PARTNERSHIP
*Clear tropical waters contain very little edible plankton. But tiny algae (seen here as green specks) living in the tissues of tropical reef corals can make sugar using the energy of sunlight. The sugar allows the corals to flourish in the food-poor water. This relationship is known as symbiosis.*

*Platelike star coral is made up of hundreds of small coral polyps.*

*Finger coral*

*Seagrass is one of the few true plants that grows in saltwater, forming dense meadows in shallow lagoons.*

*Sea urchins graze on algae and tiny creatures found on rocks.*

◄ **CORAL ARCHITECTURE**
Corals come in an incredible array of colours, shapes, and sizes. The species shown here is a brain coral. It has deep grooves that resembles the texture of a human brain. Other corals are plantlike with thin branches. These coral structures provide the perfect hiding places for reef animals.

**FACT**
The algae living in tropical reef corals provide up to 90 per cent of the coral's energy.

*Red coralline algae*

◄ **PARADISE GARDENS**
A tropical coral reef is like an oasis in a marine desert. Food is scarce in open tropical oceans, but the reef provides food and shelter for a dazzling diversity of fish, turtles, and crabs, as well as other animals. A quarter of all known marine species live on coral reefs, even though the area covered by the reefs is less than a hundredth of the total ocean area.

*Tropical coral reefs grow only in water less than 150 m (490 ft) deep.*

## COLD-WATER REEFS

Not all coral reefs grow in the sunlit shallows of the tropics, where the corals feed on sugar made by algae living in their tissues. There are also cold-water reefs that live in deeper, darker water. They survive because colder oceans contain more plankton than tropical waters, providing the corals with all the food they need. This means the corals do not rely on sugar made by algae living in their tissues, so they don't need to grow in sunlit water.

► **ORANGE SOFT CORAL**
*Many corals on cold-water reefs are soft corals without stony skeletons.*

**SHALLOW SEAS**

SHALLOW SEAS

# The Great Barrier Reef

The biggest coral reef in the world is the Great Barrier Reef, which lies off the coast of tropical northeastern Australia. It is a vast complex of 3,000 coral reefs linked together in a chain of living coral rock 2,300 km (1,430 miles) long. The barrier reef is so big it can be seen from space.

### OCEAN BARRIER
This spectacular reef gets its name because it acts as a barrier between the coast and the large waves of the open Pacific Ocean. It extends several kilometres offshore, to the edge of Australia's continental shelf. The water between the reef and the shore is relatively shallow, but beyond the reef the depth drops down from near zero to 1,000 m (3,280 ft) or more.

▶ VIEW FROM SPACE
*This view from the International Space Station, orbiting 431 km (268 miles) above Cape Flattery in northeastern Australia, shows how the Great Barrier Reef forms an almost continuous ribbon of coral along the edge of the continental shelf.*

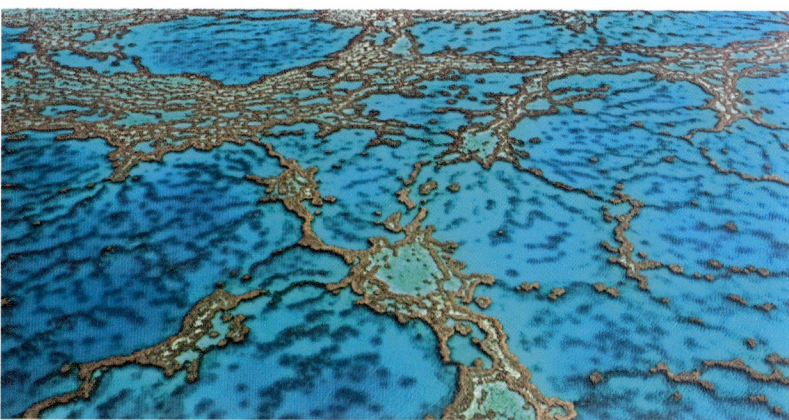

### CORAL COMPLEXITY
Although the reef makes an effective barrier against the huge waves of the Pacific, it is not a continuous wall of coral. The reef crests form a complex network of strong coral rock, enclosing thousands of small, shallow lagoons of clear blue water with soft beds of white coral sand.

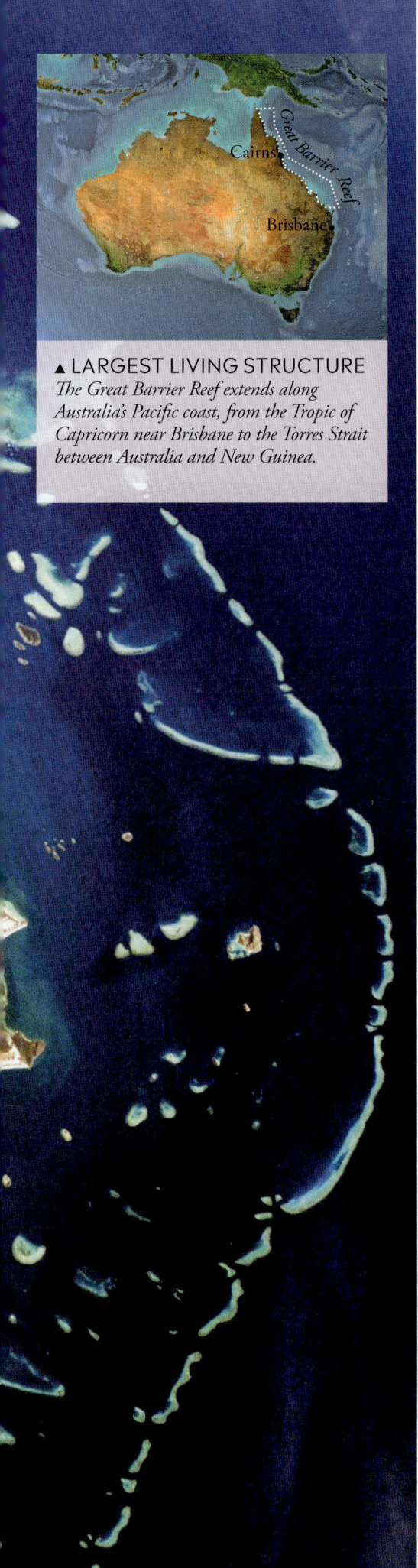

▲ **LARGEST LIVING STRUCTURE**
*The Great Barrier Reef extends along Australia's Pacific coast, from the Tropic of Capricorn near Brisbane to the Torres Strait between Australia and New Guinea.*

## BIG BUILD-UP

The organisms that created the reef consist of about 450 different types of hard corals. They have been depositing the limestone that builds up the reef for 15 million years. But the reef's development has been interrupted many times, and the current phase of growth has lasted for 6,000 years.

## FANTASTIC DIVERSITY

The Great Barrier Reef supports an amazing diversity of life, with more than 1,500 species of fish, 30 species of whales and dolphins, and at least 5,000 species of molluscs. Each has its own way of surviving on the reef, and they interact in a web of life that is one of the richest and most complex on the planet.

### FIRST SETTLERS

The First Nation Australians and the Torres Strait Islanders were the first people to live on islands and coasts along the Great Barrier Reef. The reef and surrounding seas provide these communities with everything they need, and are an important part of their cultural identity. These people continue to keep strong bonds with the reef, which is part of their Sea Country.

A First Nation man with fish caught from the Great Barrier Reef, 1925

SHALLOW SEAS

# Reef fish

**SHALLOW SEAS**

Coral reefs teem with an incredible variety of fish. Many are brightly coloured, helping them to find each other or scare away predators. Some swim in shoals as they nibble the corals, or sift edible particles from the water. Others live alone, hiding in the crevices in the reef. There are also some remarkable looking reef fish that rely on camouflage or venomous defences to protect them from predators.

## Butterflyfish
*Escape artists*

**Length** Up to 30 cm (12 in)
**Range** Atlantic, Pacific, and Indian oceans
**Diet** Corals, worms, and plankton

Many reef fish have flattened bodies that enable them to dive into narrow gaps between the corals if they are attacked by predators. They include this butterflyfish, which uses its narrow snout to pick at corals, and extract small worms and other animals from crevices in the reef.

## Angelfish
*Dazzling colours*

**Length** Up to 60 cm (24 in)
**Range** All tropical seas
**Diet** Mainly small animals

Angelfish are among the most colourful and vividly patterned of all coral reef fish, and some even change their colours and patterns as they grow. They are similar to butterflyfish, but often bigger. Found alone or in pairs, angelfish feed on tiny drifting plankton and plantlike animals such as sponges and sea squirts that cling to the reef among the corals.

## Surgeonfish
*Busy shoals*

**Length** Up to 40 cm (16 in)
**Range** All tropical seas
**Diet** Algae

Big shoals of surgeonfish swim among the reef corals searching for food. They are herbivores that use their small teeth to nibble at tiny seaweeds and other algae. A surgeonfish gets its name from the bladelike spines on each side of its tail, which are as sharp as a surgeon's scalpel.

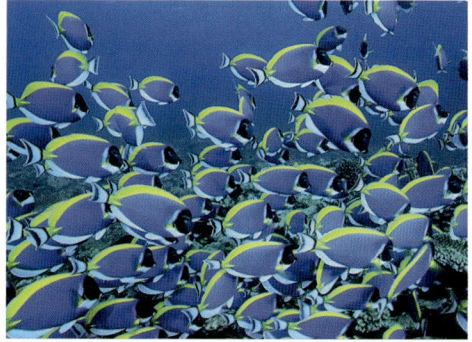

## Barracuda
*Hot pursuit*

**Length** Up to 2 m (6.5 ft)
**Range** All tropical seas
**Diet** Fish

Small fish swimming in open water are chased and caught by hunters such as barracudas, wrasses, groupers, and trevallies. Barracudas in particular are sleek, powerful killers that launch high-speed attacks on shoaling fish, ripping them to pieces with their extremely sharp teeth.

## Sharks
*Top predator*

**Length** Up to 5 m (16 ft)
**Range** All shallow tropical seas
**Diet** Fish, dolphins, and sea turtles

The reef is patrolled by sharks such as the blacktip reef shark and whitetip reef shark, as well as the much bigger, more deadly tiger shark. These top predators usually prowl the deeper waters outside the reef, but they also swim up the channels between the coral and into shallow reef lagoons.

▲ TIGER SHARK
*Armed with excellent senses of sight and smell, the tiger shark is a nocturnal hunter, attacking anything that comes across its path.*

## Cleaner wrasse
*Valet service*

**Length** Up to 12 cm (5 in)
**Range** Red Sea, Indian Ocean, and Pacific Ocean
**Diet** Fish parasites

All fish suffer from bloodsucking parasites that attach themselves to the fish's gills and skin. They get help from small reef fish called cleaner wrasses, which pick off the parasites and eat them. The wrasses often work inside their gills and even around the teeth of bigger fish, which never harm them – even if they normally feed on smaller fish. Here, a bluestreak cleaner wrasse attends to one of its clients.

## Reef stonefish
*Lurking killer*

**Length** Up to 50 cm (20 in)
**Range** Tropical Pacific and Indian oceans
**Diet** Fish and shrimps

Reef fish are often ambushed by lurking predators. They include the stonefish, camouflaged to look like a seaweed-covered rock as it lies motionless among the coral. It waits for victims to swim within range, then darts up to seize them in its gaping mouth. The stonefish is protected from its own enemies by sharp spines on its back that inject a powerful, even deadly venom.

## Damselfish
*Reef farmers*

**Length** Up to 10 cm (3.9 in)
**Range** Indian and Pacific Oceans
**Diet** Seaweed, invertebrates, and fish eggs

Many damselfish, such as this jewel damsel, are gardeners. They guard patches of coral reef and ensure the growth of desired seaweed species by removing others. Although small, damselfish bravely chase off intruders and even pick up sea urchins with their mouths to move them out of their gardens.

SHALLOW SEAS

# Reef invertebrates

▲ BARREL SPONGES
*Giant barrel sponges are found on the tropical coral reefs of the Caribbean Sea. They can measure up to 1.8 m (6 ft) across their hollow, barrel-shaped bodies.*

## LIVE SPONGE
Sea sponges live by pumping water through their spongy body walls to filter out tiny food particles. Throughout the 20th century, they were harvested on a massive scale for use as bath sponges, causing the collapse of many wild populations.

Colourful fish are the most obvious coral reef animals, but the reefs are alive with other creatures too. Most of these are various types of invertebrates (animals without backbones). They include crustaceans such as shrimps and crabs, and echinoderms such as starfish. Some of the animals look more like plants because they spend their lives rooted to one spot like the corals that build the reef. But others roam the reef searching for food, either scavenging scraps or preying on other animals.

## FILTER FEEDERS
Most of the plantlike animals on the reefs live by filtering small animals and other food from moving water. This enables them to survive without needing to roam over the reefs actively looking for food. They include the tunicates, also known as sea squirts, which pump the water through basketlike filters inside their hollow bodies. Some are solitary creatures, but most live in colonies attached to the coral rock.

*Flattened antennae sense the movement of nearby prey.*

*Rotating eyes detect the prey's exact range for an accurate strike.*

*Punching claws are folded away out of sight.*

▲ BLUE BELL TUNICATES
*Each tunicate in this colony draws water in through a "mouth" at the top of its body and pumps it out through an opening at the side.*

## SEA FAN

Some corals do not have stony skeletons, so they do not help with building the reef. Many of these soft corals are colonies of tiny, interconnected animals, just like the reef builders. They include the gorgonians (sea fans), which form branching colonies of tiny tentacled polyps. These colonies look like flattened trees growing up from the reef. Their fans grow sideways (not facing the current), increasing their chances of snaring passing food particles.

## CREEPING KILLER

The crown-of-thorns starfish has up to 21 arms bristling with long, sharp, venom-soaked spines. It feeds on living coral by turning its stomach inside-out through its central mouth to drench its prey with toxic digestive juices. These turn the coral to soup, which the starfish slowly sucks up. Sometimes swarms of these starfish overrun coral reefs, devouring the living corals and leaving behind just their dead, stony skeletons.

◆ CROWN-OF-THORNS
*This deadly enemy of coral can grow to more than 30 cm (12 in) across. The starfish shown here has unusually bright colours.*

## PUNCHING PREDATOR

The colourful mantis shrimps that live on the reef are fearsome predators. Some have claws armed with sharp, barbed tips that they use to spear passing fish. Others have clublike claws that help to crack the shells of other shellfish, punching into them with such force that the shellfish are killed instantly.

### FACT
The peacock mantis shrimp has claws that can smash into a victim at a speed of 80 kph (50 mph) – the fastest punch of any animal.

## DEADLY SNAIL

The tubular snout of a cone shell is armed with a venomous harpoon of incredible power. The poison of the bigger species can kill a human. The cone uses the venom to attack and kill small fish, which it then swallows whole. Many of the 750 species live on tropical coral reefs.

◀ PEACOCK MANTIS SHRIMP
*A relative of lobsters, this mantis shrimp lives on coral reefs in the western Pacific and Indian oceans. It hides in a burrow dug in coral sand.*

▲ TEXTILE CONE
*One of the bigger, more dangerous cone shells, the textile cone lives on coral reefs throughout the Pacific and Indian oceans, where it preys mainly on fish living on the seafloor.*

### GIANT CLAM
The magnificent giant clam is the biggest mollusc on Earth, with a huge, furrowed shell that grows up to 1.2 m (4 ft) long. The shell is lined with colourful soft tissue that is full of food-making algae, just like the tissue of reef corals. The algae supply the clam with most of the nutrients it needs.

SHALLOW SEAS

# Atolls and lagoons

Some tropical seas are dotted with islands surrounded by coral reefs. Many of the islands are extinct volcanoes that are sinking below the waves. As they sink, the coral keeps growing, and over time the original islands disappear to leave ring-shaped reefs called atolls, enclosing shallow lagoons. Other atolls have formed on ridges of rock submerged by rising sea levels.

### SINKING VOLCANOES

When an island volcano stops erupting, the rock beneath it cools and shrinks, so the island starts sinking. The coral around it grows upwards to compensate, so the fringing reef becomes a barrier reef and eventually a ring of coral – an atoll.

*Fringing reef grows in shallow water.*   *Active volcano forms island.*

▲ **1. FRINGING REEF**
*A tropical volcanic island soon develops a fringe of living coral near the shore.*

*Lagoon forms within reef.*   *Sinking volcano*

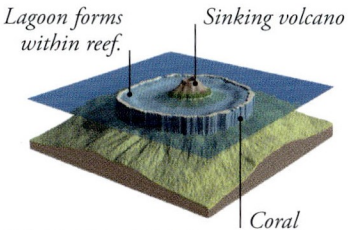

*Coral*

▲ **2. BARRIER REEF**
*When the extinct volcano starts sinking, the coral grows up towards the light.*

*Coral keeps growing as bedrock sinks.*   *Volcanic peak vanishes.*

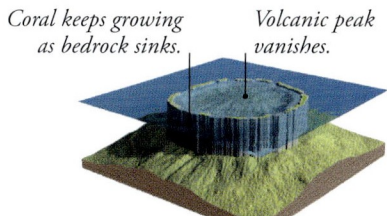

▲ **3. ATOLL**
*Over millions of years, the volcano disappears, leaving a ring of coral.*

## Tahiti
*High island*

**Location** Polynesia, western Pacific
**Type** Volcanic island with fringing reef
**Total area** 1,045 sq km (403 sq miles)

The island of Tahiti is made up of twin volcanic peaks fringed by coral reefs. The volcanoes are extinct and cooling, but still almost as high as when they were active more than 200,000 years ago. As a result, the fringing reefs still lie close to the shore.

## Bora Bora
*Sinking peak*

**Location** Polynesia, western Pacific
**Type** Volcanic island with barrier reef
**Total area** 29 sq km (11 sq miles)

Although part of the same island chain as Tahiti, Bora Bora is much older. Its central volcano last erupted more than 3 million years ago, and its extinct peak is sinking towards the ocean floor. This has created a broad lagoon between the island and the surrounding barrier reef.

## Lighthouse Reef
*Great blue hole*

**Location** Western Caribbean
**Type** Ridge reef
**Total area** 300 sq km (116 sq miles)

Lighthouse Reef lies off the coast of Belize in Central America. It did not form on an extinct volcano. Instead, it has developed on a ridge of limestone, drowned by rising sea levels as continental ice sheets melted at the end of the last ice age. The sea has flooded limestone caves that formed when the ridge was dry land. In the middle of the reef, the roof of one of these caves has collapsed to create the Great Blue Hole – a deep, dark, submerged pit in the shallow, pale blue lagoon.

## Kure Atoll
*Ring of coral*

**Location** Hawai'ian islands, Pacific
**Type** Atoll of volcanic origin
**Total area** 80 sq km (31 sq miles)

Kure is the oldest part of the island chain that includes Hawai'i. It was once an active volcano, but has been extinct and sinking for so long – 25 million years – that today the volcano has vanished. It has left behind just a ring of coral around a shallow lagoon. The only large sandy island on the atoll is a nesting site for thousands of seabirds.

## Maldives
*Atolls within atolls*

**Location** Northern Indian Ocean
**Type** Ridge reefs
**Total area** 90,000 sq km (34,750 sq miles)

Lying in the tropical Indian Ocean, the Maldives are a complex group of atolls that have formed on a ridge of volcanic rock extending south from India. Unusually, many of the atolls are chains of smaller atolls, and from space they look like strings of pearls floating in the blue ocean. The highest land is only 2.4 m (8 ft) above sea level.

▼ **PERFECT CIRCLE**
*This jewel-like atoll is one of more than 1,192 islands forming the Maldives.*

## Aldabra
*Mushroom islands*

**Location** Western Indian Ocean
**Type** Raised atoll
**Total area** 155 sq km (60 sq miles)

One of the largest coral atolls, Aldabra is unusual because the forces that build mountains have pushed up the seabed beneath it, raising the reefs into the air. The sea has carved some of these raised reefs into small mushroom-shaped islands, such as the one shown below.

# COAST AND SEASHORE

Pounded by waves and swept by the tides, the ocean shores are turbulent frontier zones, where rock is reduced to rubble and life can be a struggle for survival.

# Tides

On most seashores the sea level rises and falls every day, flooding part of the shore and then exposing it again. These high and low tides are caused by the gravity of the Moon, modified by other forces. The tidal rise and fall also create strong local currents that change direction every few hours.

▲ **LOW TIDE**
*This seashore in Vietnam experiences just one cycle of high and low tide every 24 hours, unlike most shores around the world.*

## PULLED BY THE MOON

The Moon's gravity pulls on the oceans, and drags the water into two vast tidal bulges. As Earth spins on its axis, most of its shores pass in and out of these bulges, causing high and low tides.

*Tidal bulge effect*
*Earth* *Moon*

▲ **GRAVITY EFFECT**
*Ocean water is dragged towards the Moon by the force of gravity, so sea level rises on the side facing the Moon.*

*Tidal bulge pushed up on other side*

▲ **MIRROR IMAGE**
*Earth is also orbiting the Moon very slightly, and this creates a second tidal bulge on the side of Earth facing away from the Moon.*

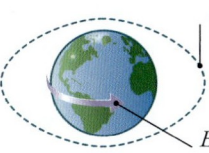 
*Combined tidal bulges*
*Earth spins one complete turn a day.*

▲ **SPINNING EARTH**
*The bulges stay in line with the Moon, so as Earth spins, any one seashore will pass through two tidal bulges each day.*

## TIDAL SHORES

When the tide level falls, it exposes parts of the shore that have been covered with seawater for several hours. On rocky shores with steep cliffs the difference may not be very obvious, but on shallow-sloping shores such as this sandy beach, a fall of a few metres can expose a vast area of tidal flat.

▲ **FLOOD TIDE**
*When the tide level starts rising again, seawater floods back to cover the sand. This can happen very quickly, transforming the beach into a glittering expanse of shallow sea.*

## LOCAL EFFECTS
Most coasts get two high tides a day. But some get just one, because the shape of the coastline alters the way the water flows. This also affects the height of the tide. On some shores, water forced into funnel-shaped bays causes very high tides.

## TIDAL RACES
As the tide rises and falls, water is moved along coasts in local currents called tidal streams. Where these are forced around headlands and between islands, the flow speeds up, and sometimes causes dangerous tidal races and whirlpools. These only appear when the tidal stream is flowing fast, halfway between high and low tide. At other times, the water can be completely calm.

◀ **STRONG CURRENTS**
The Maelstrom of Saltstraumen, on the northeast coast of Norway, is one of the world's most famous and dangerous tidal races. Twice a day, water surges through the strait at speeds of up to 40 kph (25 mph).

**COAST AND SEASHORE**

## MOON AND SUN

Every two weeks, at full Moon and new Moon, the orbiting Moon falls in line with the Sun. At these times, the gravity of the Sun and Moon combine to cause extra-large tides called spring tides, with a big difference between high and low water level.

At half Moon – the first quarter Moon and the last quarter Moon – the gravity of the Sun partially cancels out the gravity of the Moon, causing neap tides with a much smaller difference between high and low water levels.

▶ **SPRING TIDES**
The tidal bulges are bigger when the gravity of the Sun and Moon are combined. This causes spring tides.

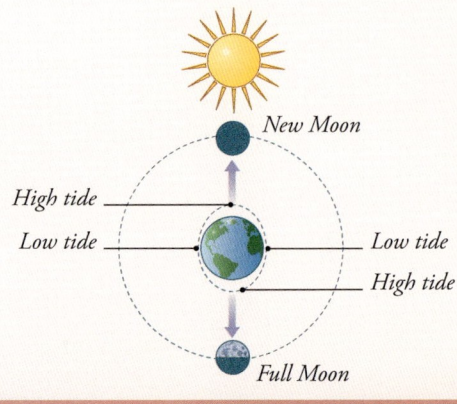

▶ **NEAP TIDES**
When the gravity of the distant Sun acts against the Moon's gravity, this makes the tidal bulges smaller.

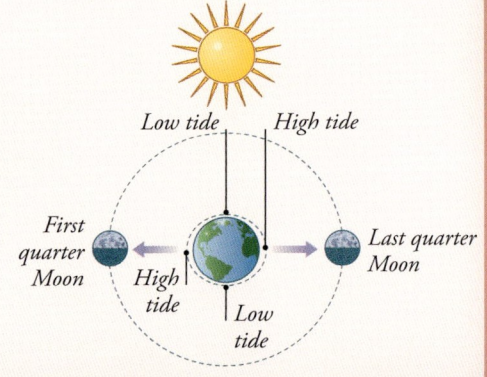

# Wave power

As waves pound exposed shores, they shatter and grind away solid rock, cutting it back at sea level to create caves, cliffs, and rocky reefs. Stones and sand are swept along the coast to more sheltered sites where the wave action is less violent. This process allows the stones and sand to settle and form shingle banks, sandy beaches, and mudflats. Therefore, as some places of the coast are being carved away, others are being built up.

**COAST AND SEASHORE**

## DESTRUCTIVE FORCE

When a wave breaks, a huge weight of water topples forward with tremendous force. On some shores most of this energy is soaked up by banks of shingle, but on rocky coasts there is nothing to stop the full force of the breaking waves slamming into the solid rock. The tumbling water hurls loose stones at the cliffs, which weakens them, and water forced into the rock can build up enough air pressure inside the cracks to blow the rock apart.

**FACT**
A big wave can hit rocks with a pressure of 500 kg per sq cm (7,000 lb per sq in) – like a car-sized hammer hitting your finger.

## COLLAPSE

The battering waves carve away coastal cliffs, and loosen big blocks of rock that eventually fall away, undermining the cliffs above. Over time the rock collapses under its own weight, dumping big boulders on the tidal shore below. These absorb most of the force of the waves until they are broken up too, exposing the cliff to further attacks.

▲ ROCKFALL
*Undercut by big storm waves, part of this chalk cliff has fallen on to the shore. The mound of rubble will not protect the cliff for long.*

## ROLLING AND TUMBLING

As soon as the rock falls onto the shore, the waves start tossing it around. This knocks the corners off, forming rounded boulders, shingle, and sand. The turbulent water sweeps the smaller fragments away, either suspended in the water or bounced and rolled over the seabed, but the large boulders remain where they fell.

## SHELTERED BEACHES

On seashores sheltered by projecting headlands, the sea is much calmer, with smaller waves. Instead of carving away the shore, the waves build it up by adding loose stones and sand carried along the coast. The relatively calm water cannot shift heavy stones, so these sheltered shores are marked by beaches of fine sand. Where the waves are bigger, they build beaches of larger stones known as shingle. Some of these beaches keep growing, but others are reshaped every year by winter storms.

## SHIFTING SAND

As moving water carries rock debris along the shore, it shifts the small, light particles more easily than the bigger, heavier ones, and carries them further from the shore where they fell from the cliff. This tends to sort the debris into different sizes, because the water drops the heaviest pebbles first, followed by smaller shingle, then sand.

# Cliffs and caves

As ocean waves break on rocky shores, they shatter and crumble the rock, and sweep the debris away to other shores. This relentless process creates a range of spectacular coastal features, including sheer cliffs, dark caves, soaring arches, isolated islands, and tall stacks. But as fast as these features are created, others are destroyed by the same forces.

## BAYS AND HEADLANDS

Where the coast is formed of different types of rock, the softer ones are destroyed first, creating a coastline made up of bays divided by headlands. The headlands shelter the bays, allowing beaches to build up and protect the softer rock. Meanwhile, the shape of the coast concentrates the wave energy on the headlands, creating caves, arches, and stacks.

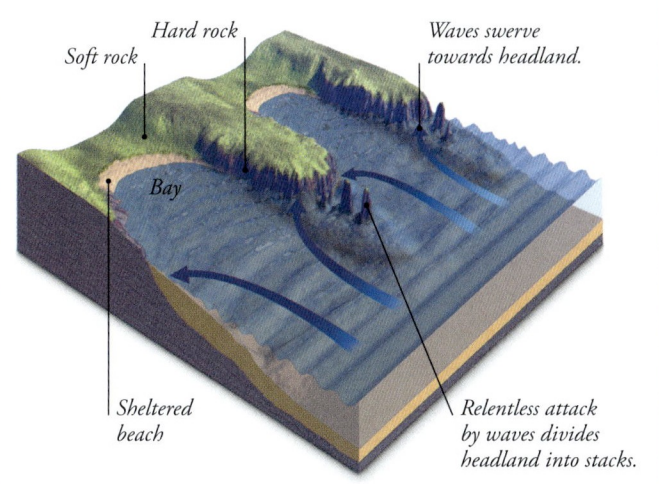

## SHEER DROP

Where high land meets the sea, the rock is cut back at sea level. This leaves the rock above without any support so it collapses under its own weight, creating a cliff. The shape of the cliff varies according to the type of rock, but the most dramatic sheer cliffs usually form in softer rock such as chalk. These chalk cliffs in southern England are known as the Seven Sisters.

## SEA CAVES

Sea caves form at the base of cliffs where hard, strong rock is undercut by wave action. Most of these sea caves are not very deep because over time the waves crashing into them makes their ceilings collapse. But this process can also create dramatic blowholes, where breaking waves are forced up through gaps in the cave roof to form fountains of salty spray.

## ROCKY ARCHES

Waves often attack a headland on both sides. They can carve away the rock near sea level to form twin caves that eventually break right through the headland, creating an arch. Arches can also form when caves in hard rock layers break through to softer layers beyond.

▼ **CURVED WONDER**
*Natural rock arches are rare because the rock usually disintegrates, but some arches have lasted for many centuries.*

COAST AND SEASHORE

## TOUGH SURVIVORS

When the sea attacks a rocky coastline, the hardest rocks tend to survive the longest. These usually take the form of long ridges that turn into headlands, but, sometimes, lumps of extra-hard rock survive as islands. These islands off Brazil – the Two Brothers – are made of volcanic basalt rock that welled up from deep within Earth long ago and hardened.

## SEA STACKS

Usually, headlands under attack from the waves crumble into heaps of rubble. But in some places, columns of extra-hard rock survive as sea stacks. Cut off from the shore, and with sheer cliff faces on all sides, these make ideal nesting sites for seabirds. Over time, most fall into the sea, leaving behind rocky stumps that may be submerged at high tide.

◄ **CRUMBLING SEA STACK**
*Gaps in the rock near sea level may mean that this sea stack is close to falling.*

## TWELVE APOSTLES
Pounding waves rolling in from the stormy Southern Ocean have carved this south Australian coastline into a complex pattern of bays, headlands, and sea stacks. The stacks are called the Twelve Apostles – there are now only eight, but more will form in the future as the waves keep battering the rocks.

# Rocky shore life

Battered by waves and partly drying out at each low tide, a rocky shore is a dangerous place for marine life. But these coastal waters are full of food, so those animals that can adapt to life in this harsh habitat often flourish in huge numbers. As a result, a typical rocky shore is packed with dense colonies of just a few species of animal life.

### IMPACT ZONE
Every wave that breaks on a rocky shore picks up loose pebbles and slams them against the rocks, and any animals that are in the way are likely to be crushed. Most of them have developed a talent for finding safe refuges in crevices, or have evolved strong armour. The thick, conical shells of these limpets are perfectly shaped to deflect the force of the waves and resist impact.

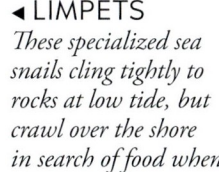

◀ **LIMPETS**
*These specialized sea snails cling tightly to rocks at low tide, but crawl over the shore in search of food when they are underwater.*

### CLAMMING UP
Every few hours, marine life on tidal shores is exposed to the air at low tide. Many shellfish cope by closing their shells or clamping down tightly to the rocks to stop themselves from drying out, which would kill them. This also ensures that they retain a supply of water containing vital oxygen.

▶ **MUSSELS**
*The hinged shells of mussels gape open when they are underwater, allowing them to feed, but seal shut at low tide.*

▼ **COLOUR CODE**
*The bands of colour on this rock are different types of organism, including yellow lichens at the top, pale barnacles in the middle, and green anemones at the bottom near the low-tide mark.*

## LIFE ZONES

Many of the organisms on rocky shores live permanently attached to the rocks. Some animals can survive for longer out of the water than others, which allows them to live higher above the low-tide mark, and have this part of the shore to themselves. As a result, many rocky shores have distinct zones of different-coloured animals, seaweeds, and other organisms living on the rocks.

▲ **FEEDING TIME**
*Submerged by the tide, these goose barnacles open their shell plates and unfurl feathery limbs to collect floating food particles.*

## HIGH WATER

When the rising tide covers the rocks, the shore is transformed. Seaweeds billow up in the water, and the animals hidden in them emerge to feed. Other animals that live attached to the rocks open up to extend tubes and tentacles that gather food from the water. Fish move in to seize what food they can before the falling tide leaves the shore once again.

## ROCKY RETREAT

Rocky shores also provide food for mobile animals such as shorebirds and crabs, which come and go as the tide allows. Seals use rocky shores as safe refuges from sharks and other marine hunters, and as places to warm up after hunting in the cold water.

▲ **SUNBATHING**
*On the tropical Galápagos Islands, marine iguanas bask on the warm rocks of the shore alongside red Sally Lightfoot crabs.*

# Tide pools

A lot of rocky-shore animals spend the hours of low tide in small rock pools that stay full of seawater, so they do not need ways of surviving on the open shore. Some of these animals, such as certain sea anemones, live in these tide pools all the time. Others, including many crabs and small fish, roam widely over the flooded shore at high water to find food, then retreat to the pools when the tide goes out.

**FACT**
Some small fish spend most of their lives in tide pools, defending them as their home territory and even breeding in them.

## SAFE REFUGES

Tide pools form in rocky depressions and crevices on the shore that have no gaps in the rock to let the water out. These act like natural marine aquariums, and the water is changed every time the tide rises to cover them. Animals and seaweeds can live in these pools just as they would in the open sea. Many of the animals are hard to spot because they are so well camouflaged.

▲ **SNAKELOCKS ANEMONE**
*Unlike the sea anemones that live higher up the shore, the snakelocks anemone cannot retract its long tentacles and close itself up to survive on the bare rock at low tide.*

## POOL RESIDENTS

Many of the animals in tide pools spend their lives attached to one spot on the rock. Since they are always submerged – either by the pool water or by the high tide – they do not need ways of surviving out of the water. They include animals such as sea squirts and the snakelocks anemone, which would dry out and die if they were exposed to the air for more than a few minutes.

▲ ROCK GUNNEL
*A north Atlantic shore fish, the rock gunnel can survive among wet seaweed at low tide, but prefers a deep pool.*

## BACK TO BASE

Some tide-pool animals, including small shore fish, shrimps, and crabs, are mobile enough to leave the pool when the rising tide floods the shore. This enables the animals to look for food among the surrounding rocks. Most return to the pools as the tide begins to fall to avoid being stranded. But some, such as shore crabs, are able to find their way back even after the tide has gone out.

### HIGH AND LOW

The richness of tide-pool life depends on the size of the pool and its position on the shore. Small pools may heat up or even freeze, so they are dangerous for marine animals. Pools on the upper shore are exposed for many hours, if not days, and may dry out or fill with rain. Big pools on the middle and lower shore are more like the open sea, and hold far more life.

Upper shore
Middle shore
Lower shore

## TIDE-POOL HUNTER

Octopuses can survive out of water for at least half an hour. Using their flexible arms covered in powerful suckers, they can pull themselves across bare rocks and climb into tide pools to hunt the animals trapped there when the tide level falls. Shrimp and fish have no way to escape the quick-moving octopus.

▲ ROCKY RETREAT
*The crystal-clear water in this tide pool in Hawai'i reveals a permanent growth of prickly sargassum, a type of edible seaweed.*

▲ COMMON OCTOPUS
*Found throughout the world, the common octopus hunts in shallow coastal seas. Remarkably, it can change its colour and patterns instantly in order to hide and blend in with its surroundings.*

◀ **COPACABANA BEACH**
*This world-renowned crescent beach forms part of the seafront of Rio de Janeiro in Brazil.*

# Beaches, dunes, and spits

The rock that is torn from exposed rocky shores by the power of the waves is smashed up and swept along the coast to quieter shores. It settles as beaches of shingle or sand, depending on how sheltered they are. These beaches are constantly reshaped by the waves, creating a variety of distinctive beach types. Meanwhile, the wind can blow beach sand way up beyond the tideline to build high coastal dunes.

## CRESCENT BAYS

Where headlands of hard rock lie on each side of a wide band of soft rock, the waves create a broad bay with a beach that forms in a sweeping curve. These crescent beaches are ideal for leisure activities such as swimming and surfing, and are often big tourist attractions. As a result, many have become famous beach resorts.

### LONGSHORE DRIFT

Waves breaking at an angle to the shore throw pebbles and sand along the beach at the same angle. Known as longshore drift, this process can carry beach material away and move it out to sea. Sometimes barriers are placed to slow the process of longshore drift. The sand and pebbles then pile up against these in a zig-zag pattern, as seen below.

## POCKET BEACHES

Projecting headlands often enclose small sandy beaches. These form where narrow bands of softer rock between the headlands have been cut back by the waves. The sand often builds up over time, but the headlands stop it from being carried along the coast by the waves, unlike on more open shores.

▲ FRASER ISLAND
*These dunes on the shore of Fraser Island, eastern Australia, are part of the longest sequence of coastal dunes in the world.*

## COASTAL DUNES

Sandy beaches that do not lie at the foot of cliffs are often backed by sand dunes. These are built up by wind blowing off the sea and rolling dry sand grains inland. The dune ridges keep moving downwind, as sand is blown up one side and down the other. But eventually, the dunes are stabilized by the roots of tough plants that can grow in the salty sand.

## LONG BEACHES

Longshore drift can create beaches that extend for incredible distances along the coast. They often form banks with the sea on one side and sheltered lagoons on the other side. These long beaches absorb the force of breaking waves during storms, protecting the true shore from erosion.

▶ 90 MILE BEACH
*Extending along a shore in the far north of New Zealand, this spectacular beach is actually 88 km (55 miles) long.*

*Sheltered lagoon forms between the beach and the land.*

## SPITS

Some long beaches extend into offshore spits. Sand and pebbles shifted along the beach by longshore drift are added to the tip of the spit, so it keeps on growing. Dungeness Spit on the Pacific coast of Washington State, US, seen here, grows by 4.5 m (15 ft) each year.

### FACT
The longest natural beach lies on the coast of southern Bangladesh. Known as Cox's Bazar, it extends for 120 km (75 miles).

COAST AND SEASHORE

# Hidden riches

A beach at low tide can look completely empty, apart from the shorebirds picking their way over the sand. But below the surface, it is often teeming with life. Many of the animals are burrowing worms and shellfish that process the sand for edible particles. Others emerge from the sand at high tide to gather plankton from the water, risking attack by predatory fish.

▲ HEART URCHIN
*When buried, a heart urchin uses its long tube feet to open up breathing and feeding channels in the sand.*

## SPINY BURROWERS

Among the animals that spend their lives hidden in beach sand are heart urchins, sometimes known as sea potatoes. These relatives of typical sea urchins have short, mobile spines that they use for digging, and long, flexible tube feet like those of starfish. They live in burrows in the wet sand, gathering and feeding on tiny fragments of dead marine life.

## HUNGRY WORMS

At low tide, many sandy beaches are dotted with the coiled casts of burrowing lugworms. These marine worms live in U-shaped burrows that allow them to draw water in at one end. They feed by swallowing sand, digesting any edible material, and ejecting the rest on the beach surface. These casts are swept away every time the tide covers them, so each one indicates the feeding activity of just a few hours.

*Tentacles*

*Shell fragments*

▲ RAZOR CLAMS
*Long-shelled razor clams sometimes emerge from the sand, but vanish if they sense danger.*

## SECRET SHELLFISH

Burrowing clams and other molluscs emerge to feed at high tide. They usually keep their bodies hidden, but extend fleshy, flexible siphon tubes to gather food. Most clams draw food-bearing seawater through a filter, while others such as tellins collect food from the flooded beach surface. When the tide level falls again, the clams retreat into the sand, so they become invisible to seabirds and other enemies.

## SPREADING FANS

Many marine worms that live in the sand must wait for the sea to flood the beach at high tide. Then they emerge from their burrows and spread fans of tentacles, which they use to collect food from the water. They include several types of tube worms that mix slime from their bodies with seashore material to make tubes. This helps to protect their soft bodies. The tubes rise above the sand's surface, enabling the worms to gather food from clear water.

▲ LESSER WEEVER
*Half-buried in the sand, this weever waits patiently in the shallows for food.*

## HIGH-TIDE HUNTERS

Burrowing animals that feed on the beach at high tide are preyed upon by fish that swim in from the sea. Many of these hunters are seafloor-feeding specialists such as weevers, flatfish, and rays, but they also include bigger fish such as sea bass and cod.

◄ SAND MASON WORM
*This worm uses shell fragments and sand to build its tube. Even the tentacles of the sand mason have tubes. The worm itself can be up to 30 cm (12 in) long.*

**COAST AND SEASHORE**

# Shorebirds

**COAST AND SEASHORE**

The hordes of marine animals that spend their lives buried in sandy tidal beaches provide a feast for shorebirds feeding on the sand at low tide. Many of these birds have long bills for probing deep into soft sand or mud, and long legs that are ideal for wading in shallow water. A few are highly adapted for a particular feeding technique. Other shorebirds specialize in eating the shellfish that live on rocky shores, or snapping up insects and other small animals feeding on the debris that wash up on beaches by the waves.

## Crab plover
*Shell cracker*

**Length** Up to 40 cm (16 in)
**Range** Indian Ocean
**Habitat** Sandy beaches and dunes

This black and white shorebird specializes in catching and eating crabs. It has an extra-strong bill that it uses to crack open shells, and even feeds crabs to its young. It lives on tropical sandy coasts all year round, breeding in dense, noisy colonies on the shore. Unusually for a shorebird, the crab plover digs nesting burrows in the sand above the high tideline.

## Ruddy turnstone
*Beachcomber*

**Length** Up to 23 cm (9 in)
**Range** Worldwide
**Habitat** Mainly stony shores

Flocks of these small coastal birds work their way along the shore, using their short, strong bills to flick pebbles and seashells aside and seize any animals that they find. They often investigate the heaps of seaweed washed up on the shore at the high-tide mark, picking at dead fish and crabs, and chasing after seaweed flies and sandhoppers.

### ▼ CAMOUFLAGE COLOURS
*Perched on a rock, a turnstone is easy to see. But its colours make it almost invisible on weed-strewn shores.*

### ▼ FINE FEATHERS
*The roseate spoonbill was once threatened by hunting for its glorious pink and white plumage.*

## Eurasian curlew
*Sensitive probe*

**Length** Up to 60 cm (24 in)
**Range** Europe, Asia, and Africa
**Habitat** Soft shores

The extremely long, slender bill of the curlew is perfect for probing soft, wet sand and mud for buried animals such as worms and clams. It can reach deeper than any other shorebird. Its bill tip is touch-sensitive, allowing it to detect invisible prey. Curlews often use their long legs to wade in shallow water, but they also pick small crabs and similar animals off the exposed shore.

## Ruff
*Dazzling display*

**Length** Up to 30 cm (12 in)
**Range** Europe, Asia, Africa, and Australia
**Habitat** Muddy estuaries

Like many shorebirds, ruffs breed on inland sites such as marshes and grasslands. Rival males perform competitive displays to attract females, showing off their flamboyant breeding plumage. At the end of the breeding season their long feathers fall out, to be replaced with modest grey and brown plumage for the winter. Ruffs feed in the salty creeks of river estuaries and further inland.

## Roseate spoonbill
*Specialist*

**Length** Up to 81 cm (32 in)
**Range** North America, Central America, and South America
**Habitat** Coastal lagoons

Some birds have highly specialized bills for feeding. They include spoonbills, which hold their spoon-shaped bills slightly open and sweep them from side to side just below the surface of the water. The roseate spoonbill uses this technique to catch shrimps as well as other small animals. Spoonbills often feed in small groups, wading in lines through the shallows.

## Oystercatcher
*Bright bill*

**Length** Up to 46 cm (18 in)
**Range** Europe, Asia, and Africa
**Habitat** Rocky and sandy shores

A few shorebirds use their bills to smash or pry open shellfish, including mussels and clams. The bright red bill of the oystercatcher is specially reinforced for hammering into their shells, and has a bladelike tip for cutting through the tough shell-closing muscles. Oystercatchers that live on rocky shores have the strongest bills; others that live on softer shores have more finely pointed bills, which they use for probing the sand, like curlews.

## Black-winged stilt
*High rise*

**Length** Up to 40 cm (16 in)
**Range** Worldwide except cold regions
**Habitat** Shallow coastal water

Many shorebirds have long legs for wading in the water in search of prey. The legs of the black-winged stilt are so long that it can feed in much deeper water than other birds, but they make feeding on land very awkward.

COAST AND SEASHORE

### OYSTERCATCHERS
In winter, hundreds and thousands of oystercatchers gather on the coastal mudflats and beaches of northern Europe. Here, they are joined by other shorebirds as they forage for food on the exposed mud and sand, and rest in tightly packed flocks at high tide.

## SHEER CLIFFS

Seabird nesting colonies attract foxes and other land predators intent on eating the eggs and chicks. This encourages the birds to choose nesting sites that the foxes cannot reach easily. Many nest on sheer cliffs with ledges just wide enough for the adult birds to sit on their eggs. When the young birds are ready to leave the nest, they drop off the ledge and flutter into the sea.

# Seabird colonies

Ocean birds cannot lay their eggs at sea. They must return to the land to nest on solid ground. They nest as close to the water as possible, relying on the shallow coastal seas to supply them with a rich source of food to raise their young. Many of these birds form large coastal breeding colonies, especially on isolated sea stacks and islands.

▲ CONICAL EGGS
*Female guillemots lay a single egg on bare cliff ledges. Like other cliff-nesters, they have conical eggs that roll in circles, so they are less likely to fall off the cliff ledges.*

▲ CLIFF COLONY
*Hundreds of Brünnich's guillemots nest on the cliff ledges of this Arctic shore. After breeding, they all fly out to sea.*

## SAFE REFUGES

The safest nesting sites for seabirds are small islands and sea stacks. Since these are cut off from the mainland, ground predators cannot get at the nests, but they are still open to attack by predatory birds such as skuas. On many of these sites, every patch of level ground is occupied, as seen on this densely packed gannet nesting colony.

## SHOWING OFF
Several ocean birds perform spectacular courtship displays on their nesting grounds. Some of the most dramatic are those of male frigatebirds, which have brilliant red inflatable throat pouches. They display in the mangrove trees on tropical coral islands, competing with each other to attract females flying overhead.

▼ STRONG GRIP
*An Atlantic puffin can catch several small fish in one dive. It uses its strong, spiny tongue to grip the fish it has caught whilst seizing more in its colourful beak.*

## GUANO ISLANDS
Some islands off the Pacific coast of South America have been used as seabird breeding colonies for centuries. The rocks are covered with incredibly deep layers of seabird droppings, known as guano. Some layers are more than 50 m (164 ft) deep. These deposits were once mined for use as fertilizer for farming and shipped all over the world.

## OUT OF SIGHT
While seabirds such as guillemots and gannets nest on rocky ledges or the flat tops of islands, others nest in burrows. They include puffins, which will often take over old rabbit burrows to avoid having to dig their own nests. The baby puffins stay hidden in their dark burrows, where they are safe from the gulls and skuas that are their main enemies. The adults hunt in the sea nearby, returning with beakfuls of fish to feed to their young.

# Sea turtles

Most marine animals breed at sea, but sea turtles must come ashore to nest. They select warm, sandy, remote beaches where the female turtles can haul themselves out of the water easily, dig holes in the sand, and bury their eggs. The warm sand incubates the eggs, and when the young hatch they make their way back to the sea. Here, they feed on marine life including shrimps and jellyfish, as well as seaweeds and seagrasses. The turtles may travel vast distances across oceans, especially when returning to their home beaches to breed.

### Olive ridley sea turtle
*Mass breeder*

**Length** Up to 70 cm (28 in)
**Range** Mainly Pacific and Indian oceans
**Diet** Fish, jellyfish, clams, and prawns

This small sea turtle starts life with a greyish heart-shaped shell that eventually changes to an olive green colour. Although they prefer to live alone, hundreds and sometimes even thousands of females return en masse to the beaches where they hatched to lay their eggs.

### Leatherback sea turtle
*Biggest turtle*

**Length** Up to 3 m (10 ft)
**Range** All warm and temperate oceans
**Diet** Jellyfish

The biggest sea turtle is the giant leatherback, which gets its name from the leathery skin that covers its ridged shell – unlike other turtles, its carapace (shell) is not made of tough keratin. Its body is highly streamlined, enabling it to swim vast distances with little effort. It is specialized for eating jellyfish; its throat is lined with fleshy, downward-pointing spikes to ensure its slippery victims cannot escape.

## Flatback sea turtle
*Shallow-water inhabitant*

**Length** Up to 1 m (3 ft)
**Range** Tropical Australian waters
**Diet** Jellyfish, clams, prawns, and seagrass

Restricted to the warm, shallow seas of northern Australia and nearby islands, the flatback seems to prefer muddy river estuaries and coral reefs over the open sea. It has a varied diet, eating almost anything it can catch, and in turn is preyed upon by saltwater crocodiles. Its name refers to the shape of its shell, which is flatter than other sea turtle shells, with upturned edges.

## Hawksbill sea turtle
*Patterned shell*

**Length** Up to 90 cm (3 ft)
**Range** All tropical oceans
**Diet** Sponges, jellyfish, clams, and prawns

The hawksbill turtle has a sharp-pointed upper jaw that looks like the beak of a hawk or eagle. It uses it to seize a wide variety of marine animals ranging from crabs to jellyfish, but its favourite prey are sponges growing on tropical coral reefs. It has a strikingly patterned shell, which was once very valuable as the source of the natural material known as tortoiseshell.

## Green sea turtle
*Undersea grazer*

**Length** Up to 1.5 m (5 ft)
**Range** All warm oceans
**Diet** Seagrass

Unlike other sea turtles, this elegant reptile is a herbivore. It feeds almost entirely on various types of seagrass and algae, which it finds growing in the shallow coastal water of bays, estuaries, and coral reef lagoons. A young green turtle, however, drifts in open water and feeds on small animals. The turtle nests on sandy beaches throughout the tropics, migrating immense distances to reach them. Its name refers to a layer of green fat beneath its skin that gets its colour from the turtle's diet. As with all sea turtles, it swims by using its long, flattened front flippers like wings to "fly" gracefully through the water at speeds of up to 3 kph (2 mph).

## Loggerhead sea turtle
*Powerful jaws*

**Length** Up to 2.1 m (7 ft)
**Range** Shallow warm oceans worldwide
**Diet** Shellfish and other marine animals

The loggerhead is an omnivore, which means that it will eat almost anything edible. It has powerful crushing jaws, but like all sea turtles it has no teeth. It usually feeds in shallow coastal seas, but loggerheads have been tracked crossing the Pacific Ocean to reach their breeding beaches.

## Kemp's ridley sea turtle
*Under threat*

**Length** Up to 75 cm (30 in)
**Range** Northwestern Atlantic
**Diet** Crabs, clams, and jellyfish

One of the smallest sea turtles, Kemp's ridley is also the rarest. Most of the females lay their eggs on a single Mexican beach, and this makes it vulnerable to any catastrophe that might wipe it out altogether. Kemp's ridley is also unusual because it feeds almost entirely on crabs, crushing them in its strong jaws.

# Shore crabs

Although crabs are sea creatures adapted for living underwater, their tough waterproof shells and strong legs allow many of them to feed on the exposed shore at low tide. They have evolved modified gills that enable them to breathe air, giving them the opportunity to spend most of their lives on the open beach, up trees, and even far inland.

**FACT**
The female red land crab can lay 100,000 eggs, so between them they release up to 2.5 trillion eggs into the ocean each year.

### HOLDING OXYGEN
Crabs gather oxygen from the water using gills, like fish. But a crab's gills are inside a cavity that holds a supply of oxygenated water. As the oxygen in the supply is used up, more seeps into it from the air. This allows a common shore crab to live out of water for many hours, provided it keeps its gills moist.

◄ SHORE CRAB
*This widespread crab feeds both in the water and on the shore, preying on mussels and other animals.*

### SCUTTLING GHOSTS
Tropical ghost crabs are so well adapted to life on the open beach that they can drown if they stay underwater for too long. They live in burrows in the sand above the high tideline, emerging to search for edible scraps and animal prey. Their flip-up eyes have sharp vision and, at the slightest alarm, they scuttle sideways into their burrows at high speed. Many are also very well camouflaged, vanishing like ghosts when they stop moving.

### LAND CRABS
Although shore crabs and ghost crabs are well equipped for living on beaches, they do not stray far from the sea. Other crabs have almost given up marine life, and are known as land crabs. They have gills, like all crabs, but their gill cavities are lined with blood vessels that extract oxygen directly from the air. These crabs live and feed on land for most of the year, but they must return to water to lay their eggs.

## RED TIDE

More than 100 million red land crabs live in the forests of Christmas Island in the Indian Ocean. In October of every year, tens of millions of them migrate to the coast to breed, swarming over the island like a red tide. A few days after reaching the shore, the females release their eggs into the ocean. The young crabs live in the sea for a month before returning to land.

▼ **PRECIOUS CARGO**
*The female crabs carry their eggs beneath their bodies for two weeks before releasing them in the sea.*

▲ **POWERFUL PINCERS**
*Robber crabs feast mainly on coconuts, using their massive pincers to crack open the hard shells. Some have been known to prey on chickens, as well as other robber crabs.*

## COCONUT MONSTER

The biggest land-living crabs are the tropical robber crabs. These giants can weigh more than 4 kg (9 lb) – as much as a domestic cat. Despite this, they climb trees, especially coconut palms growing on tropical islands. They often eat coconuts, and are sometimes known as coconut crabs. But like other land crabs, they have to return to the sea to lay their eggs.

**COAST AND SEASHORE**

# Estuaries and mudflats

Where rivers reach the sea, they often broaden out into tidal estuaries. The salty seawater makes the tiny mud particles carried in the river water settle on the bottom in thick layers, which are exposed as mudflats at low tide. The mud is salty and airless but, despite this, it is rich in food and home to huge numbers of animals.

**FACT**
Twenty-two of the world's biggest cities are located on river estuaries, including London, New York, and Shanghai.

### MUDDY RIVERS
The mud particles carried by rivers are microscopic, but the salt in seawater makes them clump together into bigger, heavier particles that sink to the river bed. When the tide is rising, the incoming flow of seawater stops the river water moving, which also encourages particles to settle.

▲ RÍO DE LA PLATA
*This view from space shows the muddy water of a South American river forming a broad estuary where it meets the sea.*

### TIDAL BORES
When the rising tide pushes water up an estuary to where the river is narrower, this can cause a funnel effect that forces the water level to rise higher and higher. On some rivers this creates a wave that surges upriver, called a tidal bore. Some of these are high enough to surf on.

### GLEAMING MUDFLATS
The muddy sediment that settles on the river bed at high tide is exposed as mudflats when the tide goes out. The falling tide allows the river flow to speed up, so it scours a narrow central channel through the gleaming mud. This is joined by many smaller channels flowing off the flats.

▶ NATURAL PATTERN
*Tiny drainage channels carry water off the mud into bigger channels, which join up to flow into the main river.*

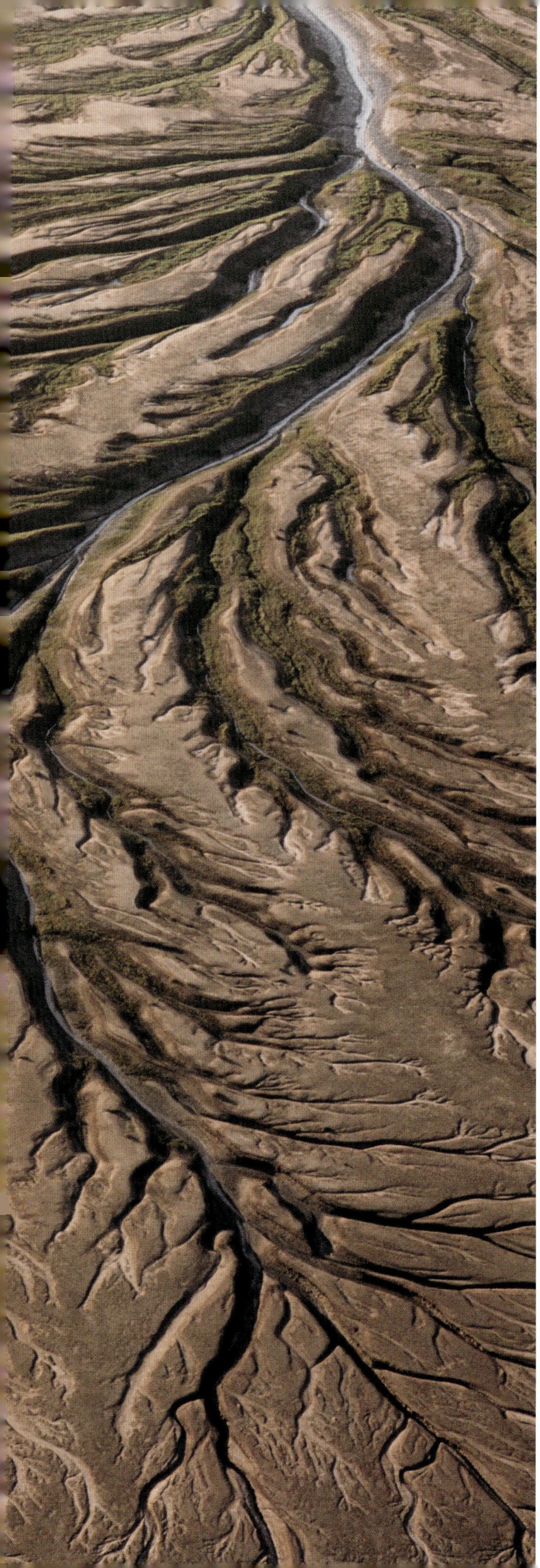

### SMELLY GAS
The tidal mud is full of microbes that live by breaking down the remains of dead plants and animals. They can survive without air, but they release a gas called hydrogen sulphide, which smells of rotten eggs. The gas bubbles up out of the mud, making the mudflats smell terrible.

### MUD PROCESSORS

The microbes in the mudflats feed millions of burrowing worms, while molluscs such as cockles and clams filter the water for food. Other animals like these tiny spire snails creep over the mud surface, nibbling at seaweeds and dead animals washed in by the tide.

### HUNGRY VISITORS
The large number of small animals that live in the mudflats attract flocks of shorebirds as well as wildfowl such as ducks and geese. The birds spread out across the mud at low tide, and retreat to the seashore when the tide comes in again. Food buried in the mud can also attract much bigger animals.

▲ GRIZZLY BEAR
*In Alaska, US, grizzly bears dig in the mud of river estuaries at low tide looking for razor clams and other shellfish.*

# Deltas

Beyond the coast, any mud and sand carried into the sea by the river water is usually swirled away by waves and currents. But if the load of sediment carried by the river is very large, or the sea is very calm, the sediment settles before it can be carried away. It builds up in layers that grow outwards from the shore, creating an extension of the land called a delta.

## SPREADING FANS

A typical river delta is a huge flat area of sand and mud. Sediment dropped by the river blocks its original course, forcing the river to spill out in many smaller channels. These soon get blocked up too, so the mud-loaded water overflows and forms even more channels, fanning out over a growing mass of soft sediment.

▲ GANGES DELTA
*This satellite image shows the Ganges Delta in eastern India and Bangladesh. Every year, the Ganges River carries about 1 billion tonnes of mud. Much of this is deposited into the sea, where it forms a submarine fan over the Bay of Bengal.*

*One of the many channels flowing off the Mississippi River Delta towards the sea*

*River water breaking through the levees fans out in a pattern that looks like the toes of a bird*

▲ MISSISSIPPI LEVEES
*Water pouring into the Gulf of Mexico from the Mississippi River is separated from the sea by levees built up from the sediment carried by the river.*

## BIRD'S FOOT DELTA

Some rivers, such as the Mississippi in the southern US, drop sand, mud, and other sediments along their edges. This forms raised banks called levees that grow out to sea. If the river breaks through one of the levees, part of it then flows off in another direction. This creates a delta in the shape of a bird's foot. Many of the levees forming the Mississippi River Delta were swept away by the storm surge of Hurricane Katrina that flooded nearby New Orleans in 2005.

## DEEP LAYERS

Deltas grow upwards and outwards as the river builds up layer after layer of mud, silt, and sand. These may extend far across the seafloor as a submarine fan. Eventually, the immense weight of the sediment warps Earth's crust downwards, and it continues to build up in very deep layers. The Bengal Fan that extends beyond the Ganges Delta is about 16 km (10 miles) thick.

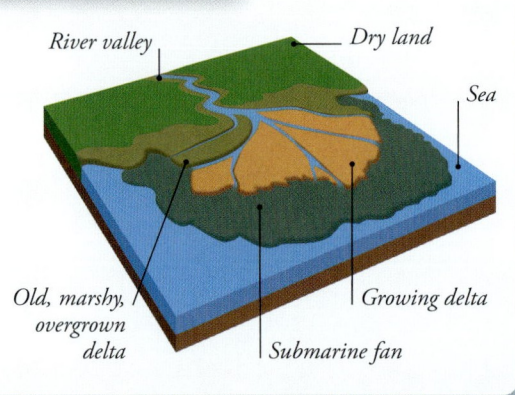

### FACT
The Ganges Delta is the biggest in the world, covering around 100,000 sq km (38,600 sq miles) – more than the total area of Tasmania.

▲ BANKS OF THE NILE
*The farmland of the Nile Delta in Egypt that once fed the ancient Egyptians remains an important food source, but is rapidly shrinking due to urbanization and climate change.*

## FERTILE LAND

The inland parts of the delta become covered with freshwater marsh plants. Over centuries, the cycle of plant growth and decay creates very fertile soil that makes rich farmland. Many ancient civilizations depended on the wealth created by farming these delta soils.

## WILDLIFE REFUGES

The inland swamps, creeks, and pools of a river delta often support a rich variety of wetland wildlife. This includes fish, turtles, and alligators, as well as birds such as herons and fish eagles. The Danube Delta in eastern Europe, for example, teems with freshwater fish. These feed vast flocks of eastern white pelicans, and so the delta is now home to 70 per cent of the world's white pelican population in the summer.

COAST AND SEASHORE

# Salt marshes

The tidal shores of estuaries and deltas are too salty for most plant life. But a few specialized plants are able to cope with the salt, and even survive being flooded by saltwater at high tide. In the cooler parts of the world, these specialists are the grasses and other low-growing plants that form salt marshes. Dotted with pools and muddy creeks, the marshes provide safe refuges for many types of coastal wildlife.

▲ GLASSWORT
*Looking like a tiny, spineless cactus, this plant lives in the wettest part of the salt marsh, flooded at every high tide.*

## PIONEER PLANTS

The first plants to take root in the tidal mudflats are cordgrass and leafless, juicy-stemmed plants such as glasswort. These plants can cope with being submerged by tidal saltwater twice a day, every day, and they have special adaptations to deal with the salt. Their roots bind the mud together. They also trap more particles from the water, slowly raising the level of the mudflat.

### QUIET LAGOONS

Salt marsh plants usually take root in quiet estuaries and lagoons that are cut off from the sea by sandy spits and islands. These natural barriers shelter the plants from the waves that might uproot them. The still water also allows fine mud to settle and build up, so it can support more and more plants. In time, the salt marsh may take over the whole area, apart from a central river channel bordered by bare mudflats.

**KEY**
- Salt marshes
- Mudflats

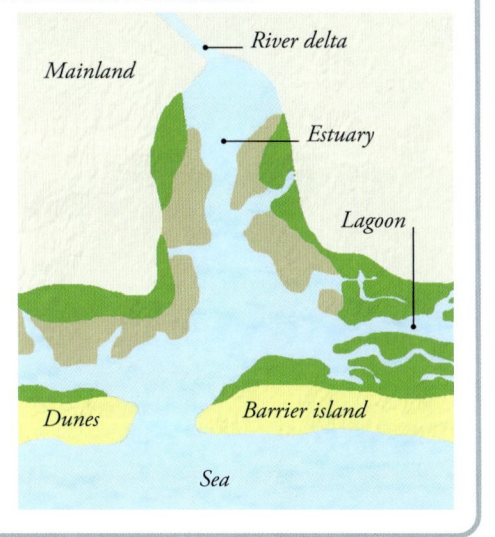

## WINDING CREEKS

A typical salt marsh is a patchwork of winding creeks, muddy pools, and dense patches of specialized salt marsh plants. At high tide, the pools and creeks fill up with saltwater, which drains away at low tide to leave shining wet mud.

▶ NATURAL PATTERN
*This view from the air shows the complex network of creeks and pools that carries water in and out of the salt marsh.*

## MARSH ZONES

Over time, the pioneer plants raise the mud level, so the lower marsh becomes drier and less salty. Different plants, such as sea lavender, take root in this higher zone, trapping sediment and raising the level even further. At the top of the marsh, the salt marsh plants give way to freshwater plants.

▶ FLOODED MARSH
*High spring tides flood the entire marsh with salty water as shown here. But during neap tides, only the lowest levels are flooded.*

COAST AND SEASHORE

## SALTY HAVENS

Remote salt marshes make ideal habitats for animals. They include insects and snails, which are eaten by frogs and small mammals. These in turn are hunted by snakes and foxes. Fish and other marine animals visit at high tide, while at low tide the muddy pools and creeks attract flocks of shorebirds.

◀ DAZZLING FLOCK
*On some warmer salt marshes, such as the Camargue in southern France, the waters support flocks of flamingos. They wade through the shallow water in their search for prey.*

### FACT
More than 400,000 wading birds, such as oystercatchers, visit The Wash salt marshes on the east coast of England every year to feed.

# Mangrove forests

The coasts of warm tropical oceans are fringed by swampy forests of salt-tolerant trees called mangroves. These tidal forests extend along more than 60 per cent of tropical shorelines, where they help stop coastal erosion and flooding by intense tropical storms. They also provide food and shelter for an amazing variety of wildlife.

### ▼ SEEDLING SPEARS
*Seeds cannot sprout in the airless tidal mud, so mangroves hang on to their seeds until they turn into tiny seedling trees. These then drop off, usually at high tide so they float away to other shores. Each seedling has a long, sharp root that stabs into the mud where it settles, enabling it to grow into a new tree.*

## FLOODED FOREST
At high tide most of the mangrove forest is flooded with seawater. Small fish swim in from the sea to feed among the tangled roots of the trees, which also provide protection from bigger predators.

### ▼ BREATHING ROOTS
*Tidal mud is full of plant nutrients, but it is also salty, waterlogged, and airless. Most plants cannot grow in this tidal mud because they need to absorb oxygen through their roots. Mangroves can survive thanks to exposed roots that absorb air through breathing pores. Some have roots that stick up from the mud as a mass of spikes. Others have aerial roots that sprout from high up the trunk and arch down through the air into the stagnant mud.*

## SHARPSHOOTER

Some fish are specialized for living among mangroves. They include the archerfish of Southeast Asia. As it swims through the flooded forest, it looks for insects on overhanging plants above the surface. When it spots its prey, the fish squirts a jet of water at it, knocking it into the water where it can snap it up.

▶ **ARCHERFISH**
*The fish's tongue fits against a groove in the roof of its mouth to form a tube. It forces water out of its mouth by pushing its tongue along the groove – it can hit a target more than 2 m (6.5 ft) away.*

## ON THE MUD

At low tide, the mangroves transform into a tangled mass of tree roots sprouting from the salty mud. Fiddler crabs swarm over the mud, gathering it up with their claws and stripping it of edible particles. The mud is also home to air-breathing fish called mudskippers. They use their front fins like crutches to haul themselves around, and some even climb into the trees.

▶ **FIDDLER CRAB**
*Male fiddler crabs have a small feeding claw, and a bigger, brightly coloured claw that they use for attracting female fiddler crabs.*

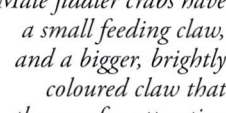

▶ **MUDSKIPPER**
*Each mudskipper lives in a burrow in the wet mud. It defends its burrow against invasion from other mudskippers, especially during the breeding season when the burrow acts as a nursery.*

## POWERFUL PREDATORS

The fiddler crabs and mudskippers foraging on the mud at low tide are hunted by a variety of land-based animals, including raccoons, monkeys, and the venomous mangrove snake. Some of these fall prey to powerful predators such as saltwater crocodiles and even tigers. The Sundarbans mangrove forest at the mouth of the River Ganges in India and Bangladesh is one of the last habitats of the Bengal tiger, and is a protected wildlife reserve.

**COAST AND SEASHORE**

## SCARLET IBIS
Perched on the mangroves growing on the tidal shores of the Caribbean, a flock of scarlet ibis waits for the falling tide to expose the mudflats below. They prey on shrimp and similar shellfish, which contain the red substance that turns their feathers scarlet.

# Seagrass beds

Nearly all the plantlike organisms that live in oceans are various forms of algae such as seaweeds, which are not true plants. The only true plants that have become adapted to life in seawater are the seagrasses that grow in sandy or muddy shallows. Seagrass beds provide sheltered habitats for small fish, and vital food for sea cows and green sea turtles.

▼ **GREEN SEA TURTLES**
*These sea turtles feed in seagrass beds in warm oceans all over the world. They are superb swimmers, travelling hundreds of kilometres every year between their feeding and nesting grounds.*

## UNDERWATER MEADOWS

Unlike seaweeds, seagrasses are true plants with proper roots and stems with internal veins. They also have flowers that open underwater. Their long grassy leaves absorb sunlight and use its energy to make food, so they only grow in shallow, relatively clear water, where they form broad underwater meadows.

Sea turtles produce salty tears to get rid of the excess salt from their bodies.

▲ QUEEN CONCH
*The big, heavy shell of the queen conch has a beautiful coral-pink glaze. It can live for up to 40 years, but many conches are caught for food and for their shells. They are also preyed on by a large number of animals.*

## GIANT SEA SNAIL

One of the most impressive animals living on seagrass beds is the queen conch – a large sea snail with a shell that can be up to 35 cm (14 in) long. It makes its home in the warm, shallow coastal waters of the Caribbean Sea and the Gulf of Mexico, using its toothed tongue to feed on seagrasses and various types of seaweed.

**FACT**
The fully aquatic and plant-eating sea cows look like walruses, but are actually more closely related to elephants.

## SEA COWS

Seagrasses are the favourite food of sea cows – large aquatic mammals that include the dugong and three species of manatees. The manatees live on both sides of the Atlantic in shallow, warm seas, as well as nearby rivers, where they eat a variety of water plants. The very similar dugong lives in the coastal waters of the tropical Indian and Pacific oceans.

▲ DUGONG
*This docile animal has few natural predators. It feeds day and night, using its strong, rubbery upper lip to dig up seagrasses, which it then swallows whole.*

## BEAKY GRAZER

In tropical coral seas, seagrasses grow in the sand of sheltered coral lagoons. They are eaten by the green sea turtle – the only species of sea turtle that is herbivorous. Seagrass is so important to this animal that some varieties are known as turtle grass. Like other turtles, the green sea turtle has no teeth, and crops the soft seagrass with its sharp-edged beak.

## CLINGING ON

Shallow seagrass beds make perfect homes for a wide variety of small fish. They include seahorses, which entwine their tails around the seagrass stems to stop themselves being swept away by the currents. Seahorses live alongside the young of many larger open-water fish. They hide among the seagrasses to avoid being eaten by predators.

▶ SEAHORSE
*When hunting for food, the seahorse waits motionless, using its long snout to catch food as it drifts by. It has excellent eyesight, and can also change colour to blend in with its surroundings.*

COAST AND SEASHORE

# Sea snakes and crocodiles

When dinosaurs ruled the land, many powerful marine hunters were reptiles. Most of these vanished long ago, and the only marine reptiles living today are sea turtles, tropical sea snakes, and a few lizards and crocodiles. A large number of them are not fully marine animals because they have to come back to land to breed, but some spend their entire lives at sea.

### SEA KRAITS
Instantly identifiable by the black bands around their bodies, sea kraits are a small group of snakes that live in the coral seas of the Indian and Pacific oceans. They hunt fish, killing them with their venomous bite. But unlike other sea snakes, they must return to land to lay their eggs.

### DEADLY PREDATOR
The fearsome saltwater crocodile hunts in rivers and along coasts. It often targets land mammals that have waded into shallow water, dragging them under to drown. Saltwater crocodiles are found in southeast Asia and Australia, and have spread to a number of small islands in the south Pacific.

*The saltwater crocodile is the world's largest reptile.*

▲ **SALTWATER CROCODILE**
*This young male saltwater crocodile can grow to at least 6.7 m (22 ft) in length. During its lifetime, its long, sharp teeth are constantly replaced.*

## DEADLY VENOM

All sea snakes apart from sea kraits are true marine reptiles because they never return to land. They even breed at sea, giving birth to live young in the water. Their venomous bite is incredibly powerful – far more deadly than a cobra's. This is because they need it to catch fish, which could easily swim away if not killed instantly.

▼ MARINE IGUANA
*The fierce-looking marine iguana normally has dark skin, but male iguanas glow with vivid colours in the breeding season.*

▲ YELLOW-BELLIED SEA SNAKE
*The yellow-bellied sea snake is found in the Indian and Pacific oceans. It hunts during the day, preying on small fish.*

## SEA-GOING LIZARDS

While some big tropical monitor lizards may swim out to sea to reach other shores, the marine iguanas of the Galápagos Islands are the only lizards specialized for ocean life. These iguanas eat seaweed, which they graze from submerged rocks. The sea around the islands is chilled by the cold Peru Current, so the iguanas often spend a long time basking in the sun after they emerge from the water.

## CARING PARENT

Widespread across Central America from the Pacific coast to the eastern Caribbean, the American crocodile has special adaptations that allow it to live in saltwater. This helps the crocodile to hunt in both freshwater and shallow tropical seas. Like all crocodiles, it lays eggs on land, burying them in a mound of sand on a river bank. The tropical climate keeps the eggs warm and helps them develop and hatch.

▶ AMERICAN CROCODILE
*American crocodiles lie in wait for hours, ready to ambush prey. They feed mainly on fish, but also use their powerful jaws to crush turtle shells.*

# POLAR SEAS

Despite being sealed beneath thick ice for part of the year, the polar seas of the Arctic and Antarctic are some of the most wildlife-rich habitats on the planet.

# Polar extremes

**POLAR SEAS**

In the Arctic and Antarctic, the Sun disappears below the horizon for most of the winter. As air temperatures plunge far below freezing point, the polar oceans freeze over, and a lot of the marine life moves away or lies dormant. But during the short summer, there is virtually continuous daylight, which melts the sea ice. Plankton multiply rapidly, causing a surge of breeding activity among polar animals before the seas freeze over again.

### FROZEN OCEANS

The Arctic Ocean is a huge sea around the North Pole, mostly surrounded by land. A large part of it is covered in ice, but the ice-free areas help warm the air. At the South Pole, Antarctica is a large icy continent surrounded by the Southern Ocean. The freezing ocean cuts off the Antarctic ice sheet from the warmth of other oceans, making the South Pole the coldest place on Earth.

▲ ROSS SEA ICE
*Dark water appears between drifting ice floes on the Ross Sea, Antarctica, as the ice breaks up in the weak summer sunshine.*

### POLAR SUNLIGHT

The winter freeze is caused by the way the Sun never rises for long in the polar winter, so there is very little sunlight to warm the surface of the ocean. By contrast, the Sun never sets in the polar summer, but it is always very low in the sky because Earth's surface does not face towards the Sun in these regions. The Sun's rays are spread over a much wider area at the poles than they are near the equator, weakening their power and allowing some ice to survive at sea level throughout the summer.

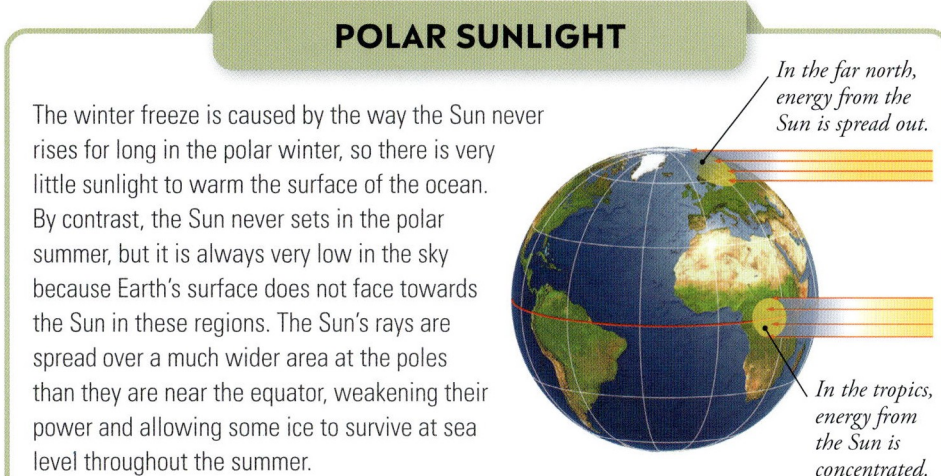

*In the far north, energy from the Sun is spread out.*

*In the tropics, energy from the Sun is concentrated.*

## THE BIG FREEZE

Winter air temperatures over the Arctic Ocean sink to below −30°C (−22°F), making the sea freeze over. The ice covers an area of up to 14.5 million sq km (5.6 million sq miles). Most of this melts in summer, leaving less than 4.3 million sq km (1.6 million sq miles) of ice near the North Pole. Around Antarctica, the winter sea ice covers 17 million sq km (6.5 million sq miles), shrinking in summer to 1 million sq km (398,000 sq miles).

◀ ICY SEAS
*As the spring Sun warms the sea near Baffin Island in Arctic Canada, the sea ice starts breaking up and drifting along the coast with the swirling currents. By midsummer (inset), all the sea ice has melted.*

## PLANKTON BLOOM

The water of cold oceans is rich in minerals stirred up from near the seabed. These are vital nutrients for the tiny algae of the phytoplankton. When the ice melts in summer, they combine with the 24-hour daylight to fuel huge blooms of phytoplankton, as seen here (blue) in the Arctic. In turn, these provide food for other marine life.

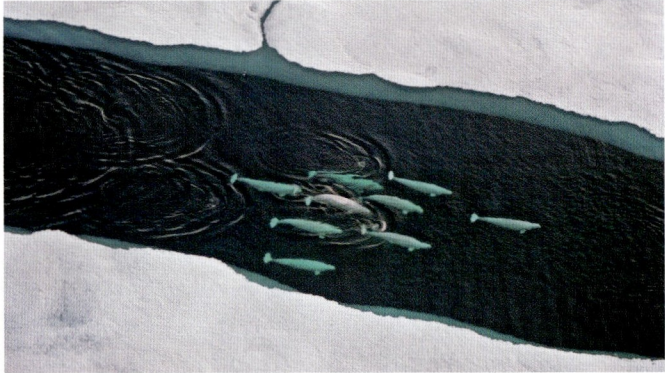

## EBB AND FLOW

As the polar sea ice forms and then melts away with the seasons, its edge is constantly moving north and south. The mobile ice front is a food-rich zone that attracts many polar animals, including these beluga whales swimming through a gap in the floating ice to reach nearby open water.

## POLAR SEAS

# Sea ice

In the polar regions, vast areas of ocean are covered with floating ice, especially in winter. The ice forms as freezing winds chill the ocean surface, creating ice crystals that fuse together into solid ice sheets that can be several metres thick. Sea ice may be frozen to the shore, so it looks like an extension of the land, but most of it drifts with the currents as pack ice.

### WHY ICE FLOATS
When water freezes, its triangular molecules go through a process of locking together and moving apart to create a three-dimensional structure with open space between them. Therefore, a litre of ice contains fewer molecules than a litre of water and also weighs less. This is why ice floats. No other substance behaves like this; it is a unique property of water.

◀ **PENGUIN PERCH**
*If ice behaved in the same way as the solid forms of other liquids, it would sink to the seabed – and these penguins would have nowhere to rest.*

### FREEZING SEAS

Sea ice does not form in a solid sheet. If the air temperature keeps falling, the water freezes in stages starting with a mass of small ice crystals called frazil or grease ice. These crystals freeze to form circular plates of pancake ice. They then fuse into thick pack ice that breaks up and freezes together again many times, but eventually becomes welded into a solid sheet.

▲ **GREASE ICE**
*Ice crystals freezing at the surface form a layer of slushy ice, like liquid mud; seals can surface through it.*

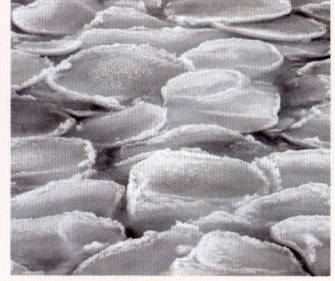

▲ **PANCAKE ICE**
*The grease ice forms plates, and as these bump together their edges turn up, like pancakes.*

▲ **MULTI-YEAR ICE**
*The ice forms a rough, tumbled sheet made up of thick ice floes pushed together by the wind.*

## DRIFTING PACK ICE

Sea ice is mostly mobile pack ice that drifts on the polar oceans. In the Arctic Ocean the currents carry the ice across the North Pole, where the low temperatures make it grow thicker over many years. Once the ice starts to drift away from the North Pole, it gets thinner, and finally melts into the ocean. This means that the marker on the ice indicating the North Pole's position is always moving with the ice, and has to be regularly relocated.

POLAR SEAS

### FROZEN VOYAGE

In the 1890s, Norwegian Fridtjof Nansen proved that sea ice drifted across the North Pole by allowing his specially strengthened ship *Fram* to become frozen into it. It took three years for the current to carry the ice and ship across the top of the world, near the North Pole. *Fram* finally broke free of the ice near Svalbard, Norway, in August 1896.

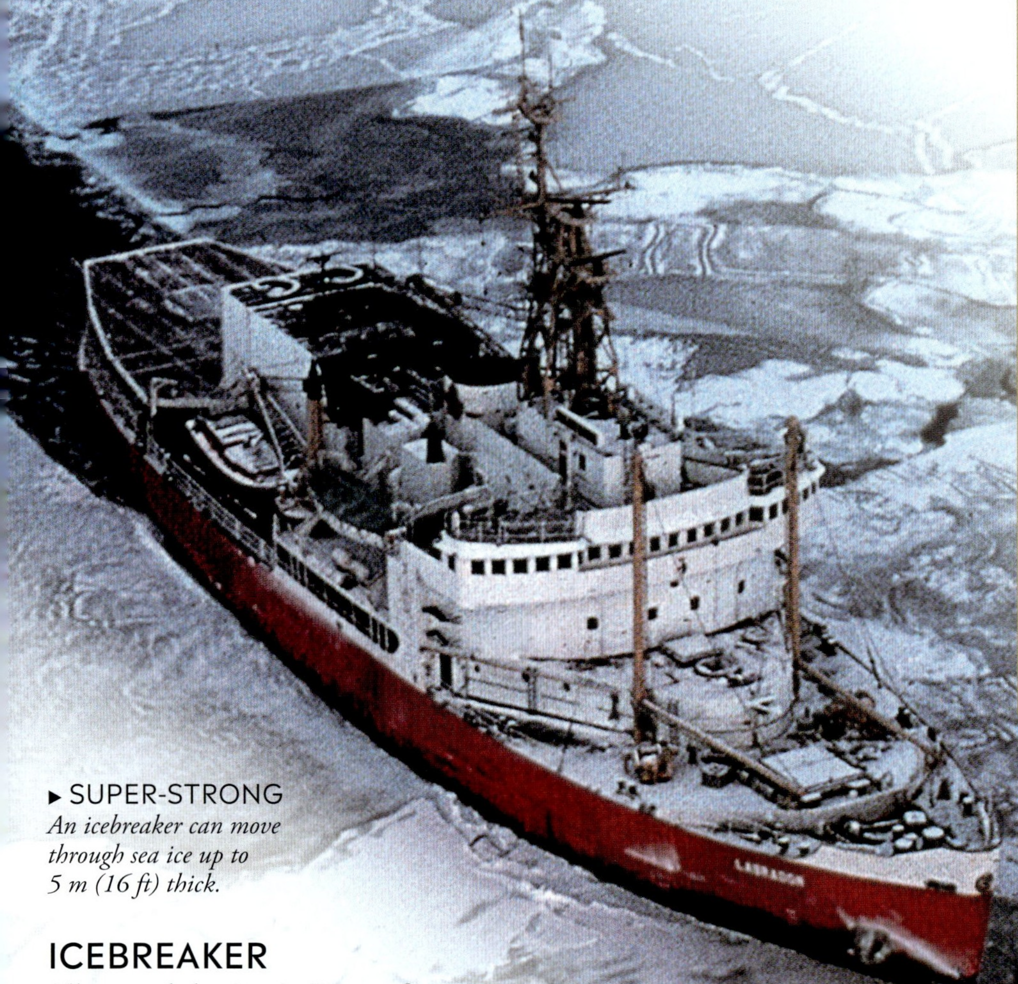

▶ **SUPER-STRONG**
*An icebreaker can move through sea ice up to 5 m (16 ft) thick.*

## ICEBREAKER

All around the Arctic Ocean, frozen seas are cleared for shipping by powerful icebreakers. These specially strengthened ships have gigantic engines that drive them up over the floating ice, so their immense weight smashes the ice. Icebreakers also work around Antarctica, but less frequently because there are no major shipping routes there.

# Life under the ice

Although the water beneath the sea ice is cold, it can be less cold than the air above. So, provided they can find food, many animals have no problem living under the ice. Tiny algae growing in the ice feed small animals that are hunted by fish and seals, and the seabed is often alive with sea urchins, starfish, and other marine invertebrates.

### ICE GARDENS
Phytoplankton is a vital food source for nearly all small creatures in polar oceans, but it does not grow in midwinter. It begins multiplying in early spring as the strengthening sunlight starts filtering through the thinning ice. Before long, the underside of the ice is covered with mats of green algae. These can be so thick that they stop the light reaching the deeper water below.

### FROZEN FOOD
The tiny algae growing under the ice feed krill, copepods, and other types of zooplankton that have survived the winter by lying dormant (asleep) beneath the ice. As soon as the algae start multiplying, the animals begin feeding intensively, and breeding. Eventually, they will form vast swarms, but not until after the ice melts.

◄ ANTARCTIC KRILL
*Green algae growing on the underside of the floating ice provides a half-frozen feast for these hungry krill in spring.*

**▼ SUPER SCAVENGERS**
*Despite the chill, these scavenging starfish thrive on the seabed beneath the floating ice of the Antarctic Weddell Sea.*

### ICE FISH  ▲ GHOSTLIKE

Salty seawater only freezes when its temperature falls to almost −2°C (28.4°F). Specialized animals such as this Antarctic ice fish have natural antifreezes in their bodies, which stop them from getting lethal frostbite.

*An ice fish looks ghostly and colourless because its blood does not have the red cells that absorb oxygen. In the oxygen-rich polar waters, its blood can carry enough oxygen without them.*

## SEABED DANGERS

The wealth of food in polar seas means that seabed animals that are able to survive the near-freezing water can flourish in huge numbers. But these animals live under constant threat of being ground to a pulp by ice floes drifting into the shallows, or being frozen solid by ice forming around them in the water.

**▲ WEDDELL SEALS**
*These seals hunt further south than any other seals, staying close to the Antarctic coast when the sea freezes over in winter.*

### HARD TIMES

Many seals hunt under the floating ice, surfacing to breathe at the ice edge or in small patches of open water. Around Antarctica, Weddell seals hunt fish and squid beneath the thick ice near the shore. They use their teeth to chip away the ice to make breathing holes.

POLAR SEAS

193

# Crabeater seals and penguins

## SEAL MILLIONS
With a population of more than 10 million, crabeater seals are the most numerous large wild mammals on Earth. They spend most of their time in the cold water or resting on the floating pack ice, sometimes in groups of up to 1,000 seals. Females give birth on the ice in spring and feed the pups on their rich milk for three weeks, until they are ready to enter the water and hunt for themselves.

The pack ice that forms on the Southern Ocean around Antarctica is home to millions of penguins and seals, the highest number of which are the crabeater seals. While most penguins leave the ice to nest on Antarctic coasts and islands when the snow melts in summer, emperor penguins breed on the coastal sea ice that extends from the shores of Antarctica in winter.

▲ FLOATING REFUGE
*A drifting ice floe makes an ideal retreat for these crabeater seals, safe from the leopard seals that are their main enemies.*

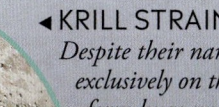

◀ KRILL STRAINER
*Despite their name, crabeater seals feed almost exclusively on the small shrimplike krill that form huge swarms in the cold Southern Ocean. They strain the krill from the water using specialized teeth that interlock with each other to form a sieve.*

## FAST FACTS

- Baby crabeater seals put on weight at the rate of 4 kg (9 lb) a day, while they are feeding on their mothers' milk.
- When breeding, krill-eating chinstrap penguins have to catch one krill every six seconds to feed their chicks.
- Male emperor penguins go without food for up to 115 days, while they are incubating their eggs. In that time, the males can lose half their body weight.

## DIVING PENGUINS

Small Antarctic penguins such as chinstrap and Adélie penguins feed mainly on krill, chasing and catching them one by one in their sharp bills. The bigger king and emperor penguins also catch fish and squid, sometimes diving to immense depths to find them. Emperor penguins may dive to a depth of 500 m (1,640 ft) or more, and stay underwater for up to 32 minutes before returning to the surface for air.

### ▲ DOWNY CHICKS
*Adélie chicks grow fast, and are soon almost as big as their parents. After about eight weeks, their soft, dark, and downy feathers are replaced by waterproof feathers, enabling them to hunt for food on their own.*

## ROCKY NURSERIES

Adélie penguins breed on the shores of Antarctica, further south than any other penguins. They wait until the relative warmth of summer has melted the snow to expose some bare rock on the coast, then form breeding colonies with hundreds or even thousands of mated pairs. Each pair makes a nest of stones, and they take turns to incubate their two eggs until the chicks hatch.

**POLAR SEAS**

### ▲ WINTER VIGIL
*Emperor penguins lay their eggs in autumn. They are incubated by the males through the bone-chilling Antarctic winter, while the females feed at sea. Each male supports his egg on his feet to keep it off the ice.*

## HUDDLING EMPERORS

Most Antarctic penguins nest on rocky shores in summer. But emperor penguins are bigger and take longer to grow up, so the summer is not long enough for them to both incubate their eggs and rear their chicks. They start breeding on the sea ice in the winter, huddling together to keep out the bitter chill. The eggs hatch in spring, so the chicks are able to develop through the summer before the winter closes in again.

**SLEEK HUNTERS**
With their short legs and waddling gait, penguins move clumsily on land. But when they dive into the water, they are transformed into sleek, fast, and elegant swimmers. Dense feathers and thick fat layers give penguins the perfect streamlined body, and keep them warm in cold seas.

# Antarctic hunters

Many of the animals that feed in the rich waters around Antarctica are hunted by leopard seals and killer whales – the most powerful predators in the Southern Ocean. Leopard seals are solitary ambush hunters, while killer whales prowl the icy seas in hunting packs that work together to outwit and overpower their prey.

### LEAP OF FAITH
Although there are no killer sharks in the icy seas around Antarctica, the water is patrolled by equally dangerous predators. The penguins and seals that spend much of their time on the floating sea ice risk death every time they enter the water to find food. A high-speed dive from an iceberg offers these Adélie penguins the best chance of avoiding attack, because they are moving so fast when they hit the water that their enemies have less time to seize them.

### AMBUSH KILLER
The powerful leopard seal eats a lot of krill, but it also preys on penguins and other Antarctic seals – especially crabeater seals. Its favourite tactic is to lurk beneath the edge of the floating ice and wait for a victim to slip into the water. If it is a penguin, the leopard seal seizes it and thrashes it around in the water to kill it. This also makes the penguin's skin and feathers peel away from its body, so the meal is easier to swallow and digest.

◀ LEOPARD SEAL
*A gentoo penguin makes a desperate bid to escape the attack of a leopard seal near Cuverville Island, Antarctica.*

## TOP PREDATOR

Killer whales, also known as orcas, are giant dolphins with jaws full of big, sharp teeth. They prey on anything they can catch and kill, including fish, penguins, seals, and even polar bears and other whales. They can rip big animals apart, but often swallow seals whole. Killer whales are found in oceans throughout the world, travelling in family groups called pods. Each pod contains about 20 members, which usually stay together for life and share the care of the young.

▼ **KILLER WHALE**
*A male killer whale leaps from the water in an icy polar sea. Males have much taller dorsal fins than females.*

## PACK HUNTERS

Like all whales and dolphins, killer whales are very intelligent, and often cooperate to hunt. Here, four killer whales have joined forces to catch a crabeater seal resting on an ice floe. Three of them are creating a wave that will wash over the ice and sweep the seal into the water, where the fourth hunter is waiting to seize it.

**POLAR SEAS**

### FACT
Each pod of killer whales specializes in hunting a particular type of prey, and even has its own unique language of sounds and calls.

POLAR SEAS

# Antarctic islands

The Southern Ocean surrounding Antarctica is dotted with islands. They are rocky, icy places, and some are active volcanoes, but they make perfect breeding sites for the seabirds and other animals that get their food from the ocean. Many have vast breeding colonies of seals and penguins. These islands are also the nesting sites of airborne wanderers such as albatrosses.

## ROCK AND ICE
Most of the Antarctic islands are rugged and hostile, with high rocky peaks smothered in ice that flows down to the sea in glaciers. Some of them are chains of volcanic islands, which have erupted from earthquake zones where two plates of Earth's crust grind together. The islands are windy and cold, with frequent snowstorms, but their bleak beaches offer easy access to an ocean teeming with fish and other food.

## BREEDING BEACHES
The beaches attract female seals, which must give birth to their pups on land. Since the seal pups cannot swim straight away, their mothers also feed them on the beaches, gathering in big groups. The male seals join them, hoping to mate with the females. But seals do not simply pair up. Each male tries to control as many females as possible, which leads to intense competition and rival males fighting each other on the beaches.

▶ SOUTHERN ELEPHANT SEALS
*These young male southern elephant seals on South Georgia Island are already practising their combat skills.*

## VAST COLONIES

Several of the penguin species that live around Antarctica nest on these islands, forming enormous breeding colonies. At least a million pairs of chinstrap penguins breed on Zavodovski, an active volcano in the South Sandwich Islands. They take advantage of the volcanic heat that melts the snow on the volcano's slopes, providing snow-free ground for nesting. This area has the largest concentration of penguins on Earth.

◀ **KINGS AND QUEENS**
*The king penguin colony at Salisbury Plain on the shores of South Georgia attracts more than 100,000 breeding pairs; each pair raises a single chick.*

## REMOTE NESTS

These black-browed albatrosses mate for life and return to the same island to breed every year. They nest on the ground near the sea in large, noisy colonies. These islands are ideal nesting grounds for these birds because they have no natural ground predators, such as foxes, to steal their eggs and young. Each pair has a single chick, which has to be fed by its parents for more than four months before it is able to fly and hunt for itself.

**FACT**
Bird Island in South Georgia is home to 130,000 fur seals and 100,000 penguins.

## WHALING STATIONS

In the past, the islands were used as bases for hunting seals and then whales. Commercial whaling was banned in 1986 to save the whales from extinction, and so the whaling stations were abandoned. Decades after the whaling ban, many whale species are recovering, including blue whales around South Georgia Island.

▼ **RUSTING RELIC**
*A beached whale-hunting ship, complete with harpoon gun, lies near the former whaling station at Grytviken, South Georgia.*

POLAR SEAS

# Glaciers and ice shelves

In cold climates, snow stays frozen throughout the year, so it gets deeper and deeper as more snow falls. Its weight compresses the lower layers of snow into solid ice, which flows slowly downhill as glaciers. Many of these melt before they reach the coast, but some polar glaciers flow all the way to the sea. Here, they form the tidewater glaciers and ice shelves that break up to create icebergs.

### Hubbard Glacier
*Crumbling cliffs*

**Location** Alaska, US
**Length** 122 km (76 miles)
**Status** Stable

This is the biggest tidewater glacier in North America. It has a huge tidewater front that extends for 10 km (6 miles), with an ice cliff up to 120 m (394 ft) high. Ice crumbling from the cliff forms a steady stream of icebergs that drift into Disenchantment Bay on the southeast Alaskan coast.

## TYPES OF GLACIERS

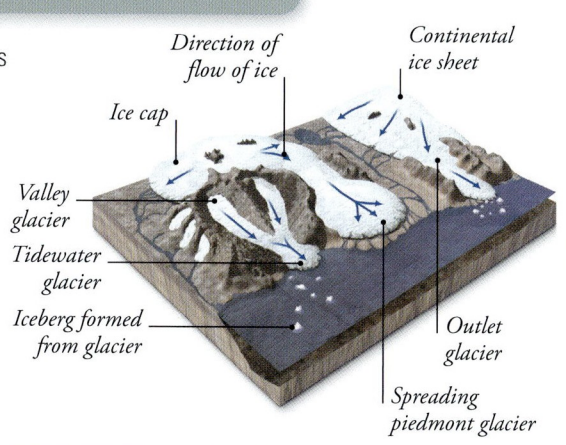

Most glaciers form in the mountains from snow that collects in a rock basin between high peaks. When the basin is full, the ice overflows and grinds its way downhill as a valley glacier. But in very cold regions, high land is covered with ice caps or huge ice sheets that feed ice into outlet glaciers. Both types can reach the sea, where they become tidewater glaciers.

### Jakobshavn Glacier
*Giant icebergs*

**Location** Greenland
**Length** More than 65 km (40 miles)
**Status** Retreating

The Jakobshavn Glacier is one of many outlet glaciers pouring off the Greenland ice sheet – a vast mass of ice that covers 80 per cent of Greenland. The glacier flows west into a fjord that opens into Disko Bay, cracking up into huge icebergs that then drift into the north Atlantic. The iceberg that sank the *Titanic* in 1912 probably came from this glacier.

### Columbia Glacier
*Iceberg factory*

**Location** Alaska, US
**Length** 51 km (32 miles)
**Status** Retreating

This tidewater glacier spills into the Gulf of Alaska in the north Pacific, and is one of the fastest-moving glaciers in the world. In 2001, it was calving icebergs into the sea at the rate of 7 cubic km (1.7 cubic miles) per year. But this prolific iceberg production is cutting back the floating ice front, which has retreated more than 20 km (12 miles) since the 1980s.

## Peters Glacier
*Island of ice*

**Location** South Georgia
**Length** 27 km (17 miles)
**Status** Retreating

At least half of the sub-Antarctic island of South Georgia is covered by permanent snow and ice, which flows downhill in about 160 glaciers. More than 100 of these reach the sea, including the spectacular Peters Glacier with its deep crevasses. Like most of South Georgia's glaciers, it is retreating as a result of climate change.

## South Sawyer Glacier
*Blue ice*

**Location** Alaska, US
**Length** 50 km (31 miles)
**Status** Retreating

The twin Sawyer Glaciers, North and South, flow off the Coast Mountains of Canada into a deep, narrow fjord on the southeast Alaskan coast called the Tracy Arm. Giant chunks of blue ice break off the glaciers and drift down the fjord, where they are used as floating refuges by harbour seals.

## Margerie Glacier
*Towering walls*

**Location** Alaska, US
**Length** 34 km (21 miles)
**Status** Stable

Glacier Bay in southeastern Alaska has a total of 16 tidewater glaciers. Named after French geographer Emmanuel de Margerie, the Margerie Glacier is one of the most spectacular, with walls of ice towering 80 m (262 ft) above the water. Unlike most of the neighbouring glaciers, it has advanced over recent years, and is now stable.

## Ross Ice Shelf
*Incredible size*

**Location** Antarctica
**Area** 487,000 sq km (188,000 sq miles)
**Status** Stable

Ice flowing off the vast Antarctic ice sheets spills out over the sea as ice shelves. The Ross Ice Shelf is the biggest – a colossal sheet of ice covering part of the Ross Sea and about the size of France. Although it is currently stable, scientists warn that it might collapse within the next century.

▼ **WHITE WALL**
*The floating ice front of the Ross Ice Shelf is more than 600 km (373 miles) long, and up to 50 m (164 ft) high.*

POLAR SEAS

**SPLASHDOWN**
As glaciers wind their way to the coast, they develop deep cracks called crevasses. When this fractured ice reaches the sea and starts floating, it becomes unstable, so it doesn't take much movement to make big chunks of ice fall away from the end of the glacier and crash into the water.

# Icebergs

Ice shelves and the snouts of tidewater glaciers float on the sea, so they move up and down with rising and falling tides. Combined with the effects of melting, this movement makes them crack up, break into pieces, and drift away as icebergs. Many of these are small, but some icebergs are vast floating islands that can drift for huge distances in the ocean currents before melting away.

**FACT**
The oceans are warming up, which is causing Greenland's melting glaciers to lose about 270 billion tonnes of ice each year, adding to rising global sea levels.

**BREAK-UP**

A tidewater glacier or an ice shelf is attached to the rock near the shore, but floats at the end nearest the ocean. The floating section of ice beyond the grounding line is thinner and, as the tide rises and falls, this flexes the floating ice until it cracks. As a result, parts of floating ice break away as icebergs – a process called calving. Since they are broken glacier ice, icebergs are made of frozen fresh water.

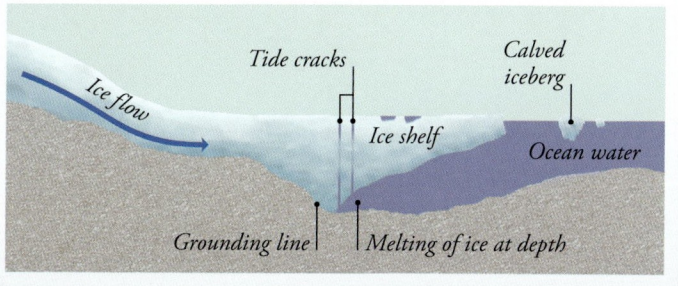

## HIDDEN MENACE

Ice expands as it freezes, so it weighs less than the same volume of liquid water. This is why an iceberg floats. But the difference in weight is only 10 per cent, meaning that 90 per cent of a drifting iceberg is hidden beneath the ocean's surface. The hidden ice may also project far beyond the visible ice above the waves.

## FLOATING ISLANDS

Enormous icebergs calve from the vast Antarctic ice shelves. In March 2000, for example, an iceberg the size of the island of Jamaica split from the Ross Ice Shelf. These immense slabs of ice, called tabular icebergs, float flat on the water and look like icy islands.

## SLOW DECLINE

As they drift at sea, icebergs start melting into strange shapes. Their weight distribution changes, so they may tip over or even turn upside down. This often reveals the green algae that have been growing on the ice beneath the waterline, as well as dark streaks of rock debris.

◀ END OF AN ICEBERG
*Beached on the coast of the Antarctic Peninsula, this iceberg is in the last stage of its life.*

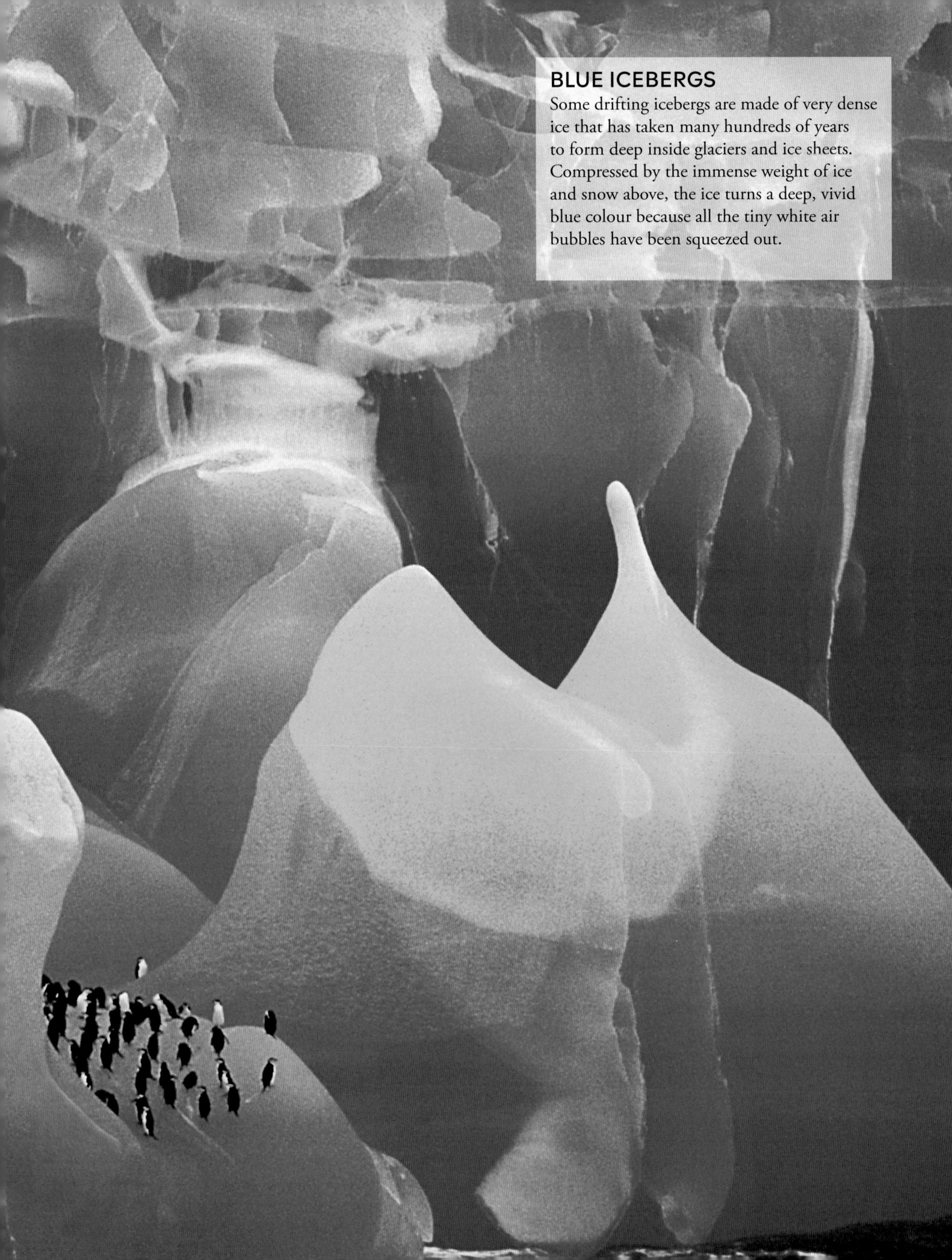

## BLUE ICEBERGS
Some drifting icebergs are made of very dense ice that has taken many hundreds of years to form deep inside glaciers and ice sheets. Compressed by the immense weight of ice and snow above, the ice turns a deep, vivid blue colour because all the tiny white air bubbles have been squeezed out.

# Arctic seals

Icy Arctic seas are home to many types of seals. Most are true seals, with back-pointing hind limbs and short flippers that are useless on land, but perfect for driving the seal through water. Fur seals, sea lions, and walruses have longer front flippers and are able to turn their hind limbs forwards, so they are more mobile on land.

## Walrus
*Tusked giant*

**Length** Male up to 3.8 m (12.5 ft)
**Weight** Male up to 1,900 kg (4,188 lb)
**Habitat** Coastal seas

The walrus is much bigger than other seals and not closely related to any of them, although it is built like an oversized sea lion. It lives all around the Arctic on rocky coasts, hunting for clams and other shellfish on the shallow seabed. The most obvious feature on both male and female walruses are the long tusks, which are extended upper canine teeth and can grow more than 1 m (3.3 ft) long. They sometimes use them for fighting, as well as for hauling themselves out of the water and on to the ice, but they are mainly a symbol of age and social importance.

▼ BASKING WALRUSES
*Walruses are very sociable and often gather in tightly packed groups to warm up after diving for food in the cold water.*

## Bearded seal
*Touch sensitive*

**Length** Up to 2.4 m (8 ft)
**Weight** Up to 360 kg (794 lb)
**Habitat** Coastal seas

The bearded seal feeds on clams and crabs, as well as squid and seafloor fish. It finds most of its prey on the seabed, locating it by touch using its very long, sensitive whiskers. This hunting technique limits the seal to shallow coastal water, but it lives all around the Arctic Ocean and nearby seas. Females give birth alone on small ice floes; unusually, the pups are able to swim and dive within a few hours of being born.

## Ringed seal
*Sleek swimmer*

**Length** Up to 1.7 m (5.5 ft)
**Weight** Up to 120 kg (265 lb)
**Habitat** Pack ice

A typical true seal, with its almost fishlike body shape, the ringed seal is one of the most widespread Arctic species. Like other seals, the ringed seal has thick layers of fat and a coat of dense fur, which allows it to swim for hours in numbingly cold water in search of prey, and rest on the ice without freezing. The favourite prey of polar bears, this seal often stays near its breathing hole in case it needs to make a quick escape.

## Steller sea lion
*Visible ears*

**Length** Male up to 3 m (10 ft)
**Weight** Male up to 1,000 kg (2,200 lb)
**Habitat** Coastal seas

Most sea lions and fur seals live further south, and include several species that live around Antarctica. But the Steller sea lion and the northern fur seal live and breed in the near-Arctic Bering Sea between Alaska and Siberia. The Steller sea lion is the biggest of all the eared seals, which get their name from their visible ear flaps. It breeds in big colonies on rocky beaches, with the bigger males fighting each other over the females. It hunts mostly at night, preying on fish, squid, crabs, and clams.

## Ribbon seal
*Distinctive pattern*

**Length** Up to 1.9 m (6 ft)
**Weight** Up to 100 kg (220 lb)
**Habitat** Pack ice

Similar to the ringed seal, the far less common ribbon seal lives in the Bering Sea and nearby Arctic Ocean between Alaska and eastern Siberia. Adult males have black or very dark coats with a pattern of white or cream bands; females are paler, with a less obvious pattern. These seals breed on floating sea ice and spend the rest of their lives hunting at sea for fish, squid, and small animals such as shrimp.

## Hooded seal
*Solitary hunter*

**Length** Male up to 2.4 m (8 ft)
**Weight** Male up to 352 kg (776 lb)
**Habitat** Pack ice

The big hooded seal hunts large fish and squid deep below the surface in the Greenland Sea and far north Atlantic. Unlike most seals, it usually lives alone. Males are much bigger than females, and rival males often fight each other.

## Harp seal
*Breeding colonies*

**Length** Up to 1.8 m (6 ft)
**Weight** Up to 136 kg (300 lb)
**Habitat** Pack ice

Named for the harp-shaped black marking on the silver-grey back of the adult, the harp seal is a slender, fast-swimming fish hunter. It spends most of its life at sea, forming big breeding colonies on the northern pack ice in late winter.

# Icy nurseries

Many seals breed on the pack ice that forms on the polar oceans, and in the Southern Ocean around Antarctica. This is a very safe strategy. In the Arctic, the threat posed by polar bears has led to the evolution of special adaptations and patterns of behaviour that reduce the risk of a deadly attack.

## SNOW CAVE
Ringed seals live near the North Pole, where they breed on snowy sea ice attached to the shore. Each female burrows up through a crack in the ice to dig a cave in the tumbled ice and snow. Her pup stays in the cave while she slips out through the secret entrance to go hunting. This means that both of them are always hidden from prowling polar bears.

### FACT
Harp seals rear their young for just 12 days, then leave them on the ice. The vulnerable pups cannot swim or hunt for another six weeks.

## ON THIN ICE
Harp seals live in big colonies. In late winter, they travel to three breeding areas on the Atlantic fringes of the Arctic, and the females gather on newly formed pack ice to have their single pups. The thin ice is strong enough for the seals, but too fragile for the polar bears that prey on them. However, the ice breaks up quickly, so the pups have to grow up fast.

▲ HARP SEAL NURSERY
*Four harp seal pups and an adult female bask on the sea ice off the eastern coast of Arctic Canada.*

## WHITE COATS

The pups of Antarctic seals are grey, like their parents. But in the Arctic, dark-coated seal pups would be easy targets for predatory polar bears. This may explain why most Arctic ice-breeding seals are born with white coats, which camouflage them against the ice and snow. The thick white fur also keeps out the cold, but soon falls away to reveal a darker, sleeker coat.

### ▶ MOULTING PUP
*Although it is only about eight weeks old, this ringed seal pup is already losing the white fur coat it was born with. It will soon look very different.*

POLAR SEAS

## INFLATABLE CHARMS

The hooded seal lives in the same Arctic regions as the harp seal. During the spring breeding season, the adult males compete with each other by performing a spectacular display. Each male seal fills the top of his black snout with air to create the swollen "hood" that gives the seal its name. They can also inflate a balloon of red skin that emerges from the left nostril, and shake it from side to side to make a loud pinging sound. The males use this display to drive off rivals, but often end up fighting instead.

# Hunters on the ice

When the Arctic Ocean freezes over, land predators are able to wander far out onto the ice in search of prey. Two Arctic hunters make a habit of this – the polar bear and the Arctic fox. Both are highly adapted for surviving the cold, but the polar bear in particular is so specialized for life on the ice that it spends more time at sea than on land.

▲ **HIDDEN PREY**
*An Arctic fox finds prey beneath the snow using its sensitive ears and acute sense of smell. It then pounces on its prey from a height to pin it down.*

### PROWLING FOX
The Arctic fox hunts mainly on land, where it preys on lemmings and other small mammals. But during the seal breeding season, in spring, it heads out on to the ice looking for seal pups. The Arctic fox also trails polar bears to feast on their leftovers. Its very dense white winter coat keeps it warm in the bitter Arctic chill, and it can even sleep on the ice.

### SUMMER COAT
In summer, the Arctic fox sheds its thick white winter coat in favour of a thinner brownish one. This stops it overheating, and also gives it better camouflage on land. Some Arctic foxes, known as blue foxes, have dark blue-grey coats that they keep all year round. But these foxes mainly live on rocky shores.

*Polar bears are the largest bears in the world.*

## SEA BEAR

The polar bear is a meat-eater that hunts at sea on the winter pack ice, protected from the cold by its dense fur and a thick layer of fat under its skin. Although polar bears can swim well, they cannot hunt in the water. When the sea ice melts in summer, they must stay ashore without eating until the sea freezes once again.

## SNOW CUBS

Each female polar bear usually has two cubs. They are born in autumn in a snow den on land. The mother feeds her tiny cubs on her milk throughout the winter, then leads them onto the sea ice in early spring in search of prey. The cubs stay with their mother until they are about two years old.

## ICE HUNTER

Polar bears eat seals – especially ringed seals that breed in isolated snow caves on the floating pack ice. The bears locate these hidden seal nurseries by smell, and are able to detect them from at least a kilometre (0.6 miles) away. When a bear finds a seal nursery, it uses its weight to punch down through the snow and seize the seal before it can escape – killing it with a single swipe of its huge paw.

◀ FAMILY MEAL
*Polar bears roam the drifting pack ice in search of prey. The cubs follow their mother so that they can learn how to hunt for themselves.*

# Humans on the ice

The Inuit and Yupiit have lived near the Arctic for thousands of years by adapting to the intense cold and darkness. They hunt well on the sea ice, and use equipment crafted from the skins and bones of the animals they hunt, as well as modern technology, to survive the harsh environment. Today, many of them work in local industries, but continue to hunt, herd, and fish.

### KEEPING WARM

In winter, the temperature in the Arctic rarely rises above freezing point and can plunge to below −50°C (−58°F). The Inuit are used to the chill, but they could not survive without their extra-warm clothes made of furry animal skins. Traditionally, the warmest clothes are made of caribou (reindeer) skins, but sealskin and even polar bear fur are also used.

**FACT**
Inside their iglus, Inuit hunters sleep on beds made of solid ice that are covered with furry caribou skins.

### SNOW HOUSES

In the past, many Arctic peoples lived in houses made of stones, animal bones, and driftwood, or animal-skin tents in summer. But Inuit hunters staying out on the sea ice in winter would camp for the night in small shelters made of snow blocks called iglus. The walls of snow kept out the bitterly cold wind, while the heat from the sleeping people kept the inside surprisingly warm. The Inuit still build iglus when hunting, but their families usually live in modern houses.

### HUNTING AT SEA
Inuit hunters use one-person canoes called kayaks to hunt seals and whales at sea. Kayaks originally had whalebone or timber frames covered with sewn sealskins. The plastic kayaks now used all over the world are based on this Inuit design. To hunt, the Inuit use bows, arrows, harpoons, and guns.

### DOG POWER
More than 4,000 years ago, the Inuit began using sleds hauled by teams of husky-type dogs to travel over the sea ice and snowy terrain. Traditional dog sleds are made of wood or bone held together with strips of leather rather than nails.

### MODERN TIMES
In the 21st century, many Arctic peoples wear ready-made cold-weather clothes, and their houses have modern conveniences such as central heating. They even travel by motorized sleds, but still hunt out on the sea ice like their ancestors.

A well-built iglu can support the weight of a person standing on its roof.

POLAR SEAS

# OCEANS AND US

Once seen as barriers to exploration, oceans have now become rich sources of food and mineral wealth. But there is also an awareness of the need to protect the oceans from harm.

# Seafarers and explorers

Humans have travelled on the seas for thousands of years. Indigenous peoples crafted special boats for seafaring and were the first explorers. They began by looking for food and seeking new places to live. As people made bigger and more robust ships, they set out to travel greater distances to explore and map out the world.

## Polynesian settlers
*Exploring the Pacific*

**Date** 1500 BCE–1200 CE
**Object of voyage** Settlement
**Distance travelled** Tens of thousands of kilometres

The scattered Pacific islands were settled by people who originally came from southeast Asia. From about 3,500 years ago, they spread from island to island until they reached Easter Island (Rapa Nui) in about 1200. The settlers made their incredible journeys across vast tracts of the Pacific Ocean in big double-hulled sailing canoes, navigating by the stars. According to the oral tradition of the Māori people of Aotearoa (New Zealand), their island was discovered by Polynesian explorer Kupe. He found Aotearoa while chasing a beast across the Pacific Ocean.

▼ MĀORI CANOE
*Traditional Māori canoes are called waka. They are carved from tree trunks and can have either one hull or two, with sails to catch the wind.*

## Thule migration
*Arctic life*

**Date** 1–1500 CE
**Object of voyage** Hunting
**Distance travelled** Thousands of kilometres

The Thule people, who lived in the Arctic, travelled around the region using boats to cross the water and dog sledges to skim across snow and ice on land. They lived seasonally, transporting their belongings around with them throughout the year as they hunted seals and whales. To track down whales they used boats called umiaqs. Each umiaq could seat up to 15 people, and was light enough to be carried over the ice.

## Makah travellers
*Coastal explorers*

**Date** 500 CE onwards
**Object of voyage** Whale hunting
**Distance travelled** Thousands of kilometres

The Makah are an Indigenous people, who live in the far northwestern US. They have had a close relationship with the sea for thousands of years, exploring the Pacific Ocean and vast inland lakes in canoes carved from cedar wood. These vessels were used for fishing, whaling, carrying cargo, and going to war. The Makah people continue to whale and fish on these traditional canoes.

▲ ROCK ART
*Whales were an important part of the Makah diet, and are still hunted today. This Makah rock carving of a whale is from what is now the state of Washington, US.*

## Viking raiders
*Across the Atlantic*

**Date** 700–1100
**Object of voyage** Settlement
**Distance travelled** Tens of thousands of kilometres

More than a thousand years ago, the Vikings from Scandinavia were mounting armed raids on the coasts of northern Europe, crossing the seas in their sleek longships. But over time, they began settling in new lands, including Iceland and the southern tip of Greenland. Eventually, they reached Newfoundland on the eastern fringes of North America, settling there 500 years before Christopher Columbus crossed the Atlantic.

▲ **VIKING LONGSHIP**
*Built for speed, Viking longships were used for raiding. The Vikings built bigger boats for crossing the Atlantic.*

## Ferdinand Magellan
*Around the world*

**Date** 1519–1522
**Object of voyage** Trade route
**Distance travelled** 60,000 km (37,000 miles)

Portuguese explorer Ferdinand Magellan hoped to reach the rich trading ports of Eastern Asia by sailing west. He left Spain in 1519 with five ships and around 260 crew, and had to sail around the southern tip of South America before he could cross the vast Pacific. The journey took far longer than expected, and when Magellan was killed in the Philippines, his surviving crew decided to cross the Indian Ocean and sail home around Africa. They got back to Spain in 1522, having sailed around the world.

**OCEANS AND US**

▲ **VALUABLE GOODS**
*Zheng He returned to China with military successes, treasure, and goods never seen before. One African ruler even sent the Chinese emperor a giraffe.*

## Zheng He
*Chinese fleets*

**Date** 1405–1433
**Object of voyage** Exploration
**Distance travelled** 200,000 km (124,000 miles)

One of the first explorers of the Indian Ocean, Chinese admiral Zheng He made seven epic voyages in the early 1400s, visiting India, Arabia, and east Africa. Unlike European explorers, he had huge fleets of ships, and on his first voyage in 1405 he took a fleet of more than 300. They included several nine-masted Chinese junk ships estimated at 120 m (400 ft) long – far bigger than European ships of the time.

▲ **MAGELLAN'S SHIPS**
*Only two of Magellan's five ships completed the journey around the world. They were led by Magellan's second-in-command, Juan Sebastian de Elcano.*

▼ **GALÁPAGOS ISLANDS**
*Some of Darwin's most important discoveries were made on the eastern Pacific Galápagos Islands. The data he collected here was vital to his later work on evolution. This inlet on San Cristóbal island is named Darwin Cove in his honour.*

## HMS Beagle
*Charting the coasts*

**Date** 1831–1836
**Object of voyage** Coastal surveying
**Distance travelled** 64,400 km (40,000 miles)

The world's oceans were charted by many European surveying expeditions in the 18th and 19th centuries. They included the five-year voyage of HMS *Beagle* around the world, for which the captain hired the young British naturalist Charles Darwin. While on board, Darwin made serious studies of marine life, ocean water, and coral reefs.

# Ocean science

People have travelled and studied the oceans for thousands of years, developing an understanding of marine environments. The observations of European naturalists such as Charles Darwin and the scientific voyage of HMS *Challenger* in the late 19th century laid the foundation for modern oceanography. Today, ocean scientists use ships, submersibles (deep-sea crafts), and satellites to relay data to researchers that study all aspects of the oceans, from the ocean floor to the causes of oceanic storms.

National Oceanography Centre in Southampton

### OCEAN SCIENCE
Oceanography is one of the most complex sciences, involving physics, chemistry, geology, marine biology, and meteorology. These subjects are studied at oceanographic research institutes around the world. These institutes operate research ships of their own, including this one docked at Southampton in England.

### RESEARCH SHIPS
Oceanographic research ships are specially built for the job. As well as having laboratories, sampling equipment, and surveying gear, many carry deep-sea submersibles. These need special handling equipment, shown in action here as the Woods Hole research ship *Atlantis* hoists the submersible *Alvin* from the water after a dive.

### OCEAN-FLOOR DRILLING
The nature of the ocean floor has been probed by deep-sea drilling, which collects samples of the rocks to develop an understanding of its geology. The Japanese drilling ship *Chikyū*, shown here, can drill to the amazing depth of 7,000 m (23,000 ft) below the ocean floor, in water 2,500 m (8,200 ft) deep. These drilling projects have provided us with new information about the planet.

## SONAR SURVEYS

The early research ships spent a lot of time measuring ocean depths using huge lengths of weighted cable. Today, however, research vessels use sonar technology, which produces a detailed image of the seafloor. Large areas of the ocean have been surveyed in this way, including this region around the North Pole, colour-coded for depth; the landmass is shown as grey.

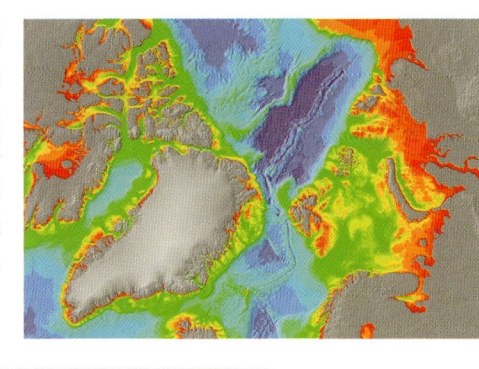

## EYES IN THE SKY

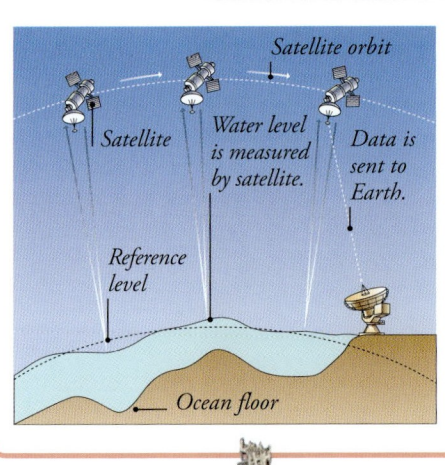

Orbiting satellites give us vital information about oceanic weather systems such as hurricanes. They can also map ocean currents, ice cover, water temperature, and plankton growth. Amazingly, measurements of the ocean surface compared to a reference level show that the water is not flat, but piles up above raised ocean floor features. Detected by satellites, these surface measurements can be used to create graphic, detailed images of the ocean floor.

OCEANS AND US

### FACT
The maximum drilling depth of the *Chikyū* is greater than the height of Mount Everest, the world's highest mountain.

# Scuba diving

Our understanding of the oceans has been helped a lot by our ability to dive beneath the surface and see the oceanic world for ourselves. This was made practical with the development of scuba diving gear in the mid-20th century. By providing divers with the means to swim freely to depths of around 40 m (130 ft), it opened a new era of underwater exploration.

### HARD HAT DIVERS
In the past, a diver was equipped with a waterproof suit sealed to a metal helmet, which was filled with air supplied through a rubber tube from a boat. Weighted boots stopped divers from floating to the surface, but forced them to walk on the seabed. The system worked well enough for static jobs such as inspecting harbour walls, but it was less useful for exploring the underwater world.

**FACT**
The face masks worn by scuba divers make fish and other objects look much bigger and closer than they really are.

### CLOSE ENCOUNTERS
Since the invention of the scuba system, divers have seen and photographed many types of marine life that were once known only from dead and dying specimens brought up by fishing lines and nets. Divers have also been able to watch the behaviour of these animals, and record it on video. Most of the images of marine life that we see on television have been captured by scuba divers equipped with specialized underwater cameras such as the one seen here.

Long fins on the diver's feet increase swimming speed.

## AQUA-LUNG
The letters of the word scuba stand for self-contained underwater breathing apparatus — a system that uses cylinders of compressed air carried on the diver's back. It was invented in 1942 by French ocean explorer Jacques Cousteau and French engineer Émile Gagnan, and was originally called the Aqua-Lung. Unlike the earlier hard hat system, it enables a diver to swim in open water, and does not require a special suit; scuba divers usually wear suits, but only for warmth and protection against stinging organisms in the water.

Cylinder holds enough air to last at least 30 minutes.

Buoyancy jacket can be inflated with air to adjust buoyancy underwater.

Diver draws in air through a tube from the cylinder.

### ▼ ANCIENT GLASS
In the 11th century, a ship sank off the coast of Turkey with a cargo of glassware on board. Known as the Glass Wreck, the shipwreck was excavated, and many of the glass jars were found intact.

## DIVING INTO THE PAST
Scuba diving has also revolutionized underwater archaeology. Ancient cities and shipwrecks are often hidden under layers of sediment, and many have been discovered by amateur scuba divers. Such finds are painstakingly excavated by teams of expert divers using the same basic scuba equipment. The position of every find is recorded by photographs and special underwater drawing techniques before it is taken to the surface. These finds provide a unique insight into the past.

## UNDER THE ICE
Scuba divers have even explored beneath floating polar sea ice, encountering some amazing creatures such as this beluga whale. Divers need special protective suits to combat the cold, but since the water temperature can never be lower than freezing point, it's not much colder than any other cold ocean — and warmer than the air above the ice.

OCEANS AND US

# Deep-sea exploration

Scuba divers cannot dive very deep below the surface, because a diver's unprotected body cannot cope with the effects of the intense pressure in deep water. Exploring the deep ocean requires special craft called deep-sea submersibles. These are designed for scientific work on the ocean floor, and they can dive much deeper than military submarines. Some carry people, but others are remotely controlled from ships on the surface using video technology.

### INTO THE DEEP
The first submersible capable of resisting the intense pressure in the ocean depths was called the *Bathysphere*, designed in 1928 by US engineer Otis Barton. It was made of steel with 76-mm- (3-in-) thick windows, and suspended from a ship by a steel cable. Naturalist William Beebe (left) and Barton (right) used it to make the first studies of life in the twilight zone.

### FULL CONTROL
Modern deep-sea exploration began with the fully controllable *Alvin*. Owned by the US Navy, but operated by the Woods Hole Oceanographic Institution, *Alvin* made its first deep dive in 1965. *Alvin* has a spherical pressure-proof cabin mounted inside a motorized hull that is equipped with lights, cameras, grabs, and sample baskets. It is still in use following modifications, and has made more than 4,600 dives – including the first crewed survey of the shipwrecked ocean liner *Titanic*.

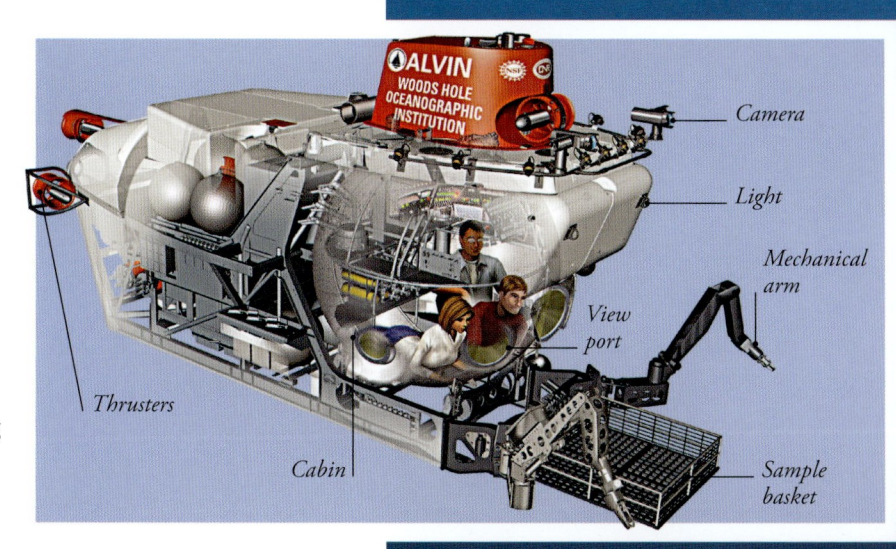

## DEEP DIVERS

*Alvin* is one of several similar submersibles that include the Japanese *Shinkai 6500*, the two Russian *Mir* craft, and the Australian *Deepsea Challenger*, designed to make a crewed descent to the Mariana Trench – the deepest part of the Pacific Ocean.

◀ **DEEPSEA CHALLENGER**
In 2012, film director James Cameron used this submersible to dive 10,908 m (35,787 ft) to the bottom of the Mariana Trench.

*The tall upper part of the* Deepsea Challenger *contains its batteries and hi-tech lighting arrays.*

*Two mobile booms controlled by the pilot carry a powerful spotlight and a 3-D camera.*

*The pressure-proof cabin is a steel sphere 109 cm (43 in) wide – just big enough for one cramped pilot.*

## REMOTE VIEW

Only a few crewed submersibles have been built because making them safe for the crew is very expensive. It is often easier to use a remotely operated vehicle (ROV), pictured above, controlled via a video link to a screen on a mother ship. These craft can also explore shipwrecks and other places that are too dangerous for crewed vehicles to visit. Some deep-sea exploration vessels, such as the *Okeanos Explorer* and *Nautilus*, broadcast live footage from their explorations over the internet.

## NEW DISCOVERIES

Without deep-sea submersibles, we would have little idea of what the deep ocean floor is like and what lives there. In the 1970s, for example, scientists aboard *Alvin* were the first to discover the black smokers that erupt on mid-ocean ridges, and the first to see and collect the amazing wildlife that lives around them.

▶ **HIDDEN WORLD**
*This view through the porthole of* Alvin *shows its mechanical arm in action. It is sampling the minerals pouring out of a black smoker on the Juan de Fuca Ridge on the floor of the northeastern Pacific.*

# Historic shipwrecks

One of the most exciting forms of exploration at sea is finding, excavating, and even raising historic shipwrecks. Many of these wrecks lie in shallow coastal waters, which are accessible to scuba divers. But others have plunged into the deep ocean, and have only recently been rediscovered using deep-sea submersibles.

### Kyrenia ship
*Ancient timber*

**Date of sinking** Between 286 and 272 BCE
**Depth of water** 33 m (108 ft)
**Rediscovery date** 1965

Discovered by a scuba diver near Kyrenia on the Mediterranean island of Cyprus, these timbers are the remains of a Greek merchant ship that sank more than 2,300 years ago. Salvaged along with its cargo of wine jars and many other objects, it gives us a glimpse into the ancient world.

### Mary Rose
*Tudor warship*

**Date of sinking** 1545
**Depth of water** 11 m (36 ft)
**Rediscovery date** 1971

One of the biggest ships in the navy of King Henry VIII of England, the *Mary Rose* sank just off the English coast during a sea battle. It settled on its side, half-buried in the mud. The exposed timber was soon eaten away, but the buried side was preserved with all its contents, and was raised in 1982.

### Vasa
*Amazing survival*

**Date of sinking** 1628
**Depth of water** 32 m (105 ft)
**Rediscovery date** 1956

The Swedish warship *Vasa* sank on its very first voyage after sailing just 1.3 km (0.80 miles) from the dockside in Stockholm harbour. It was a national disaster. The wooden ship lay on the seabed for 333 years, but thanks to the cold, airless water of the Baltic Sea the exposed timber was not destroyed by marine life. This allowed the ship to be raised almost intact in 1961, along with most of its equipment and the ornate carvings that had adorned it.

◀ **SHIP MUSEUM**
*The restored* Vasa *is now housed in a special museum in Stockholm, Sweden. Most of the timber is original, but has been treated with chemicals designed to stop it decaying.*

## Geldermalsen
*Sunken treasure*

**Date of sinking** 1752
**Depth of water** 40 m (132 ft)
**Rediscovery date** 1985

The cargo of a wrecked ship can be very valuable. When the 18th-century Dutch trading ship *Geldermalsen* sank near Singapore, it was carrying Chinese porcelain and gold that were salvaged and sold in 1986 for more than 10 million pounds. The ship was also carrying tea, which, at that time, was more valuable than its cargo of gold.

## Central America
*Lost gold*

**Date of sinking** 1857
**Depth of water** 2,200 m (7,220 ft)
**Rediscovery date** 1988

When the paddle steamer *Central America* sank in a hurricane off the Atlantic coast of the US, it was carrying 21 tonnes of gold. A part of the shipwreck's cargo (seen here) was recovered from deep water using a remotely operated submersible. The gold is estimated to be worth up to 120 million pounds.

**OCEANS AND US**

## Titanic
*Into the deep*

**Date of sinking** 1912
**Depth of water** 3,784 m (12,415 ft)
**Rediscovery date** 1985

The most famous shipwreck of all is the *Titanic*. On its maiden voyage, it hit a north Atlantic iceberg at full speed and sank to the ocean floor. The ship was found using a remotely controlled submersible, but crewed submersibles including *Alvin* and the two *Mir* craft were then used to explore, photograph, and film it. Some items have also been recovered from the site.

▶ **GHOST SHIP**
*The vast rusting hull of the* Titanic *is very fragile and may be close to collapse.*

# Minerals from the oceans

Oceans are an important source of useful minerals. These minerals range from the sand and gravel needed for the construction industry, to incredibly valuable diamonds. Some minerals have been harvested for centuries. Others, however, are found in much deeper parts of the ocean and there is still no way of retrieving them without spending more than the minerals are worth.

## SEA SALT

For hundreds of years, people living near the seashore have turned salty ocean water into edible sea salt. The water is let into shallow pools called salt pans, which dry out under the Sun. As the water evaporates, it leaves the salt crystals behind. These can then be heaped up and shovelled into sacks. This industry is still important to many coastal communities.

▼ **SALT PAN WORKERS**
*Rubber boots and gloves protect the skin of these salt gatherers on the coast of Vietnam.*

## DESALINATION

The salt in seawater makes it undrinkable. But the salt can be removed to obtain fresh water – a process called desalination. It uses a lot of energy, but this is not a problem for the oil-rich desert states of the Middle East, where it is often the only source of fresh water. This aerial view shows one of these desert-shore desalination plants. Some recent installations make use of solar energy, which is freely available in hot, dry countries, but this technology is still being perfected.

## VALUABLE METALS

Huge areas of the deep seabed are dotted with dark rocks that look like lumps of coal – these are called polymetallic nodules. They form over millions of years from minerals dissolved in seawater that settle onto hard particles and very slowly grow bigger. While mining companies are planning to harvest these nodules for their metals, conservationists are concerned about the damage this may cause to the environment.

## GLITTERING PRIZES

Off the southwest coast of Africa, diamonds are mined from the sea. These gemstones were originally formed in rocks on land, which have weathered over time. The diamonds were eventually carried down rivers to the coast, where they are found scattered among the gravel of the shallow seabed. Dredged up by special ships, and then separated from the gravel, many have the eight-sided form of perfect diamond crystals.

### FACT
Namibia, in southwest Africa, has the richest known resource of marine diamonds in the world.

## SAND AND GRAVEL

All over the world, huge quantities of sand and gravel are scooped from shallow seabeds, shipped back to shore, and unloaded, as seen here. These materials are used for making concrete and other building materials, and for road construction. The sand is also used for glass-making, because it is often pure quartz – the main ingredient of glass.

OCEANS AND US

# Energy from the oceans

**OCEANS AND US**

The oceans provide us with energy to fuel many aspects of our lives. The seabed rocks of shallow coastal seas are stores of fossil fuels such as oil and gas, which when used excessively can contribute to climate change. Environmentally friendly energy sources include oceanic winds, which can drive turbines that generate electricity. The power of tides, currents, and waves is also being used in the same way.

## WIND POWER
The winds blowing over the sea are stronger and steadier than the winds that blow over land. This makes shallow coastal seas good places to install wind turbines for producing electricity. Some of these offshore wind farms have more than 100 giant turbines, each generating enough power for 100,000 electric kettles.

▶ **OFFSHORE WIND FARM**
*Anchored to the seabed in shallow water, these wind turbines are connected to the shore by undersea electricity cables.*

## OIL AND GAS
Fossil remains of marine life locked in rocks on the seabed can turn into oil and natural gas – fuels and raw materials for industry. They are extracted using drilling rigs such as this one, which either stand on shallow seabeds or float in much deeper water. Modern oil and gas rigs can work in water depths of more than 3,000 m (9,800 ft), and drill up to around 10,000 m (32,800 ft) below the seabed.

▶ **LA RANCE BARRAGE**
*Opened in 1966, La Rance Barrage in St Malo was the world's first tidal power station, and has been running reliably ever since.*

**FACT**
The rotating blades of an offshore wind turbine can span more than 100 m (330 ft) – the length of seven school buses.

## TIDAL FLOW

Moving water is incredibly powerful, but it is difficult to harness at sea. The most effective way is to use the power of the tides as they flow in and out of a river estuary. At St Malo in France, the rising tide is allowed through a dam across the river mouth, and when the tide falls again the water pouring out through the dam generates electricity.

## OCEAN CURRENTS

Currents in oceans are like giant rivers flowing across the globe. In the future, it may be possible to use a powerful current such as the Gulf Stream to drive submerged rotors linked to electric generators.

▶ **RAISED ROTORS**
*This pair of current turbines has been raised above sea level for maintenance.*

**OCEANS AND US**

## WAVE ENERGY

Ocean waves are very powerful, but can be very destructive. Turning that power into useful energy is not easy. The most successful systems use waves to pump air through pipes, creating high pressure that drives turbine generators. These generators produce electricity in both directions – when the wave washes into the system, and when it washes back out again.

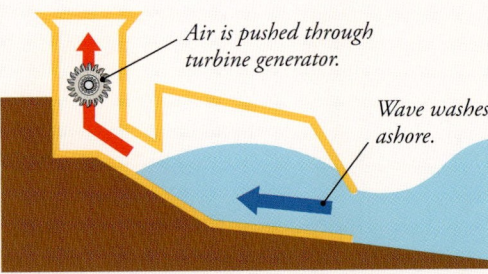

*Air is pushed through turbine generator.*
*Wave washes ashore.*
Inflow phase

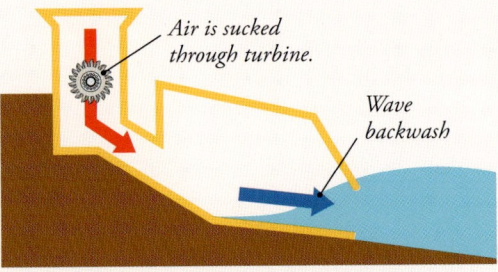

*Air is sucked through turbine.*
*Wave backwash*
Outflow phase

# Fishing

Sea fish have been part of our diet for thousands of years, and in some parts of the world, traditional techniques continue to be used to harvest enough fish to meet the local demand. Far greater quantities of fish can be caught using boats and nets, and so sea fishing has now become a major industry involving big ships supported by advanced technology. However, overfishing can threaten the stocks of many species. An alternative is to farm the fish, shellfish, and other types of seafood.

### TRADITIONAL METHODS
These Fijians are using a net supported by floats to encircle a small shoal of fish in shallow water near the shore. People living on sea coasts have traditionally used simple ways of catching fish, such as hand-worked nets, baited lines, and spears.

### INSHORE FISHING
Many coastal communities have fleets of small fishing boats that go to sea for a few hours, and return each day to unload their catch. The fishermen use simple nets and lines, and if they catch just enough fish to supply local markets, they may have little impact on fish stocks.

▶ A GOOD CATCH
*With the fleet lying safely at harbour, villagers collect the morning catch that has been brought in by the fishermen in Mui Ne on the central south coast of Vietnam.*

### FARMING SHELLFISH
Wild clams, limpets, and other wild shellfish have probably been harvested since humans first walked on Earth, but many shellfish are also well suited to being farmed. Mussels in particular naturally attach themselves to rocks and other hard surfaces. They will readily cling to timber piles, rafts, and ropes provided for them, and will gather their own food. Mussels are also very easy to harvest when their supports are exposed at low tide or when ropes are pulled out of the water.

◀ MUSSEL FARM
*Ropes made of natural fibre are wound around posts to support thousands of farmed mussels on this French beach.*

## FISH FARMS
Salmon and some other sea fish can be farmed by keeping them in submerged cages near coasts. Tidal water sweeping through the cages helps keep the fish healthy. But they have to be supplied with food, and the large numbers of farmed fish can affect local wildlife.

## OCEAN FLEETS
Most of the fish that are eaten worldwide are caught by fleets of big boats or by special factory ships. These stay at sea for months at a time and catch vast numbers of fish, which they process and freeze on board. Such fleets are even fishing in stormy seas.

◂ **INDUSTRIAL SCALE**
*This Alaskan purse-seining boat uses a bag-shaped net to scoop an entire shoal of wild salmon out of the sea.*

OCEANS AND US

**FACT**
Every year, the world's fishing fleets catch up to 2.2 trillion fish, weighing more than 80 million tonnes.

## STILT FISHING

Balanced on wooden poles above the waves, these Sri Lankan fishermen hope to catch fish swimming in shoals in the shallow water below. They use simple rods with baited lines, and store their catch in bags tied around the poles or their waist.

# Ocean trade

The oceans have been trading routes for centuries, providing vital links between nations. Ships are still the best way of transporting heavy cargoes such as oil and cars, but they also carry many other trade goods. These are often loaded into big steel containers that are easily lifted off the ship and on to trucks for distribution by road.

### TRADE ROUTES

For centuries, the main trading routes between the continents were dictated by the oceanic winds that drove sailing ships. For example, ships such as the one above would cross from east to west in the tropics, using the easterly trade winds, and from west to east using the westerly winds that blow over cooler oceans. Modern ships no longer rely on the wind to direct them, but it still pays to take advantage of ocean currents.

### CONTAINER SHIPS

Lightweight goods traded over long distances are often carried by air, especially perishable foods such as fruit. But heavy loads are best sent by sea, because ships are supported by the water, allowing them to carry a huge weight of cargo. Ships are slow, but for many types of cargo this is not a problem. A fleet of ships can also act like a floating conveyor belt, delivering an almost continuous supply of goods.

*A big cargo ship can carry more than 24,000 containers.*

▶ **HEAVY LOAD**
*A colossal load of shipping containers full of heavy freight is a standard cargo for this specialized container ship.*

## TRADING PORTS

Most of the world's coastal cities were built on wealth created by ocean trade. Many still have thriving ports, but most modern cargo ships dock at dedicated terminals equipped for dealing with particular types of freight (cargo). This port has special cranes designed for loading and unloading containers.

### FACT
The biggest cargo ship in the world, MSC *Irina*, measures just under the length of four football pitches.

## FLOATING HOTELS

Big, slow ocean liners were once the only way to travel between continents. Today, most people travel by air, which is much quicker, but passenger ships have become popular for cruise holidays. They are like giant floating hotels, which carry tourists in luxury to a series of exotic locations over a number of days.

*About 90 per cent of the world's cargo is transported by sea in shipping containers.*

## THREAT OF PIRATES

Ocean trade is much safer than it used to be, thanks to accurate charting of coastal hazards and the development of electronic navigation systems. But in some parts of the world, ships still risk attack by heavily armed pirates in small speedboats. If attacked, this ship sets off its fire hoses to stop pirates climbing aboard and seizing command.

OCEANS AND US

# Climate crisis

Records show that the world is getting warmer, and this change in climate threatens marine habitats and coastal cities. Runaway climate change, which is a small increase in global temperatures, is melting the polar ice and raising sea levels, making it likely that some islands will disappear underwater. Warmer oceans are increasing the frequency and strength of hurricanes and other storms, as well as causing damage to coral reefs. The rising level of carbon dioxide in the air, which is the main cause of global warming, is also increasing the acidity of the oceans, and this could be catastrophic for a lot of marine life.

## MELTING ICE
The polar ice sheets in Antarctica and Greenland are melting, and the sea ice at the North Pole is getting thinner. The Arctic has been losing more than 12 per cent of its sea ice every decade since the 1980s. The dwindling ice cover could have a big impact on Arctic wildlife, especially on polar bears that rely on the pack ice to hunt.

▲ FLOODED STREET
*Many cities in Bangladesh already suffer flooding due to heavy monsoon rain, as seen here in Dhaka, the capital. But rising sea levels could make some coastal cities uninhabitable.*

## RISING SEA LEVELS
As continental ice sheets melt, meltwater flowing off the land is increasing global sea levels. It is likely that they will rise by at least a metre (3 ft) over the next century. This one-metre rise would flood 17 per cent of Bangladesh. It would also expose coastal cities such as New York City, London, and Shanghai to the risk of serious flooding. What's more, several low-lying island nations could vanish completely.

▲ NORTHERN HURRICANE
*In 2012, Hurricane Sandy swept so far north from the Caribbean that storms battered the coast of Maine in the northeastern US.*

## STORM FORCE

Hurricanes are fuelled by water evaporating from warm tropical oceans in late summer. As global temperatures are rising, the surface waters of the oceans are warming up, so more water vapour is forming over a broader area, and for longer each year. Climate change is causing more storms, and where temperatures are highest, the storms are strongest. As cooler oceans warm up, hurricanes will also start to affect regions that currently lie outside the hurricane zone.

OCEANS AND US

**FACT**
Some scientists predict that by the year 2050, all the summer ice at the North Pole will melt away because of global warming.

## CORAL BLEACHING

High ocean temperatures known as marine heatwaves make reef corals expel the tiny algae that supply them with food, making them turn white. If the water cools down again, the corals can recover, but if not, they die. Recently, this process has become more frequent. Scientists warn that this coral bleaching could destroy most of the world's coral reefs within 100 years.

## ACID BATH

Global climate change is being caused by more carbon dioxide in the atmosphere. A lot of this gas is absorbed by ocean water, and mixes with it to form carbonic acid. The acid makes the oceans less alkaline, which means there's less chalky minerals for shellfish and corals to make their shells and skeletons. This could be fatal to many types of sea life, and to all the animals that rely on them for food.

▶ THREAT TO SHELLS
*These washed-up shells are made of alkaline minerals that could become scarce in the oceans of the future.*

# Harming the oceans

Human activity has a devastating effect on the oceans – we pour our waste into marine waters, destroy animal habitats, and deplete populations of wild animals. Industries and settlements dump plastic and other forms of chemical waste into seas and oceans, while oil spills harm entire ecosystems.

▼ **ENVIRONMENTAL DISASTER**
In April 2010, an explosion 1,500 m (4,920 ft) underwater on the Deepwater Horizon offshore drilling rig sent oil spilling out into the Gulf of Mexico. Here, boats can be seen dragging a floating oil "boom" to prevent the oil from spreading further.

### POISONED WATERS
Accidental oil spills out at sea are very dangerous to marine habitats. Oil spills poison the water, and in some cases cause harm to fish and wipe out their eggs. They coat the feathers of sea birds, preventing them from flying, and can pollute shallow waters and beaches.

### WASTE FROM INDUSTRIES
Industrial waste and sewage are sometimes illegally dumped into the oceans. These contain harmful substances that can kill animals, and include chemicals that take a long time to decompose. Over time these chemicals build up in food webs as they are passed from one animal to another.

### COASTAL DEVELOPMENT
The world's seashores are magnets for tourists, and many wild habitats have been destroyed to make way for beach resorts. Coastal development can also lead to increased amounts of sewage and rubbish that end up poisoning the sea and smothering nearby seagrass beds and coral reefs.

## PLASTIC POLLUTION

Vast amounts of rubbish find their way into the oceans, and some of it drifts in the currents for years. Plastic in particular does not rust away or decay, but it is swept up on beaches all over the world. It forms deadly traps for animals such as seabirds and turtles.

**OCEANS AND US**

### FACT
The Deepwater Horizon disaster was the largest oil spill in US history, with around 507 million litres (134 million gal) of crude oil spilled into the waters.

## OVERFISHING

Modern fishing trawlers can capture a huge number of fish at one time. A big modern fishing boat can catch an entire shoal of fish in one net, so none of the fish can escape to breed. Heavy fishing gear dragged across the seabed also damages and destroys important habitats.

## INVASIVE SPECIES

The spread of animal and plant species away from their native areas can be very dangerous for their new habitats. One of the most damaging invasive species is the European green crab, which first reached North America on merchant ships in the 1800s. Since then, its numbers have rapidly multiplied, leading to the destruction of seagrass meadows, which the crab feeds on.

# Oceans in danger

The oceans once seemed too big to be affected by human activity, but pollution, overfishing, and coastal development are wreaking havoc on marine habitats and sea life. Some parts of the seabed have turned into poisoned underwater deserts, and the damage to the oceans is leading to the rise of extreme weather events.

OCEANS AND US

### MICROPLASTICS
Pieces of plastic less than 5 mm (0.2 in) in size are known as microplastics. They are used in cosmetics or form when larger plastics break down. Across the globe, they can be found in food, soil, and water. Microplastics pollute habitats and can cause health problems for animals that consume them.

### BLEACHED CORAL
Pollutants and temperature shifts can have severe effects on marine ecosystems. Corals rely on algae, which live on them, for food. If the water warms by even a few degrees, the algae leave the corals. Without food, the coral becomes weaker and turns white in a process known as "bleaching".

## GREENHOUSE GASES

Earth is surrounded by a layer of gases, including carbon dioxide ($CO_2$), which trap heat around the planet, much like a greenhouse. Many human activities, such as burning fossil fuels and excessive farming, cause the levels of these gases in our atmosphere to increase. The oceans absorb more heat as a result and warm up. Carbon dioxide also turns the waters acidic, making the environment unfit for marine organisms.

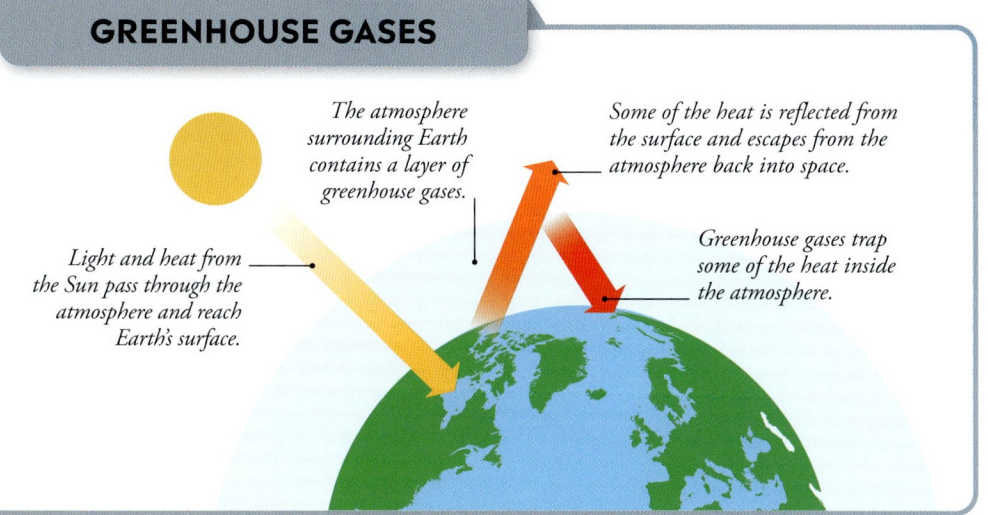

*The atmosphere surrounding Earth contains a layer of greenhouse gases.*

*Some of the heat is reflected from the surface and escapes from the atmosphere back into space.*

*Light and heat from the Sun pass through the atmosphere and reach Earth's surface.*

*Greenhouse gases trap some of the heat inside the atmosphere.*

### WEATHER EXTREMES
Human-driven climate change has led to an increase in extreme weather events. Hurricanes, thunderstorms, and tornados are becoming common and more intense. In 2024, Hurricane Helene swept across Florida, US, leaving a trail of destruction in its wake.

### SINKING COASTLINES
Water levels in the seas and oceans are rising around the world because global warming is melting the ice caps in the North and South Poles. The rising levels are a danger to low-lying coastal areas, which are beginning to sink beneath the waters. Frequent flooding in Pantai Bahagia in Indonesia, shown below, has forced hundreds of families to relocate.

OCEANS AND US

### ▼ TURNED WHITE
*In 2019, a marine heat wave in the tropical Pacific waters bleached coral reefs in Mo'orea, Society Islands, French Polynesia.*

### HARM TO LIFE
The health of marine life is seriously affected by pollution in the water, which reaches from the surface all the way down to the deep sea. Chemicals and microplastics poison animals, and in extreme cases, cause them to die or develop life-altering conditions, such as cancer and the loss of the ability to breed.

### ALGAL BLOOM
When sewage and run-off from farms are dumped into the oceans, they can introduce excess nutrients in the water. Algae feed on these nutrients and grow rapidly, creating an "algal bloom". By the time the algae die and break down, they have consumed all the oxygen in the water, suffocating other species. This process is known as eutrophication.

# Marine conservation

**OCEANS AND US**

Our future depends on the health of our oceans. These bodies of water support countless food chains that sustain not only humans but also plants and other animals on land. Many individuals, communities, and organizations are playing a vital role in protecting marine life and trying to save and restore ocean environments.

### TACKLING WASTE
Ocean clean-up projects, such as Keep Britain Tidy, focus on removing waste material, including fishing nets and other plastic items, from the ocean. They recover and recycle as much of this waste as possible, but in the long run they suggest producing less plastic in the first place.

### CLEANING RIVERS
Any pollution and litter that rivers carry eventually finds itself in the oceans, so cleaning up rivers can help us save the oceans. A device called Mr Trash Wheel (above) scoops up rubbish from the Jones Falls River in Baltimore, US, before it can enter the ocean at Baltimore harbour.

### RESTORING CORALS
Monitoring corals and the water they live in is essential for restoring the health of our reefs. Scientists may scuba dive to study corals in reefs, collect samples for study, plant healthy corals, or remove debris from the reef.

## PROTECTING THE OCEAN

Protected areas of the oceans are safeguarded regions where human activities such as fishing are restricted. This allows sea life to recover and thrive. There are more than 5,000 marine protected areas, covering just over 8 per cent of the global ocean waters. The Great Barrier Reef Marine Park (above) in Australia protects more than 344,400 sq km (132,973 sq miles) of a coral reef ecosystem.

**FACT**
To restore a reef, scientists may grow corals in nurseries before planting them back in the reef.

## YOUNG CHAMPIONS

Around the world, many young people are dedicating their time to saving the oceans and protecting marine habitats.

◀ **RESTORATION**
*Steve Misati from Kenya began a project to restore mangroves along the coast of Mombasa, Africa, to save the coastal ecosystem.*

◀ **CONSERVATION**
*Scottish champion Finlay Pringle raises awareness on the need to protect sharks, which are essential to marine food chains.*

◀ **CLEAN-UP**
*Australian conservationist Bronte Halden organizes beach clean-ups to remove harmful debris that washes up from the ocean.*

## OIL CLEANUP

When oil is spilled into an ocean habitat, environmental organizations rush to stop the spread of the damage. They use floating "booms" to contain the oil, industrial vacuums to suck the oil off beaches, and even absorbent pads and pillows to soak up the oil. Protective gear is worn during these operations, as seen above on the volunteer cleaning a beach in Thailand.

OCEANS AND US

# Glossary

**Abyssal plain** A flat area on the floor of the deep ocean, beyond the continental shelf, at a depth of 3,000–6,000 m (10,000–20,000 ft).

**Algae** Plantlike organisms that can make food using solar energy. Most algae are single-celled, but they also include larger seaweeds.

**Anemone** A marine animal related to jellyfish that clings to a hard surface and uses stinging tentacles to catch food.

**Antennae** Long sensory organs that detect movement and sometimes chemicals in the water or air.

**Archaea** Bacterialike microscopic organisms that have a different biology, and form a separate kingdom of life.

**Archaeology** The study of human history by the scientific excavation and analysis of ancient remains.

**Atoll** A ring-shaped island, often formed from a coral reef based on a sunken extinct volcano.

**Atom** The smallest unit of an element, such as iron.

**Bacteria** Microscopic organisms with a simple single-celled form, and some distinct internal structures.

**Baleen** The fibrous material that certain large whales have in place of teeth, used for filtering small animals from seawater.

**Barnacle** A relative of shrimps and crabs that cements itself to a hard surface.

**Basalt** A dark, heavy volcanic rock that erupts as molten lava from oceanic volcanoes and forms oceanic crust.

**Bedrock** The solid rock that lies beneath more recent, softer material (sediments).

**Bioluminescence** A form of light produced by living things.

**Bivalve** A mollusc such as a clam with two shells joined by a hinge.

**Buoyant** Able to float.

**Calving** The process by which icebergs break off from the floating ends of glaciers.

**Camouflage** A pattern, body shape, or colour that living things use to hide themselves from predators.

**Carbon dioxide** A gas naturally present in the atmosphere produced by the respiration of living things and by human activities, such as burning fossil fuels.

**Cell** The smallest unit of life. It can exist as a single cell, or form part of a more complex multi-celled organism.

**Cephalopod** A type of mollusc, such as an octopus, with several sucker-covered arms and a relatively large brain.

**Chalk** A soft type of limestone rock formed from the skeletons of microscopic marine organisms (coccolithophores).

**Chitin** The substance that forms the tough external skeleton of a crustacean.

**Chlorophyll** A substance that absorbs the energy of sunlight, used by many living things to make sugar in the process of photosynthesis.

**Chloroplast** A microscopic organ within a plant cell or algal cell that contains chlorophyll, and makes sugar.

**Cnidarian** One of a group of marine animals that includes jellyfish and corals.

**Coccolithophore** A microscopic marine organism with a chalky skeleton.

**Colony** A group of animals or other organisms that live together.

**Compound** A substance that is made of the chemically bonded atoms of two or more elements. Sugar is a compound of carbon, hydrogen, and oxygen.

**Continent** A large landmass.

**Continental crust** A thick slab of relatively light rock that "floats" on the heavier rock of Earth's mantle and forms a continent.

**Continental drift** The process by which continents are slowly dragged around the globe by the mobile plates of Earth's crust.

**Continental shelf** The submerged fringe of a continent, forming the relatively shallow floor of a coastal sea.

**Continental slope** The edge of the continental shelf, which slopes down to the ocean floor.

**Convection** Circulating currents in gases or liquids such as air and water, and even hot, mobile rock, driven by differences in temperature.

**Convergent boundary** A boundary between two plates of Earth's crust that are moving together, marked by earthquakes and volcanoes.

**Copepod** A tiny crustacean that lives in large swarms.

**Coral** A small sea animal that often has a hard skeleton made of limestone and forms colonies. Over many years the limestone can build up into a coral reef.

**Coral reef** A rocky mass built up by corals with stony skeletons, which supports many other kinds of marine life.

**Courtship** Animal behaviour, usually by males, designed to win a breeding partner.

**Crustacean** An animal with a hard external skeleton and jointed legs, such as a crab or shrimp.

**Cyclone** A weather system of clouds, rain, and strong winds caused by air swirling into a region of warm, moist, rising air.

**Diatom** A single-celled oceanic organism that drifts as part of the phytoplankton. It has a skeleton of glassy silica.

**Dinoflagellate** A different type of single-celled oceanic organism that drifts as part of the phytoplankton.

**Divergent boundary** A boundary between two plates of Earth's crust that are moving apart.

**Dorsal fin** The single fin on the back of a fish or whale.

**Echinoderm** One of a group of spiny-skinned animals that includes starfish and sea urchins.

**Echolocation** Locating prey or other objects in water or air by transmitting sound pulses and detecting the echoes. The echoes create an image of the target.

**Echo-sounding** Finding the depth of water by transmitting a sound pulse and detecting the echo from the seabed. The time taken by the echo gives the depth.

**Ecosystem** An interacting community of living things in their natural environment.

**Ekman transport** The way moving water swerves increasingly to the right or left with depth, so that it moves in a different direction to the surface water.

**Estuary** A river mouth.

**Evaporate** To turn from a liquid to a gas or vapour.

**Evolution** The process by which living things change over time.

**Excavate** Dig up, often carefully and systematically, to reveal buried remains.

**Extinct** Having died out, or, in the case of a volcano, completely stopped erupting.

**Fault** A fracture in rock, where the rock on one side of the fracture has moved relative to the rock on the other side.

**Fjord** A deep valley gouged by a glacier, which is now flooded by the sea.

**Fossil** The remains or traces of any living thing that have survived the normal processes of decay, and have been preserved by being turned to stone.

**Fracture zone** An area of oceanic transform faults, which are sliding breaks in the ocean crust. These breaks extend away from spreading mid-ocean ridges.

**Gastropod** A type of mollusc that crawls on a long muscular foot, such as a snail.

**Geyser** A jet of hot water and steam that erupts from volcanically heated rocks.

**Glacier** A mass of ice made of compacted snow that flows slowly downhill.

**Granite** A hard rock that is one of the main rocks found in continental crust.

**Gravity** The force of attraction exerted by a large object such as Earth, which holds things on the planet's surface and in orbit.

**Greenhouse gases** The gases in Earth's atmosphere that trap heat, warming the planet's land and oceans. They include carbon dioxide, methane, and nitrous oxide.

**Gyre** A large-scale circular pattern of ocean currents, rotating clockwise north of the equator, and anticlockwise south of the equator.

**Herbivore** An animal that eats plants or algae, rather than other animals.

**Hotspot** A zone of volcanic activity caused by a stationary plume of heat beneath Earth's crust.

**Hurricane** A severe tropical storm.

**Iceberg** Part of a glacier or ice shelf that has broken off and floated out to sea.

**Ice floe** A floating fragment of sea ice.

**Ice sheet** A very large, deep covering of ice over a continent.

**Immune** Not affected by something.

**Incubate** To keep an egg warm so it develops and hatches.

**Invertebrate** An animal that does not have a jointed internal skeleton.

**Island arc** A line of islands marking a boundary between two plates of Earth's crust. It is created by volcanic activity as one plate plunges beneath the other and is destroyed.

**Keratin** The natural substance that forms fingernails, hair, and turtle shells.

**Lagoon** An area of shallow water that has been cut off from the sea.

**Lava** Molten rock that erupts from a volcano.

**Limestone** A rock composed of calcium carbonate (lime) that can be made by reef corals.

**Magma** Molten rock that lies within or beneath Earth's crust.

**Mammal** One of a group of warm-blooded, often hairy vertebrates that feed their young on milk supplied by the mother.

**Mangrove** Any of various trees growing on muddy shores in the tropics and adapted to live with their roots and lower trunks immersed in salt water.

**Mantle** The deep layer of hot rock that lies between Earth's crust and the core.

**Meteorite** A fragment of space rock that plunges through the atmosphere and hits the ground.

**Microbe** A microscopic living thing.

**Microbial** Something formed of microbes.

**Mid-ocean ridge** A ridge of submarine mountains on the ocean floor, created by a spreading rift between two plates of Earth's crust.

**Migrate** To make a regular, often annual journey in search of food or a suitable place to breed.

**Mineral** A natural solid made of one or more elements in fixed proportions, usually with a distinctive crystal structure.

**Molecule** A particle formed from a fixed number of atoms. One oxygen and two hydrogen atoms form a water molecule.

**Mollusc** A soft-bodied animal that may have a shell, such as a snail or a clam. An octopus is a type of shell-free mollusc.

**Molten** The state of having melted, as in hot, liquid rock.

**Naturalist** Someone who studies the natural world.

**Northern hemisphere** The region of Earth that lies north of the equator.

**Nutrients** Substances that living things need to build their tissues.

**Oceanic crust** The relatively thin crust of solid basalt that lies above Earth's mantle and forms the bedrock of the ocean floor.

**Oceanography** The study of the oceans.

**Omnivore** An animal that feeds on both plants and animals.

**Ooze** A soft sediment formed from the remains of living things such as plankton.

**Organism** A living thing.

**Outlet glacier** A glacier that drains ice from a much bigger ice sheet.

**Pack ice** Thick floating ice that has been formed by the freezing of the ocean surface. It can take the form of separate ice floes or a virtually solid sheet.

**Parasite** A living thing that feeds off other live organisms without killing them first.

**Pectoral fins** Paired fins on either side of a fish near the gills.

**Peridotite** The rock that forms much of Earth's deep mantle.

**Photophore** An organ that produces light.

**Photosynthesis** The process by which plants and algae use light to make sugar from carbon dioxide and water.

**Phytoplankton** Microscopic, single-celled organisms that drift in the sunlit surface waters of oceans and lakes. They carry out photosynthesis to make food.

**Plankton** Living things that drift in lakes and oceans, usually near the surface.

**Pollution** Waste substances that have been dumped or escape into water, air, or on land. They can often have a harmful effect on the environment.

**Polyp** The tubular body form of a sea anemone or single coral. Colonial corals are made up of many polyps.

**Predator** An animal that kills other animals for food.

**Prevailing wind** A wind that blows from a particular direction for most of the time.

**Protein** A complex substance that a living thing makes out of simpler nutrients, and uses to form its tissues.

**Protist** Usually a type of single-celled organism that is more complex than bacteria, but also includes multi-celled marine algae (seaweeds).

**Protozoan** An animal-like single-celled organism, usually microscopic.

**Radiolarian** A single-celled oceanic organism that feeds like an animal and drifts as part of the zooplankton.

**Reef** A ridge of submerged rock, often created by marine animals called corals.

**Reptile** One of the group of animals that includes turtles, lizards, crocodiles, snakes, and dinosaurs.

**Rift** A crack in rocks or Earth's crust, caused by the rocks pulling apart.

**Rift valley** A region where part of Earth's crust has dropped into the gap formed by the crust pulling apart.

**Rorqual** A type of large filter-feeding whale with an expandable throat that can hold a lot of water containing food.

**Satellite** Something that orbits a planet, such as Earth, in space.

**Scavenger** An animal that eats the remains of dead animals and other scraps.

**School** A shoal of fish that swims in perfect formation.

**Seamount** An ocean-floor volcano, active or extinct, that does not break the ocean surface to form an island.

**Sediment** Solid particles such as sand, silt, or mud that have settled on the seabed or ocean floor.

**Shelf sea** A shallow sea covering a continental shelf.

**Shellfish** A term for marine animals with either hard shells or external skeletons.

**Shoal** A group of fish that live together.

**Silica** A mineral made of oxygen and silicon, the main ingredient of sand.

**Single-celled** An organism made up of a single living cell.

**Siphon tube** A tube used by a clam, squid, or other mollusc to draw water into its body or pump it out.

**Solar system** The system of planets, moons, asteroids, and other bodies orbiting the Sun.

**Southern hemisphere** The region of Earth that lies south of the equator.

**Subduction** The process of one plate of Earth's crust diving beneath another, creating an ocean trench, causing earthquakes, and fuelling volcanoes.

**Temperate** A climate that is neither very hot nor very cold, or a region that has such a climate.

**Tentacle** A long, boneless extension of an animal's body, sometimes armed with stinging cells.

**Thermocline** The boundary between deep, cold, dense water and a layer of warmer, less dense water that floats at the surface of oceans.

**Tidal** To do with the tides.

**Tidal race** A fast-moving tidal current that has chaotic waves and whirlpools.

**Tidal stream** A horizontal flow of water created by the rise and fall of the tide.

**Tidewater glacier** A glacier that flows all the way to the coast and out to sea, so that its end floats on tidal seawater.

**Tissue** In biology, living material such as bone, muscle, or plant material.

**Trade wind** A wind that blows steadily from east to west over a tropical ocean.

**Tsunami** An unusually large and destructive series of sea waves typically produced by an earthquake, but which can also be caused by volcanic eruptions and submarine landslides.

**Tube feet** Tubular, water-filled, mobile projections from the body of an echinoderm animal such as a starfish.

**Tube worm** A type of marine worm that lives in a protective tube.

**Turbine** A rotor driven by a flow of water or air, which can be used to turn an electricity generator.

**Upwelling zone** A part of the ocean where deep water that is rich in plant nutrients is drawn up to the surface.

**Urbanization** The increasing movement of people from rural areas to cities.

**Venom** Poison that a biting or stinging animal uses for hunting or defence.

**Water vapour** The gas that forms when liquid water is warmed and evaporates.

**Westerly wind** A wind that blows from west to east.

**Zooplankton** Animals that mainly drift in the water, although some swim actively.

# Index

Page numbers in **bold** refer to main entries.

## A
abyss 70
acidity 239
adaptations 71, 82, 176, 210
air circulation 52, 54
air currents 52
air pressure 55
albatrosses 96–97, 201
Aldabra 143
Aleutian Arc 34–35
algae 72, 73, 74, 78, 112, 132, 133, 141, 182, 192, 205, 243
*Alvin* 220, 224, 225
Andes 34
angelfish 136
anglerfish 100, 118
Antarctic Bottom Water 66
Antarctic Convergence 18
Antarctica 18, **188–189**
  islands **200–201**
antifreeze, natural 193
Aqua-Lung 223
archaea 104
archaeology, underwater 223
archerfish 179
arches 150, 151
Arctic **188–189**
  humans in **214–215**
Arctic Ocean 9, **10–11**, 188, 189, 191
Ascension Island 41
Atlantic Ocean **12–13**, 36, 37
atmosphere 22, 25, 52, 239, 242
atolls 15, **142–143**
auks 97

## B
bacteria 71, 72, 78
bait balls 84–85
baleen plates 90
barnacles 127, 155
barracudas 136
barrier reefs 134–135, 142
Barton, Otis 224
basalt 24, 25, 30, 42, 151
basket stars 103
*Bathysphere* 224
bays 150, 153, 158
beaches 146, **158–159**
  waves and 149
  wildlife **160–161**
*Beagle*, HMS 219
bears
  grizzly 173
  polar 210–211, 238
Beebe, William 224

Bengal Fan 175
Benguela Current 61
billfish 82, 83
bioluminescence 73, 98, 99, 100
birds
  ocean **96–97**
  salt marshes 177
  seabird colonies **166–167**
  shorebirds **162–165**, 173, 177
bivalves 120, 121
black smokers 30–31, 225
  wildlife **104–105**
blooms, algal 73, 243
blowholes 93, 150
blue colour 50
blue light 72
blue planet 21, 22
boobies 96
Bora Bora 142–143
Brazil Current 61
breathing holes 193
brittlestars 129
bubble-net feeding 91, 92–93
butterfly fish 136

## C
calm zones 53
calving 204, 205
camouflage 99, 155, 162, 211, 212
Canary Current 60
canyons, submarine 45
carbon dioxide 73, 238, 239, 242
carbonic acid 239
cargo ships 236–237
cartilage 87
caves 148, **150–151**
*Central America* 227
cephalopods 122–123
Challenger Deep 33
*Challenger*, HMS 220
chlorophyll 73
chloroplasts 73
chop 56
clams 104, **120–121**, 173
  giant 140–141
  razor 161
cliffs 148, 149, **150–151**
  ice 18
  seabird colonies 166
climate 50, 51
climate change 10, 46, 67, **238–239**, 242, 243
clones 77
clothing, Arctic peoples 214, 215
clouds 48
  storm 54, 55
clownfish 131
cnidarians **130–131**
coast and seashore 144–185
coastal development 240
coccolithophores 73
cockles 173

colonies
  corals 132, 139
  penguin 195, 201
  seabird **166–167**, 201
  seal 200, 210
Columbia Glacier (US) 202
comb jellies 76, 77
comets 25
communications
  dolphins 94, 95
  twilight-zone animals 99
  whales 90, 95
conches, queen 183
cone shells 139
conservation, marine **244–245**
consumers 78
container ships 236–237
continental drift 36
continental fringe 34
continental plates 12
continental rise 44
continental shelves 28, **44–45**, 46, 61
continental slope 44
continents 24, 25, 26, 36–37, 44
convergent boundaries 31
copepods 74, 75
coral islands 17
coral reefs 78, 107, **132–135**
  atolls and lagoons **142–143**
  cold-water 133
  conservation 244–245
  fish **136–137**
  invertebrates **138–141**
corals 102, 130, **132–133**, 139
  bleaching 239, 242–243
  brain 133
cordgrass 176
core, Earth's 24
cormorants 96
courtship displays 167
Cousteau, Jacques 223
crabs 78, 118, **126–127**, 156, 157
  fiddler 179
  ghost 170
  Japanese giant spider 127
  land 170–171
  robber 171
  sargassum 63
  shore **170–171**
  white 104
craters, volcanic 41
creeks 176
crescent bays 158
crevasses 204
crocodiles **184–185**
  American 185
  saltwater 184
cruises 237
crust
  Earth's 24, 25, 32, 35, 37
  oceanic 24, 30
crustaceans 126–127
curlews, Eurasian 163

currents 50, 147, 221, 231
  deepwater 18, **66–67**
  global air 52
  surface **60–61**, 62, 66
  turbidity 45
cuttlefish **122–123**
cyclones 54, 55

## D
damselfish 137
Darwin, Charles 219, 220
*Deepsea Challenger* 224–225
deltas **174–175**
depth, measuring 28, 45
depth zones **70–71**
desalination 228
detritivores 102
diamonds 229
diatoms 73
dinoflagellates 73
diving **222–223**
dog sleds 215
Doggerland 47
doldrums 53
dolphins **94–95**
  bottlenose 94
  common 84–85
downwelling 65
drilling, ocean-floor 220–221, 230
dugong 183
dunes **158–159**

## E
Earth
  planet ocean **22–23**
  spin 60, 146
earthquakes 15, 17, 34, 35
  earthquake zones 37
  oceanic 37, 38, 39
Easter Island 41
easterlies 53
echinoderms **128–129**
echolocation 95
eels 62
  gulper 100–101
  moray 118
eggs 75
Ekman transport 60, 65
El Niño 65
electricity, generating 230–231
electroreception 87
erosion
  coastal 44, 45
  waves 148–149
estuaries **172–173**
eutrophication 243
Everest, Mount 32, 33
exoskeletons 126, 127
explorers **218–219**

## F
feather stars 103, 129
feeding frenzies 83
filter feeders 79, 80, **88–89**, 90–91, 111, 138, 161, 173
First Nations Australians 135

250

fish
   oceanic hunters **82–83**
   reef 133, **136–137**
   seafloor **118–119**
   shoals **80–81**
fish farms 233
fishing industry 109, **232–235**
fjords 47
flame shells 111
flamingos 177
floods 38, 39, 55, 238, 243
flounders 119
food chain **78–79**
food pyramids 78
food webs 79
fossils 46, 49
foxes, Arctic 212
*Fram* 191
frazil 190
frigatebirds 97, 167
fringing reefs 142
frontal storms 55
fusiliers 81

## G
Galápagos 41
Ganges, River 174, 175, 179
gannets 96, 166, 167
gas 230
gastropods 120, 121
*Geldermalsen* 227
gill rakers 80, 88
gill slits 88
gills 80, 82
glaciers 18, 47, **202–203**, 204
glasswort 176
global conveyor 66, 67
global ocean 25, 26
global warming 67, 238, 242
Gondwana 37
gorgonians 139
Grand Canyon (US) 46
granite 24
gravel 229
gravity 146, 147
grease ice 190
Great Barrier Reef (Australia) **134–135**, 190, 245
greenhouse gases 242
guano 167
guillemots, Brünnich's 166
Gulf Stream 60, 61, 62, 67, 231
gurnards, red 118
gyres 60, 62

## H
habitats 22, 23, 49
hatchetfish 99
Hawai'i 26, 40, 42–43
headlands 150, 151, 153, 158
heat **50–51**
Heezen, Bruce 29
herrings 75, 80, 81, 83
holdfasts 114
hotspots 14, **40–41**, 42
Hubbard Glacier (US) 202

Human activity **240–241**, 242–243
Humboldt Current 61
hunters
   Arctic peoples 214–215
   food chain 79
   large fish **82–83**
hurricanes 55, 56, 174, 239, 243
hydrogen sulphide 173
hydrothermal vents
   *see* black smokers

## I
ibises, scarlet 180–181
ice 49
   floating 190
   humans on **214–215**
   life under **192–193**
Ice Age, last 46, 47
ice fish 193
ice floes 188, 193
ice sheets 190, 202, 205
   Antarctic 18, 188, 203, 238
   Greenland 202, 238
   melting 47, 143, 238
ice shelves 38, **202–203**, 204
icebergs 202, **204–207**
icebreakers 191
Iceland 40
iglus 214–215
iguanas, marine 155, 185
impact zone 155
Indian Ocean **14–15**
industrial waste 240
Inuit 214–215
invasive species 241
invertebrates, reef **138–139**
islands
   Antarctic **200–201**
   climate crisis 238
   seabird colonies 166, 167

## JK
Jakobshavn Glacier (Greenland) 202
Japan, natural disasters 35, 39
Java Trench 15
jaws, sharks 87
jellyfish **76–77**, 98–99, **130–131**
   *Atolla* 98–99
   box 131
   lion's mane 76–77
   luminous 101
   mauve stinger 131
Jurassic Period 37

kayaks 215
kelp forests 107, **114–115**
krill 74–75, 79, 126, 192, 194, 195, 198
Kure Atoll 143
Kuril Trench 33
Kyrenia ship 226

## L
La Rance Barrage (France) 231
lagoons **142–143**, 159, 176
land, rising 46, 47
landslides, coastal 38
lantern fish 98
larvae 75, 126
Laurasia 37
lava 30, 42–43
Lesser Antilles Volcanic Arc 12
levees 174
lichen 155
life on Earth 23, 49
light **50–51**, 72, 73, 108
Lighthouse Reef 143
limestone 46, 132, 135
limpets 78, 154
liners, ocean 237
lobsters **126–127**
longshore drift 158, 159
lures 100

## M
mackerel 80, 84–85
Magellan, Ferdinand 219
magma 34
Makah travellers 218
Maldives 15, 143
mangrove forests **178–181**
mantle, Earth's 24, 36
mapping, ocean floor 7, 23, 29
Margerie Glacier (US) 203
Mariana Trench 32–33, 225
*Mary Rose* 226
Mediterranean Sea 8
medusas 130
Mesozoic age 36
metals 229
meteorites 24

methane 105
microbes 104, 105, 173
microplastics 242
Mid-Atlantic Ridge 12, 29
mid-ocean ridges 12, 17, 28, **30–31**, 36, 37, 104, 225
midnight zone 70, 71, **100–101**
minerals 49, 108, 132, **228–229**
mining 229
Mississippi, River 174–175
molecules, water 48, 49
molluscs 111, 120–23, 135, 161, 173
monsoons 15
Moon, and tides 146, 147
mountains
   continental 34
   underwater 17, 28, 29, 30, 31, 34
mud 102
mudflats **172–173**, 176
mudflows 45
mudskippers 179
multi-year ice 190
mussels 104, 154
   fan 120

## NO
Nansen, Fridtjof 191
narwhals 95
nautiluses, shelled 122
neap tides 147
Nile, River 175
North Atlantic Deep Water 66, 67
North Pole 10, 188, 189, 191, 221, 238, 239
Nunavut 10
nutrients 64, 65, 67, 71, 109
ocean floor 24, 25, 26, **28–29**
   coastal seabed **110–111**
   creation and destruction 36
   mapping 7, 23, 29
   surveying 220–221

ocean trenches 28, 29, **32–33**, 34, 35, 36, 37
oceanography 220
oceans
  ancient 46
  area covered by 8, 22
  deep-sea exploration **224–225**
  energy from **230–231**
  evolving **36–37**
  formation of **24–25**
  harming **240–241**
  in danger **242–243**
  minerals from **228–229**
  science **220–221**
  size of 9
octopods 101
octopuses 79, **122–125**
  common 157
  Dumbo 101
  giant 123
  Pacific giant 115, **124–125**
oil 230
oil spills 240, 241, 245
ooze 102
open ocean **68–105**
orcas 198, 199
otters, sea 115, **116–117**
outlet glaciers 202
overfishing 109, 232, 241, 242
oxygen levels 71, 78
oystercatchers 163, **164–165**, 177

**P**
Pacific Ocean 9, **16–17**, 36
Pacific Ring of Fire 34, 35, 36
pack hunting 199
pack ice 18, 190, 191, 194, 210
pancake ice 190
Pangaea 36
parrotfish 113
penguins 97, **194–197**, 198, 201
  Adélie 195, 198
  chinstrap 194, 201
  emperor 194, 195
  king 201
peridotite 24

Peters Glacier (South Georgia) 203
photophores 98, 99
photosynthesis 73, 74, 112
phytoplankton 64, 72, 73, 74, 75, 77, 78, 98, 108, 109, 112, 189, 192
Piccard, Jacques 33
pillow lava 30
piracy 237
plaice 119
plankton 18, 61, 64, 65, 67, 70, 71, 102, 111, 133, 188, 189, 221
plants, salt marshes 176, 177
plastic pollution 241, 242, 244
plovers, crab 162
polar seas 53, **186–215**
pollution 240–241, 242, 243, 244
polymetallic nodules 229
Polynesian settlers 218
polyps 130, 132
ports 237
Portuguese man-of-war 76, 77
prawns **126–127**
  red deep-sea 100
primary consumers 78
producers 78
protected areas 245
protists 112
protozoans 74
Puerto Rico Trench 12
puffins, Atlantic 167

**R**
radioactive elements 24
rain 25, 48, 54
rays
  giant 89
  manta 79, 89
  spotted eagle 119
  torpedo 119
recycling 244
Red Sea 8, 15
reefs 45, 110
regeneration 129

remotely operated vehicles (ROV) 224, 225
research ships 220
Réunion 40
rift zone 30
ripples 56
rivers
  cleaning 244
  deltas **174–175**
  estuaries and mudflats **172–173**
rock 24
  age of 37
rock gunnels 157
rockfalls 149
rocky shores 146
  wildlife **154–155**
rogue waves 56, 57
roots, exposed 178
rorquals 90
Ross Ice Shelf (Antarctica) 203, 205
Ross Sea 53, 188
rubbish patches 63
ruffs 163

**S**
sailfish 82, 83
salps 77
salt marshes **176–177**
salt water 9, 49
sand 45, 110, 149, 229
sandbanks 45
sandstone 46
Sargasso Sea **62–63**
sargassum fish 63
satellites 221
scallops 121
scavengers 102
schooling 81
scuba diving **222–223**, 224
sea anemones **130–131**, 155, 156
  snakelocks 131, 156
sea cows 183
sea cucumbers 102, **128–129**
sea fans 139

sea ice 10, 66, 188, 189, **190–191**
  life under **192–193**
  scuba diving under 223
sea levels
  changing **46–47**, 142, 204, 238, 243
  tides **146–147**
sea lions
  Galápagos 111
  Steller 209
sea pens 103
sea salt 228
sea slugs 77, 121
sea snails **120–121**
  bubble snail 120
  cone shells 139
  giant 183
  spire snail 173
sea snakes **184–185**
  sea kraits 184
  yellow-bellied 185
sea squirts 138
sea stacks 151, **152–153**, 166
sea stars 115
sea temperatures 50, 221
  rising 10, 204, 238, 239
sea turtles **168–169**
  flatback 169
  green 169, **182–183**
  hawksbill 169
  Kemp's ridley 169
  leatherback 63, 168
  loggerhead 169
  olive ridley 168
sea urchins 115, **128–129**, 160
seafarers **218–219**
seagrass beds 72, 133, **182–183**
seahorses 183
seals 111, 155
  Antarctic 200–201, **210–211**
  Arctic **208–211**
  bearded 208
  crabeater **194**
  harp 209, 210
  hooded 209, 211
  leopard 198

REFERENCE SECTION

seals cont.
  ribbon 209
  ringed 209, 210, 213
  southern elephant 200–201
  Weddell 193
seamounts 17, 29, 65
seas 8
  coastal 44
seawater 8, 9, 23, **48–49**
seaweeds 62–3, 72, 73, 78, **112–115**
secondary consumers 78
sediments 29, 45, 46, 102, 110, 174, 175, 177
sewage 240, 243
shale 46
shallow seas 106–143
sharks 79, **86–89**, 137
  basking 88
  frilled 86
  great white 86–87
  hammerhead 64
  megamouth 89
  saw 86
  thresher 86
  tiger 137
  whale 88–89, 109
  wobbegong 86
shellfish, farming 232
shells
  climate crisis 239
  sea snails and clams 121
  shedding and regrowth 127
shipwrecks 45, 110–111, 223, 224
  historic **226–227**
shoals **80–81**, 82
shrimps
  peacock mantis 138–139
  pistol 51
  white 104
Silfra fissure 12
snow caves 210
sodium chloride 49
soils, delta 175
sonar surveys 221
sound **50–51**
South Pole 188
South Sawyer Glacier (USA) 203
Southern Ocean **18–19**, 57, 188
spits **158–159**
sponges, barrel 138
spoonbills, roseate 162–163
spring tides 147
squid **122–123**
  firefly 98, 99
  giant 101
  vampire 71
starfish **128–129**, 193
  crown of thorns 139
stargazers, marbled 118
stilt fishing **234–235**
stilts, black-winged 163
stinging cells 130, 131
stingrays, ribbon-tailed 110

stonefish, reef 137
stoplight loosejaw fish 100
storm petrels 97
storm surges 55, 174
storms, oceanic **54–55**, 109, 239
streamlining 82
subduction zones 12, 33, 34, 35, 36, 37
submersibles 33, 220, **224–225**
sugar 72, 73, 132, 133
Sun
  and tides 32, 147
  polar regions 188
Sundarbans 179
sunlight
  and depth zones 70, 72
  and food chain 78
  coral reefs 132
  polar 188
sunlit zone 70, **72–73**
  shallow seas **108–109**
superorganisms 81
surgeonfish 136
swells 56, 57
swordfish 83
symbiosis 132

## T
Tahiti 142
tectonic plates 12, 24, 30, 31, 32, **34–35**, 36, 38
teeth
  sharks 87
  whales 94
temperate zones 52, 53, 55
tentacles, stinging 76, 77, 130, 131, 132
terns, Arctic 18
Tethys Ocean 37
Tharp, Marie 29
thermocline 71
thermohaline circulation 67
Thule migration 218
tidal bores 172
tidal flow 231
tidal races 147
tide pools **156–157**
tides **146–147**
tidewater glaciers 202, 204
tigers, Bengal 179
*Titanic* 224, 227
top predators 79, 87
Torres Strait Islanders 135
trade **236–237**
trade winds 52, 60, 65
tripodfish 103
tropical zones 52, 55, 71, 78
tsunamis 15, 34, **38–39**, 55
tuna 82, 83
tunicates, blue bell 138
turnstones, ruddy 162
Twelve Apostles (Australia) 152–153
twilight zone 70, 71, **98–99**

## UV
upwelling zones **64–65**
valley glaciers 202
*Vasa* 226
venom 76, 77, 118, 123, 131, 139, 185
Venus comb 120
Vescovo, Victor 33
Viking raiders 219
viperfish 99
volcanic chains 40
volcanic islands 16, 26, 34, 200, 201
volcanoes 12, 25, 28, 30, 34, 35, 38, 40–43
  sinking islands 142

## WYZ
walruses 208
Walsh, Don 33
waste material 244
water
  density 66
  ocean **48–49**
  states of 49
water cycle 48
water, liquid 22, 23, 49
water vapour 25, 48, 49, 54, 239
wave energy 231
waves **56–57**
  breakers 56, 58–59
  cliffs and caves **150–151**
  coastal erosion 44
  power of **148–149**
  tsunamis **38–39**
weather, extreme 243
weather systems 54
Weddell Sea 53
weevers, lesser 161
westerlies 53
whale fall 102
whales 79
  baleen **90–91**
  beluga 189
  blue 91
  bowhead 90
  Bryde's 79
  gray 90
  horned 95
  humpback 51, 67, 91, 92–93
  killer 198, 199
  minke 91
  narwhal 95

whales cont.
  pygmy right 91
  sperm 95, 101
  toothed **94–95**
whaling stations 201
whirlpools 147
wildlife
  coast and seashore 145, 154–157, 160–171, 173, 175, 177, 179–185
  depth zones 70
  ocean habitats 23
  open ocean 69–105
  photography 222
  polar seas 187, 192–201, 208–213
  prehistoric 46
  shallow seas 107, 109–141
wind power 230–31
winds
  dunes 158, 159
  monsoon 15
  oceanic **52–53**, 54
  prevailing 60, 64
  Southern Ocean 18
  trade routes 236
  waves 56, 57
worms
  bone-eating 102
  marine 118, 160–161, 173
  peacock 111
  Pompeii 104
  sand mason 161
  tube 105, 161
wrasse, cleaner 137
Yupiit 214
Zheng He 219
zooids 76
zooplankton **74–75**, 76, 80

# Acknowledgments

**The publisher would like to thank the following for their help with making the book:** Philip Parker for consultancy; Dr Pearl Brower and Timothy K Topper for sensitivity reading; Lizzie Munsey for writing text; Bharti Bedi, Vandana Likhmania, and Shahid Qureshi for editorial assistance; Vagisha Pushp and Samrajkumar S for picture research admin support; Caroline Stamps for proofreading; and Helen Peters for the index.

**For the first edition:** Shaila Brown, Vanessa Daubney, Pakshalika Jayaprakash, Antara Moitra, Tejaswita Payal, Ira Pundeer, Paula Regan, and Joanna Shock for editorial assistance; Vaibhav Fauzdar, Parul Gambhir, Meenal Goel, Owen Peyton Jones, Roshni Kapur, Vansh Kohli, Namita, Pooja Pipil, Chhaya Sajwan, Neha Sharma, Astha Singh, Riti Sodhi, Smiljka Surla, Arunesh Talapatra, Priyansha Tuli, and Steve Woosnam-Savage for design assistance; Simon Mumford for cartographic assistance; Sumedha Chopra, Deepak Negi, Rob Nunn, and Nishwan Rasool for picture research assistance; and Nand Kishor Acharya, Dheeraj Singh, Bimlesh Tiwary, and Mohammas Usman for DTP assistance.

**The publisher would like to thank the following for their kind permission to reproduce their photographs:**

(Key: a-above; b-below/bottom; c-centre; f-far; l-left; r-right; t-top)

**1 Alamy Stock Photo:** Photoshot Holdings Ltd. **2–3 Getty Images:** Alexander Safonov. **4 Alamy Stock Photo:** Aquascopic (cr/shipwreck). **Corbis:** Layne Kennedy (cra). **Dreamstime.com:** Steven Melanson (crb/jellyfish). **Getty Images:** Handout (tr). **NASA:** Hal Pierce (crb). **naturepl.com:** Jurgen Freund (br). **Robert Harding Picture Library:** Frans Lanting (cr). **Science Photo Library:** NASA (cra/Sea). **5 Alamy Stock Photo:** Reinhard Dirscherl (ca/kelp); blickwinkel / Schmidbauer (tc); nagelestock.com (cb); Universal Images Group Limited (bc); Ariadne Van Zandbergen (cra/seal); Avalon.red / Oceans Image (ca); Jean-Michel Mille / Biosphoto (c/damselfish). **Shutterstock.com:** Tigergallery (br). **Corbis:** Jurgen Freund / Nature Picture Library (cb/crabs); Ralph White / Encyclopedia (cra); GM Visuals / Blend Images (cr/diver); Paul Souders (crb/polar bear). **Dreamstime.com:** Dibrova (tr). **Getty Images:** Georgette Douwma (c). **Photoshot:** Ashley Cooper (crb). **Robert Harding Picture Library:** Pete Ryan (cr). **6–7 NASA**. **10 Dreamstime.com:** Ute Eisenlohr (ca). **naturepl.com:** Bryan and Cherry Alexander (bl). **NASA:** Jacques Descloitres, MODIS Land Rapid Response Team, NASA / GSFC (cl). **12 Alamy Stock Photo:** Alex Mustard / naturepl.com (ca). **iStockphoto.com:** MichaelUtech (cl). **naturepl.com:** Wild Wonders of Europe / Lundgre (bl). **15 Dreamstime.com:** Ekaterina Vysotina (cra). **Getty Images:** Priit Vesilind (br). **Science Photo Library:** NASA (cb). **17 naturepl.com:** Shane Gross (tl). **SeaPics.com:** Michael S. Nolan (crb). **18 FLPA:** Terry Whittaker (bl). **Getty Images:** Handout (cb). **Shutterstock.com:** glen photo (cl). **20–21 Getty Images:** Aaron Foster. **22 123RF.com:** Artem Mykhaylichenko (bl). **Getty Images:** Liane Cary (tl). **22–23 Dorling Kindersley:** Surya Sarangi / NASA / USGS (cb). **23 Alamy Stock Photo:** Norbert Probst / imageBROKER (cra). **Getty Images:** valentinrussanov / E+ (b). **iStockphoto.com:** BrendanHunter (cr). **24 Trustees of the National Museums of Scotland:** (br). **25 Robert Harding Picture Library:** Guy Edwardes (bl); Last Refuge (t). **26–27 Corbis:** epa / Bruce Omori. **28 Science Photo Library:** (c); Dr Ken Macdonald (cr). **29 Copyright by Marie Tharp 1977/2003. Reproduced by permission of Marie Tharp:** (tr). **NASA:** Norman Kuring, SeaWiFS Project / Visible Earth (tl). **Science Photo Library:** Dr Ken Macdonald (cl); Worldsat International (cr). **30 NOAA:** NSF (tr). **31 Dreamstime.com:** Galih Wisnu. **32 Science Photo Library:** Martin Jakobsson (bc). **33 Science Photo Library:** NOAA (tr). **34 Alamy Stock Photo:** Nigel Hicks (cb). **Getty Images:** Øystein Lund Andersen / E+ (cl). **34–35 Science Photo Library:** NASA (c). **35 Corbis:** Michael S. Yamashita (crb). **36 Getty Images:** Fuse (clb). **36 Dorling Kindersley:** Ed Merritt (br). **37 Dorling Kindersley:** Ed Merritt (bl, br). **39 Getty Images:** JIJI Press (t); Athit Perawongmetha (bl). **40 Corbis:** Jim Sugar (c); Bernd Vogel (cra). **41 Alamy Stock Photo:** Ken Welsh (cr). **Corbis:** John Farmar / Ecoscene (tl). **Robert Harding Picture Library:** Frans Lanting (b). **42–43 Getty Images:** Paul Souders. **44 Getty Images:** Juan Jose Herreo Garcia / Moment Open (cl). **44–45 Alamy Stock Photo:** Aquascopic (c). **45 Getty Images:** Fotosearch (tr). **46 Alamy Stock Photo:** Klaus Lang / age fotostock (t). **Dorling Kindersley:** Natural History Museum, London (crb). **47 Getty Images:** Brian Lawrence (b). **Science Photo Library:** Gary Hincks (tc, tr). **49 Corbis:** Paule Seux / Hemis (tl). **Dreamstime.com:** Richard Carey (br). **Getty Images:** Paul Souders / Stone (cra). **50 Alamy Stock Photo:** Brandon Cole Marine Photography (cla); Reinhard Dirscherl (clb). **NASA:** MODIS Instrument Team, NASA / GSFC (cb). **50–51 Getty Images:** Linda Mckie (bc). **51 Alamy Stock Photo:** RGB Ventures / SuperStock (tr). **OceanwideImages.com:** Gary Bell (crb). **52–53 Alamy Stock Photo:** Tsuneo Nakamura / Volvox Inc (c). **53 Alamy Stock Photo:** Chris Cameron (br); David Tipling (cra). **Getty Images:** Mike Hill (tr). **54-55 Alamy Stock Photo:** Micheko Productions, Inh. Michele Vitucci / beyond / Yevgen Timashov. **55 Alamy Stock Photo:** keith morris news (tr). **Getty Images:** Helifilms Australia (br). **NASA:** Hal Pierce (cla). **56 Alamy Stock Photo:** david gregs (clb); ImagePix (bl). **iStockphoto.com:** DanBrandenburg (cla). **Science Photo Library:** Duncan Shaw (c). **56–57 Alamy Stock Photo:** Nature Picture Library / Philip Stephen. **57 Corbis:** Seth Resnick / Science Faction (tl). **58–59 Robert Harding Picture Library:** Eric Sanford. **60–61 NASA:** Goddard Space Flight Center, and ORBIMAGE (c). **61 123RF.com:** Andrew Roland (cra). **62–63 OceanwideImages.com:** Michael Patrick O'Neill. **62 Corbis:** Wil Meinderts / Buiten-beeld / Minden Pictures (br). **63 Alamy Stock Photo:** Masa Ushioda (crb). **Corbis:** Jurgen Freund / Nature Picture Library (clb). **NOAA:** (cra). **Science Photo Library:** Dante Fenolio (cb). **64–65 SeaPics.com:** Bob Cranston (t). **Science Photo Library:** Dr Gene Feldman, NASA GSFC (bl). **65 FLPA:** Tui De Roy / Minden Pictures (bl). **66 Corbis:** Kike Calvo / National Geographic Society (b). **67 Alamy Stock Photo:** robertharding / Roberto Moiola (crb); John Hyde / Design Pics (bl). **68–69 naturepl.com:** Henley Spiers. **71 Alamy Stock Photo:** Amana images inc. (cra). **Nature Picture Library / David Shale (clb). **naturepl.com:** Solvin Zankl (cb, crb). **72–73 Corbis:** Ralph A. Clevenger. **73 Corbis:** Doug Perrine / Nature Picture Library (bc); Norbert Wu / Minden Pictures (cr). **Science Photo Library:** John Durham (cl); Jan Hinsch (tc). **74 Corbis:** Visuals Unlimited (clb). **imagequestmarine.com:** (c). **74–75 SeaPics.com:** Richard Herrmann (c). **75 Alamy Stock Photo:** blickwinkel / A. Hartl (bc). **Corbis:** Gerald & Buff Corsi / Visuals Unlimited (ca). **Getty Images:** Franco Banfi (crb). **76-77 Dreamstime.com:** Steven Melanson. **76 Alamy Stock Photo:** Franco Banfi / Biosphoto (bl). **77 Getty Images:** Visuals Unlimited, Inc. / Richard Herrmann (bc). **Alamy Stock Photo:** Jeff Milisen (tr); Richard Herrmann / Minden Pictures (cr). **78 Alamy Stock Photo:** SCHMITT / BSIP (cr); **naturepl.com:** Franco Banfi (c); Alex Mustard (cl). **79 Alamy Stock Photo:** Image Source (c). **Getty Images:** Marevision / age fotostock (cl). **SeaPics.com:** Doug Perrine (t). **80-81 naturepl.com:** Jurgen Freund (t). **80 Alamy Stock Photo:** WaterFrame (c). **Dreamstime.com:** Peter Leahy (bl). **81 Barcroft Media Ltd:** Alexey Stoyda (br). **82 Alamy Stock Photo:** Mark Conlin (bl). **Corbis:** Doug Perrine / Nature Picture Library (cr). **FLPA:** Jon Baldur Hlidberg / Minden Pictures (cl). **83 Alamy Stock Photo:** Design Pics Inc (tl). **Corbis:** Doug Perrine / Nature Picture Library (bl). **naturepl.com:** Doug Perrine (c). **84–85 Science Photo Library:** Christopher Swann. **86 Alamy**

imageBROKER (cl); Stephen Frink Collection (cla). **Corbis:** Fred Bavendam / Minden Pictures (clb). **Getty Images:** Awashima Marine Park (bl). **86–87 Corbis:** Visuals Unlimited (c). **87 Getty Images / iStock:** tswinner (cr). **Robert Harding Picture Library:** Jody Watt (tr). **88 Corbis:** Dan Burton / Nature Picture Library (cl). **Robert Harding Picture Library:** Alan James (c). **88–89 Alamy Stock Photo:** YAY Media AS. **Corbis:** Mauricio Handler / National Geographic Society (bc). **89 naturepl.com:** Alex Mustard (br). **SeaPics.com:** Bruce Rasner (tr). **90 Alamy Stock Photo:** John Tunney (bl). **Corbis:** Mike Paterson / National Geographic Creative (br). **Getty Images:** Paul Nicklen (cb). **90–91 naturepl.com:** Sue Flood (tr). **91 Alamy Stock Photo:** Nature Picture Library / Alex Mustard (br). **SeaPics.com:** Mark Carwardine (cb). **92–93 Alamy Stock Photo:** Danita Delimont. **94–95 Alamy Stock Photo:** blickwinkel / Schmidbauer (bc). **94 Alamy Stock Photo:** Douglas Fisher (cra). **95 Getty Images:** Paul Nicklen (crb). **SeaPics.com:** Doug Perrine (cl). **96 Robert Harding Picture Library:** Michael Nolan (br); Malcolm Schuyl (bl). **96–97 Alamy Stock Photo:** Bill Coster (tl). **97 (c) Mat & Cathy Gilfedder:** (br). **naturepl.com:** Alex Mustard / 2020VISION (c); Markus Varesvuo (clb). **Robert Harding Picture Library:** Michael Nolan (tr). **98 NOAA:** Deep East 2001, NOAA / OER (clb). **98–99 FLPA:** Photo Researchers (b). **SeaPics.com:** Michael Aw (t). **99 Corbis:** Michael Ready / Visuals Unlimited (clb); David Shale / Nature Picture Library (tc). **Getty Images:** Paul A. Zahl (br). **100 Getty Images:** Oxford Scientific / Photodisc (bc). **Science Photo Library:** Dante Fenolio (c). **100–101 Corbis:** Norbert Wu / Minden Pictures (ca). **imagequestmarine.com:** Peter Herring (b). **101 Alamy Stock Photo:** Nicemonkey (br). **NOAA OKEANOS EXPLORER Program, Gulf of Mexico 2014 Expedition / Lee Dalton (tr). 102–103 Alamy Stock Photo:** Avalon.red / Oceans Image. **102 Alamy Stock Photo:** Nature Picture Library / David Shale (cra); Adisha Pramod (bc). **Shutterstock.com:** John A. Anderson (clb). **103 Alamy Stock Photo:** Ralph Bixler / age fotostock (cra). **NOAA:** OER (crb). **104 Corbis:** Ralph White (cla). **imagequestmarine.com:** (clb). **naturepl.com:** David Shale (cr) **Woods Hole Oceanographic Instititution:** Photo by HOV Alvin (bc). **105 Ocean Networks Canada:** CSSF-ROPOS. **SeaPics.com:** Susan Dabritz (cr). **106–107 OceanwideImages.com:** Gary Bell. **108–109 Getty Images:** Ellen van Bodegom. **108 NASA:** Robert Simmon (bl). **109 naturepl.com:** Inaki Relanzon (clb). **SuperStock:** John Hyde / Alaska Stock - Design Pics (br). **110 Corbis:** Tor / imageBROKER (tr). **Getty Images:** Lisa Collins (clb). **110–111 Robert Harding Picture Library:** Lawson Wood (bc). **111 Alamy Stock Photo:** National Geographic Image Collection (cr). **Photoshot:** Gordon MacSkimming / PictureNature (cla). **Robert Harding Picture Library:** Sue Daly (tc). **112 Alamy Stock Photo:** Reinhard Dirscherl (l). **Getty Images:** Darryl Torckler (crb). **113 Alamy Stock Photo:** Steve Bloom Images (tc). **Adrian P. Ashworth:** (c). **naturepl.com:** Brandon Cole (cr). **Robert Harding Picture Library:** Marevision (crb, br). **114 OceanwideImages.com:** Gary Bell (bl). **114–115 Alamy Stock Photo:** Mark Conlin. **115 Corbis:** Fred Bavendam / Minden Pictures (br); Norbert Wu / Minden Pictures (tc, cr). **Alamy Stock Photo:** Reuben Reynoso (cl). **116–117 Alamy Stock Photo:** Steve Bly. **118 Alamy Stock Photo:** Reinhard Dirscherl (bl). **Corbis:** Visuals Unlimited (cra). **SeaPics.com:** (cl). **119 FLPA:** Pierre Lobel. **imagequestmarine.com:** (tl). **120 Alamy Stock Photo:** cbimages (cra). **Getty Images:** Reinhard Dirscherl (bl). **imagequestmarine.com:** (c). **120–121 Alamy Stock Photo:** cbpix. **121 Dorling Kindersley:** The Natural History Museum, London (c). **122 Robert Harding Picture Library:** Reinhard Dirscherl (t); Marevision (crb). **122–123 Photoshot:** NHPA (b). **123 Getty Images:** Jeff Rotman (cr). **Dreamstime.com:** Pics516 (tl). **124-125 FLPA:** Fred Bavendam / Minden Pictures. **126–127 OceanwideImages.com:** Gary Bell (c). **126 Flickr / Derek Haslam:** (cl). **naturepl.com:** Kim Taylor (cb). **127 naturepl.com:** Mark Carwardine (crb); Nature Production (ca, cra); Bertie Gregory (cr). **128 naturepl.com:** Georgette Douwma (clb). **128–129 Getty Images:** Michael Aw (c). **129 Dreamstime.com:** Olga Khoroshunova (cb). **Getty Images:** Paul Kay (tr). **130–131 Science Photo Library:** Alexander Semenov (c). **131 Ardea:** Auscape, ardea.com (ca). **OceanwideImages.com:** Gary Bell (crb, bc). **132 Alamy Stock Photo:** Terry Moore / Stocktrek Images (cb). **Robert Harding Picture Library:** Andre Seale (cb). **133 Corbis:** Todd Winner / Stocktrek Images (bc). **Getty Images:** Georgette Douwma (cb). **Alamy Stock Photo:** Nature Picture Library / Pascal Kobeh (tc). **134 Corbis:** Ingo Arndt / Minden Pictures (clb). **134-135 NASA:** (c). **135 Getty Images:** Bristol Archives / Universal Images Group (crb). **OceanwideImages.com:** Gary Bell (cra, br). **136 Alamy Stock Photo:** Connect Images / Zac Macaulay (tr). **Corbis:** Aflo (bc). **Dreamstime.com:** Mikhail Blajenov (clb). **SeaPics.com:** David B. Fleetham (c). **136–137 Alamy Stock Photo:** SeaTops (b). **137 Alamy Stock Photo:** Erik Schlogl (cra); Jean-Michel Mille / Biosphoto (crb). **Getty Images:** Image Source (tc). **138 Alamy Stock Photo:** Michael Patrick O'Neill (tl). **Corbis:** Hal Beral / Visuals Unlimited (bl). **138–139 Robert Harding Picture Library:** J. W. Alker. **139 OceanwideImages.com:** Gary Bell (br). **Robert Harding Picture Library:** Reinhard Dirscherl (tr); Dave Fleetham (cla). **140–141 Dreamstime.com:** Izanbar. **142 Alamy Stock Photo:** F1online digitale Bildagentur GmbH (c). **142–143 Alamy Stock Photo:** Ian Bottle (tc). **Getty Images:** Mint Images - Frans Lanting (bc). **143 Alamy Stock Photo:** WaterFrame (br). **Corbis:** Yann Arthus-Bertrand (cra). **NASA:** (cb). **144–145 OceanwideImages.com:** Gary Bell. **146–147 Alamy Stock Photo:** nobleIMAGES. **Corbis:** Topic Photo Agency (tc). **146 Corbis:** Lee Frost / Robert Harding World Imagery (cb). **147 Corbis:** Wild Wonders of Europe / Lundgren / Nature Picture Library (ca). **148 Alamy Stock Photo:** Mike VanDeWalker. **149 Alamy Stock Photo:** nagelestock.com (clb). **Corbis:** Ron Dahlquist (bc). **Rex Features:** John McLellan (tl). **150 Corbis:** Aflo (cr); Image Source (b). **151 Alamy Stock Photo:** (t, b). **Getty Images:** Alex Robinson (c). **152–153 Dreamstime.com:** Steveheap. **154 Alamy Stock Photo:** Stuart Hall (c). **Getty Images:** Design Pics / John Doornkamp (bc). **154–155 Bcasterline / English Wikipedia Project. 155 Corbis:** Tui De Roy / Minden Pictures (br). **SeaPics.com:** David B. Fleetham (cra). **156–157 Alamy Stock Photo:** David Fleetham (b). **156 Alamy Stock Photo:** Steve. Trewhella (cl). **157 Dreamstime.com:** Pnwnature (t). **naturepl.com:** Jose B. Ruiz (crb). **158 Corbis:** Larry Dale Gordon (t). **Dreamstime.com:** Michael Thompson (bl); Susan Robinson (br). **159 Aurora Photos:** Peter Essick (tl). **Corbis:** Neil Rabinowitz (cl); Skyscan. **160 Ardea:** David Kilbey (bl). **SeaPics.com:** Marc Chamberlain (cl). **160–161 Photoshot:** Laurie Campbell. **161 Flickr / Derek Haslam:** (crb). **Arne Hückelheim:** (tr). **162 Alamy Stock Photo:** Genevieve Vallee (bl). **Manjeet & Yograj Jadeja:** (tr). **162–163 Dreamstime.com:** Kevin Winkler. **163 Alamy Stock Photo:** Cal Vornberger (cb). **Ardea:** M. Watson (tr). **Getty Images:** Javier Tajuelo (br). **Photoshot:** Jordi Bas Casas (cl). **164–165 Corbis:** Flip de Nooyer / Minden Pictures. **166 Alamy Stock Photo:** Ann and Steve Toon (cl); Rolf Hicker Photography (b). **Photoshot:** Alan Barnes (cr). **167 Dreamstime.com:** Hecke01 (c). **Getty Images:** Steve Ward Nature Photography (br); Tui De Roy (t). **168 Alamy Stock Photo:** Visual&Written SL (bl). **Robert Harding Picture Library:** Jason Bazzano (tr). **168–169 Corbis:** Tim Fitzharris / Minden Pictures. **169 Alamy Stock Photo:** Nature Picture Library / Claudio Contreras (tr).**OceanwideImages.com:** Michael Patrick O'Neill (br). **170 Alamy Stock Photo:** Natural Visions (c); Peter Johnson (b). **OceanwideImages.com:** Gary Bell (cr). **170–171 Corbis:** Jurgen Freund / Nature Picture Library. **171 Getty Images:** Morales (t). **naturepl.com:** Ingo Arndt (c). **172 Sergio Moraes / Reuters (bl). NASA:** Jacques Descloitres, MODISRapid Response Team, NASA / GSFC (c). **172–173 Corbis:** Annie Griffiths Belt. **173 Corbis:** Michael Freeman (t); Paul Souders (b). **FLPA:** Steve Trewhella (c). **174 NASA:** NASA image created by Jesse Allen, Earth Observatory, using data obtained from the University of Maryland's (bl). **174–175 Alamy Stock Photo:** Universal Images Group Limited. **175 Alamy Stock Photo:** Barry Iverson (c). **Corbis:** Wild Wonders of Europe / Presti / Nature Picture Library (b). **176 Robert Harding Picture Library:** Sabine Lubenow (tl). **176–177 FLPA:** Ingo Arndt / Minden Pictures (b). **177 Corbis:** Theo Allofs / Terra (cl). **Alamy Stock Photo:** Chris Herring (tr). **178 Alamy Stock Photo:** Tom Stack (cra). **Dreamstime.com:** Dibrova (bl). **178–179 Dreamstime.com:** Seadam (b). **179 Alamy Stock Photo:** Nature Picture Library / Daniel Heuclin (crb). **Corbis:** Stephen Dalton / Minden Pictures (tc). **Dreamstime.com:** Feathercollector (cra); James Shearing / Jimbomp44 (bc). **180–181 FLPA:** Konrad Wothe / Minden Pictures. **182 OceanwideImages.com:** Gary Bell (cra). **182–183 Getty Images:** M Swiet Productions / Moment. **183 Alamy Stock Photo:** Brandon Cole Marine Photography (tl). **Dreamstime.com:** Dmytro Pylypenko / Pilipenkod (cr). **SeaPics.com:** D. R. Schrichte (br). **184 scubazoo.com:** Jason Isley (tr). **Robert Harding Picture Library:** Reinhard Dirscherl (b). **185 Alamy Stock Photo:** MichaelGrantWildlife (cla); Rosanne Tackaberry (tr). **Photoshot:** NHPA / Adrian Hepworth (br). **186–187 FLPA:** Jean-Jacques Pangrazi / Biosphoto. **Getty Images:** Kim Westerskov / Photographer's Choice RF (cl). **188–189 NASA:** NASA image by Jeff Schmaltz, MODIS Rapid Response Team, Goddard Space Flight Center. Caption by Michon Scott. **189 Alamy Stock Photo:** Doug Allan / Nature Picture Library (crb). **NASA:** NASA image courtesy Jeff Schmaltz, MODIS Rapid Response Team at NASA GSFC. Caption by Mike Carlowicz and Holli Riebeek, with interpretation from Barney Balch (Bigelow Laboratory) and Norman Kuring and Sergio Signorini of NASA's Goddard Space Flight Center. (cr); World Wind (tl). **190 Corbis:** Flip Nicklin / Minden Pictures (bc); Rick Price / Documentary Value (bl). **Robert Harding Picture Library:** Colin Monteath (cl); Michael Nolan (br). **190–191 Corbis:** Ralph White / Encyclopedia. **191 Corbis:** Topic Photo Agency / Passage (tr). **Getty Images:** Oesterreichsches Volkshochschularchiv / Imagno / Hulton Archive (cr). **192 Alamy Stock Photo:** Kim Westerskov (c). **Corbis:** Flip Nicklin / Minden Pictures (bl). **192–193 Corbis:** Norbert Wu / Minden Pictures. **193 Corbis:** Norbert Wu / Minden Pictures (crb/background). **Getty Images:** Maria Stenzel / National Geographic (crb/seals). **Science Photo Library:** British Antarctic Survey (tc). **194 Corbis:** Momatiuk - Eastcott / Ramble (cl). **Robert Harding Picture Library:** Michael Nolan (c). **194–195 Alamy Stock Photo:** Juniors Bildarchiv GmbH. **195 Corbis:** Stefan Christmann / Latitude (cb); Tim Davis / DLILLC (tl); Frans Lemmens / Flame (tr). **196–197 Getty Images:** Paul Nicklen. **198–199 Alamy Stock Photo:** Tom Brakefield (main). **199 SuperStock:** MIVA Stock (tr). **200 Dreamstime.com:** Dmytro Pylypenko / Pilipenkod (tl). **Getty Images:** Specialist Stock / Barcroft Media (b). **201 Corbis:** Fotofeeling / Westend61 (br). **naturepl.com:** Andy Rouse (cr). **Robert Harding Picture Library:** Michael Nolan (tl). **202 Getty Images:** Steven L. Raymer / National Geographic (bc). **Science Photo Library:** (tr). **SuperStock:** Radius (crb). **203 Corbis:** Andy Rouse / Nature Picture Library (cla). **Dreamstime.com:** Davis2247 (tr). **Getty Images:** Ben Cranke / The Image Bank (b). **Robert Harding Picture Library:** Mike Hill (c). **204 Dreamstime.com:** Philip Dickson / Psdphotography (tl, tc, tr, ftr). **204–205 FLPA:** Wil Meinderts / Minden Pictures. **205 Corbis:** Ralph A. Clevenger / Crave (tl); Colin Monteath / Hedgehog House / Minden Pictures (cra). **206–207 Corbis:** Frans Lanting / Latitude. **208 Alamy Stock Photo:** Ariadne Van Zandbergen (cra). **208–209 Alamy Stock Photo:** Wayne Lynch / All Canada Photos. **209 Alamy Stock Photo:** Natural History Library (cra). **Corbis:** C. Huetter / Encyclopedia (tc). **210 Corbis:** Flip Nicklin / Minden Pictures (cl); **210–211 SuperStock:** age fotostock. **211 Alamy Stock Photo:** Wildlife GmbH (br). **naturepl.com:** Doug Allan (tr). **212 Alamy Stock Photo:** Roberta Olenick / All Canada Photos (cr). **FLPA:** Sergey Gorshkov / Minden Pictures (cl). **212–213 Alamy Stock Photo:** Paulette Sinclair. **213 Getty Images:** Wayne R. Bilenduke / Stone (cra). **naturepl.com:** Steven Kazlowski (tl). **214 Corbis:** Michael DeYoung / Design Pics / Canopy (bl). **Getty Images:** Michael Sewell / Photolibrary (c). **214–215 Corbis:** Beat Glanzmann / Comet. **215 Alamy Stock Photo:** Jeff Schultz / Design Pics Inc (cr). **Getty Images:** Werner Forman / Universal Images Group Editorial (tr). **Robert Harding Picture Library:** Pete Ryan (tl). **216–217 OceanwideImages.com:** Gary Bell. **218 Alamy Stock Photo:** Sentilo Media (bl); George Ostertag (br). **219 Alamy Stock Photo:** North Wind Picture Archives (cr). **Bridgeman Images:** Pictures From History (cl). **Getty Images:** Henning Bagger / AFP (tc); Paul Kennedy / Lonely Planet Images (bl). **220 National Oceanography Centre, Southampton:** (cla). **Woods Hole Oceanographic Instititution:** Photo by Rod Catanach © 2013 (cb). **220–221 Photoshot. 221 Science Photo Library:** NOAA (tr). **222 Alamy Stock Photo:** WaterFrame (cl). **Robert Harding Picture Library:** Len Deeley (br) **222–223 Corbis:** GM Visuals / Blend Images. **223 Corbis:** Jonathan Blair / Latitude (tr). **Robert Harding Picture Library:** Andrey Nekrasov (cr). **224 Corbis:** Ralph White / Historical (clb). **Woods Hole Oceanographic Instititution:** Illustration by E. Paul Oberlander © 2013 (bc). **224–225 National Geographic Stock:** Handout. **225 Shutterstock.com:** lego 19861111 (tr). **Woods Hole Oceanographic Instititution:** (br). **226 Alamy Stock Photo:** Stefan Auth / imageBROKER (cl); Jan Greune / LOOK Die Bildagentur der Fotografen GmbH (bl); Neil Holmes / Holmes Garden Photos (cra). **227 Corbis:** Heritage Images / Fine Art (cl). **Rex Features:** Sipa Press (tc). **Science Photo Library:** NOAA (b). **228 Siemens AG, Munich/Berlin:** (bl). **228–229 Getty Images:** Pham Le Huong Son / Moment Open. **229 Corbis:** Olivier Polet / Corbis News (c); STR / SRI LANKA / Reuters (br). **Science Photo Library:** NOAA Office Of Ocean Exploration And Research, 2019 Southeastern Us Deep-Sea Exploration (tr). **230 Corbis:** Eric Kulin / First Light (cl). **230–231 Photoshot:** Ashley Cooper. **231 Marine Current Turbines Limited / A Siemens Business:** (cr). **Rex Features:** Sipa Press (tr). **232 FLPA:** Robert Henno / Biosphoto (bl). **Getty Images:** Luis Marden / Contributor / National Geographic (tr). **Robert Harding Picture Library:** Gavin Hellier (cr). **233 Corbis:** Bill Broadhurst / FLPA / Minden Pictures (tr). **Robert Harding Picture Library:** Michael Nolan (b). **234–235 Magnum Photos:** Steve McCurry. **236-237 Corbis:** Kike Calvo / National Geographic Creative. **236 Alamy Stock Photo:** Dalgleish Images (tl). **237 Corbis:** Ron Chapple (tl); HO / Reuters (crb). **Dreamstime.com:** Ruth Peterkin (cra). **238 Getty Images:** Pacific Press / LightRocket (cl). **238–239 Corbis:** Paul Souders (cr). **239 Alamy Stock Photo:** Imagebroker / Helmut Corneli (c); Luc Hoogenstein / Buiten-Beeld (br). **Getty Images:** Portland Press Herald (tl). **240 Depositphotos Inc:** stockfoto-graf (bl). **Dreamstime.com:** Barmalini (br). **240–241 Alamy Stock Photo:** Louisiana Governors Office. **241 Getty Images:** Suryanto Suryanto / Anadolu (tl). **naturepl.com:** Shane Gross (br). **NOAA:** NOAA Fisheries (bl). **242 Adobe Stock:** Pcess609 (tr). **243 Dreamstime.com:** Jillian Cain (bl). **Getty Images:** AFP / Chandan Khanna (tl); Jefri Tarigan / Jefta Images / Future Publishing (cra); AFP (bc). **244 Dreamstime.com:** Avictorero (tr); Joe Benning (cl). **244–245 Shutterstock.com:** Mike Workman (b). **245 Alamy Stock Photo:** imageBROKER.com / Norbert Probst (tl). **Shutterstock.com:** Tigergallery (crb). **246 Corbis:** Larry Dale Gordon (t). **249 Alamy Stock Photo:** cbpix (b). **252 Getty Images:** M Swiet Productions / Moment (b). **253 Photolibrary:** Image Source (b).

**Cover images:** *Front:* **FLPA:** Reinhard Dirscherl; *Back:* **Dreamstime.com:** Vilainecrevette c; *Spine:* **Dreamstime.com:** Vilainecrevette b. **FLPA:** Reinhard Dirscherl t.

# WHAT WILL YOU DISCOVER NEXT?

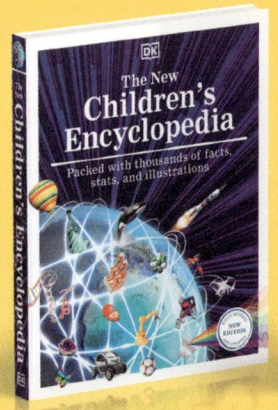 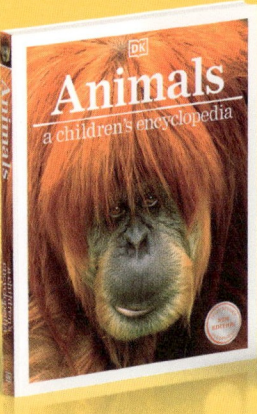 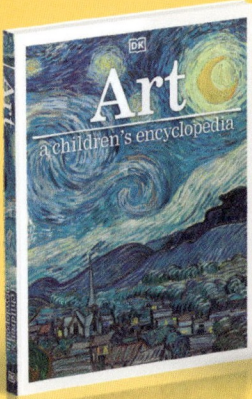 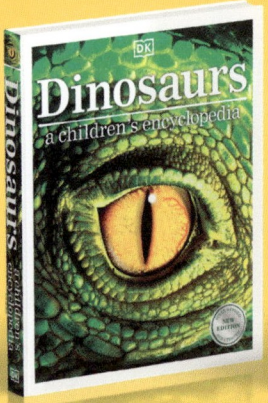 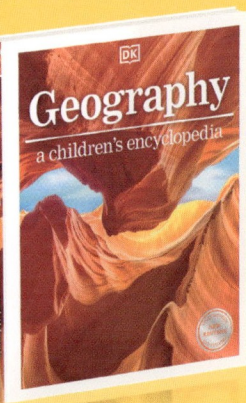

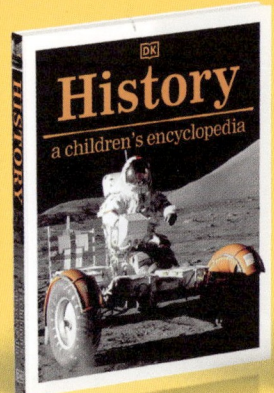 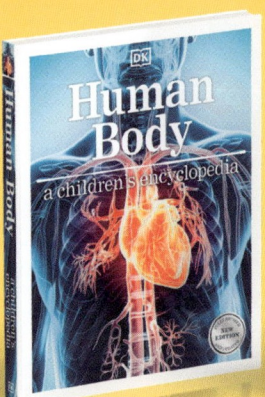 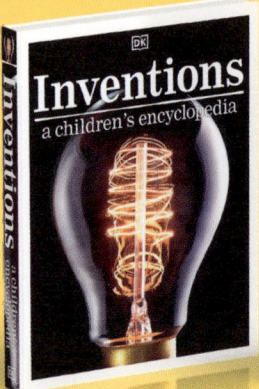 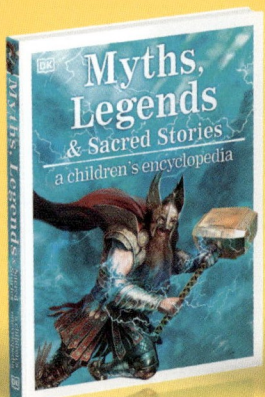 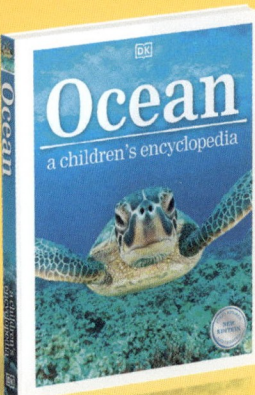

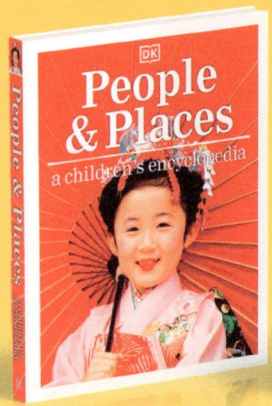  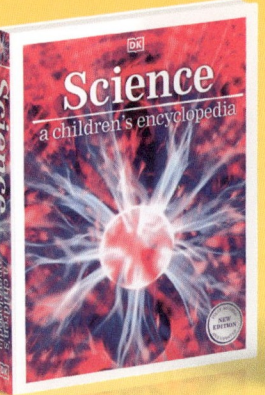